# Punch Bowl
## OPTIONAL

Johnson County Young Matrons Cookbook

WIMMER
COOKBOOKS

A CONSOLIDATED GRAPHICS COMPANY

800.548.2537   wimmerco.com

# Table of Contents

# Dedication

This 50th Anniversary cookbook is dedicated to the amazing women of JCYM — those who came before us, those who are currently members and those to come. Your commitment to bettering our community with your time and support is inspiring. Your friendship and caring are timeless. You are an awe-inspiring group of ladies and leaders.

# JCYM Mission Statement

To promote and foster charitable, literary and educational purposes, by and through uniting congenial women of the community in friendship and intellectual development in the futherance of community improvement activities.

# JCYM Collect for Club Women

Keep us, O God, from pettiness;
let us be large in thought, in word, in deed.

Let us be done with fault-finding,
and leave off self-seeking.

May we put away all pretense and meet each
other face to face without self-pity and
without prejudice.

Let us take time for all things;
make us grow calm, serene, gentle.

Teach us to put into action
our better impluses,
straightforward and unafraid.

Grant that we may realize it is the little
things that create differences;
that in the big things of life we are at one.

And may we strive to touch and to know the
great common human heart of us all;
and O Lord God,
let us forget not…to be kind.

Mary Stuart

# Introduction

The year 1961 was the time of white gloves, pillbox hats, and afternoon teas. It was a time for celebrating peace, prosperity and growth. It was a time of change, change that would alter forever the future of the world. John F. Kennedy was inaugurated as our 35th president and challenged us to "ask not what your country can do for you—ask what you can do for your country".

Fifty-one women in our area met that challenge by establishing JCYM (Johnson County Young Matrons) on June 22, 1961. Their mission statement clearly stated their goals—to be a philanthropic, civic, and social organization with an emphasis on giving back to and improving our community. To that end they offered support to numerous area philanthropies, often creating programs to fill needs identified by the community. Included among this establishment of programs was the founding and developing of TLC for Children and Families (now KidsTLC), originally an emergency shelter for children but now grown to provide a wide variety of support systems for area youth.

Other events occurring in 1961 included: the first American (Alan Shepherd) in space and the stated goal (by Kennedy) of reaching the moon within the decade, the establishment of the Peace Corps, the construction of the Berlin Wall, the introduction of "Ken" as Barbie's boyfriend, the development of the Freedom Riders in promoting integration of our society, the awarding of the Pulitzer Prize to Harper Lee for <u>To Kill a Mockingbird</u>, the debut of the Beach Boys, the introduction of the "Poppin' Fresh Doughboy" by Pillsbury, the on-air broadcasting of KCPT in Kansas City, the opening of the world's first revolving restaurant (Top of the Space Needle in Seattle) and the first in-flight movie shown by TWA. Each of these events affected our community and was indicative of changes to come.

These charter members of JCYM looked into the future and saw the need for continued support for our community. They created an organization that continues to reach out to this day with both financial and philanthropic support of non-profit organizations that serve others. We are proud to carry on that fine tradition with ways and means earnings and hands-on service. We are equally proud to continue to provide a social networking for like-minded women—our membership today reflects this as well as our dedication to serving our community.

To this end, JCYM thanks you for your support of our philanthropic efforts with your purchase of this cookbook. And we know that you will enjoy our celebration suggestions as well as the many fine recipes that were submitted by our members and friends.

# Cookbook Committee

| | |
|---|---|
| Ruth Cousins | Sheila Sanders |
| Paula Humphries | Suellen Smith |
| Vida Leming | Diana Willman |
| Desi Miller | Martha Wofford |
| Robin O'Hara | Doris Yantis |
| Joy Padley | |

# Acknowledgements

Our thanks to these women who spent many hours
making this the best cookbook possible.

### TYPISTS:

| | |
|---|---|
| Maryln Golub | Ginger Waters |
| Dottie Marr | Poppy Zurcher |

### PROOFREADERS:

| | |
|---|---|
| Winky Bergeson | Cathy Vicklund |
| Margie Ray | Barbara Wilson |

We wish to express our deepest appreciation
to all those who so generously shared their favorite recipes.
Without you this book wouldn't have been published.
We regret that we were unable to publish all recipes
due to similarity or availability of space.

# Autumn Offerings

# BACK TO SCHOOL BRUNCH

## Substitutions

# SOUP BUFFET

## Substitutions

# FALL BACK DINNER

Mulled Cider and Wine, page 26
Avoid the Tomatoes Bruschetta, page 26
Sun-Dried Tomato and Spinach Torta, page 27
Fennel and Red Onion Salad, page 28
Chicken in a Hurry, page 27
Baked Apricot Casserole, page 29
Cheese Grits Soufflé, page 28
Sweet Potato Biscuits and Butter, page 30
Apple-Pecan Pie Cobbler, page 29
Chocolate-Praline Pecan Cake, page 31

## Substitutions

Honey Gingered Pork Tenderloin, page 30
Indian Summer Gratin, page 32

# IT'S A HOOT PARTY

Hot Mexican Cider, page 33
Tangy Herb Cheese Spread, page 33
Crab and Artichoke Appetizer Pizza, page 34
Tijuana Tidbits, page 34
Buffalo Chicken Dip, page 33
Roasted Butternut Squash & Curry Soup, page 35
French Dip Sandwiches, page 35
Peanut Butter and Toffee Candy Bark, page 36
Candy Corn Popcorn Balls, page 36

# GAME DAY TAILGATE

## Substitutions

# AWESOME AUTUMN

# FALL FEST

Red Wine Sangría, page 51
Cowboy Caviar, page 52
Salsa Cheesecake, page 51
Taco Chicken Soup, page 53
Southwest Sweet Potato Hash, page 52
Green Onion Cornbread, page 54
Bourbon Panna Cotta, page 53
Kahlúa Cake, page 54
Peanut Butter Fudge Bars, page 55

## Substitutions
Autumn Soup, page 56
Famous French Onion Soup, page 55

# SOUTH OF THE BORDER

Amazing Margaritas, page 57
Homemade Kahlúa, page 57
Passion Fruit Rum Punch, page 57
Chopped Mexican Salad with Veggies and Avocado, page 58
Baby Romaine Salad with Spicy Chicken, page 59
White Enchiladas, page 60
Chili-Rubbed Rib-Eye Steak with Corn and Green Chili Ragoût, page 60
South of the Border Veggie-Chili and Fixins, page 61
Rice with Green Chilies, page 62
Southwestern-Style Potato Salad, page 63
Grilled Fish Tacos, page 64

# Blushing Mimosas

2 cups orange juice (not concentrate)
1 cup pineapple juice, chilled
2 tablespoons grenadine

1 (750 milliliter) bottle champagne or sparkling wine, chilled

Stir together orange juice, pineapple juice and grenadine. Pour equal parts orange juice mixture and champagne into champagne flutes.

*SERVES 6*

# Almond Crusted French Toast

½ cup butter, melted.
3 tablespoons white corn syrup
1 cup firmly packed brown sugar
1 cup sliced almonds
1 loaf unsliced French bread

8 eggs
2 cups milk
1 teaspoon almond extract
1 teaspoon vanilla extract

Spray a 9x13 inch pan with non-stick spray. Combine butter, corn syrup and brown sugar. Place in prepared pan. Add sliced almonds. Slice bread into 1½ inch slices. Place on top of butter mixture. Beat eggs, milk, almond and vanilla. Pour over bread. Cover and set overnight in refrigerator. Preheat oven to 350°. Bake covered for 25 minutes. Invert on a large platter or another 9x13 inch pan.

*SERVES 8-10*

# Grape Surprises

1 (8 ounce) package cream cheese, softened
1 (8 ounce) package sharp Cheddar cheese, shredded
½ cup butter, softened
1 tablespoon prepared mustard

½ teaspoon Worcestershire sauce
Fresh seedless grapes (about 50)
Paprika
3 cups (or more if needed) pecans or walnuts, chopped

Beat together cheeses, butter, mustard and Worcestershire sauce. With damp hands, form 1 inch balls of dough around individual grapes. Roll each ball in paprika and then in chopped nuts. Chill.

*SERVES 50*

# Tomato Potato Onion Bake

2 large white or yellow onions, peeled and thinly sliced into rings

2 pounds potatoes, thinly sliced

1 pound fresh tomatoes, thinly sliced

6 fresh basil leaves, thinly cut chiffonade style

6 tablespoons extra virgin olive oil, divided

1 teaspoon salt, divided

½ teaspoon freshly ground pepper, divided

1½ cups freshly grated Parmesan cheese, divided

Preheat oven to 350°. Generously coat a 9x13 inch baking dish with non-stick cooking spray. Arrange half of the onion rings in the bottom of prepared baking dish. Carefully place half of the potato slices on top of the onion rings. Place half of the tomato slices on top of the potatoes, adding any tomato juice from slicing into the dish. Top with 3 cut basil leaves. Pour 3 tablespoons of olive oil over and season with ½ teaspoon salt and ¼ teaspoon pepper. Sprinkle with ¾ cup cheese. Repeat. Place uncovered in oven and bake 60 minutes or until potatoes are fork-tender. If the top begins to brown too much place a sheet of aluminum foil over the top of the dish. Serve hot.

*SERVES 6-8*

# Albuquerque Quiche

One frozen pie shell or pre-made pie crust

¾ cup grated Cheddar cheese

½ cup grated Monterey Jack cheese

3 eggs, at room temperature, lightly beaten

¼ teaspoon salt

12 ounces half and half

1 (4 ounce) can chopped green chilies

1 (2.25 ounce) can sliced black olives

2 tablespoons diced green onions

Preheat oven to 350°. Place pie dough in a 9 inch pie plate or use the pie shell that is ready to go. Combine the cheeses and place evenly in the pie shell. Combine the eggs, salt, half and half, green chilies, black olives and green onions. Pour over the cheese mixture. Bake for 40 minutes or until a knife comes out clean after being inserted into the center of the quiche. Serve immediately.

*SERVES 4 AS MAIN DISH OR 8 AS APPETIZER*

# Zesty Fresh Orange Breakfast Cake

2 tablespoons butter, melted, plus more for the pan

1 (16.3 ounce) can refrigerated biscuits, preferably the large sized ones

¼ cup minced walnuts

⅓ cup sugar

2 teaspoons orange zest

**GLAZE**

½ cup powdered sugar

2 ounces cream cheese, softened

2 tablespoons orange juice or more as necessary

Preheat the oven to 350°. Butter a 9 inch round cake pan. Separate the biscuit dough into 8 biscuits. Place 1 biscuit in the center of the pan. Cut the remaining biscuits in half, forming 14 half-circles. Arrange the pieces around the center biscuit with cut sides facing in the same direction. Brush melted butter over the tops of the biscuits. In a small bowl, combine the walnuts, sugar and orange zest. Mix well and sprinkle over the biscuits. Bake for 20 minutes or until golden brown. Meanwhile, in a small bowl combine powdered sugar, cream cheese and orange juice. Blend until smooth adding more orange juice, if needed, to thin. Drizzle glaze over the warm breakfast cake and serve.

*SERVES 8*

# French Muffins

⅓ cup butter

½ cup sugar

1 egg, beaten

1½ cups all-purpose flour

½ teaspoon salt

½ cup milk

1½ teaspoons baking powder

¼ teaspoon nutmeg

**DIPPING MIXTURE**

¼ cup butter, melted

¼ cup sugar

1 teaspoon cinnamon

Preheat oven to 350°. Cream together butter, sugar and egg. Mix together flour, salt, baking powder and nutmeg. Add dry ingredients and alternate with milk. Bake the muffins for 20 minutes. When baked, dip muffins in melted butter and a mixture of sugar and cinnamon.

*SERVES 12 MUFFINS*

# Cream Scones

3 cups bread flour
½ cup sugar
2 tablespoons baking powder
½ teaspoon salt

**CLOTTED CREAM**
2 cups heavy cream

2 cups heavy cream
2 tablespoons milk
3 tablespoons sugar for the tops

Cut 2 (10 inch) circles of parchment paper. Use 1 to line a 10 inch round cake pan. Reserve second piece. Sift together flour, sugar, baking powder and salt into a mixing bowl. Make a well in the center of the flour mixture, add 2 cups heavy cream and stir by hand just until the batter is evenly moistened. Place dough in lined cake pan and press into an even layer. Cover the dough with second parchment circle. Freeze dough until very firm, at least 12 hours. (Leaving dough in freezer overnight makes a more tender scone.) Preheat oven to 350°. Prepare a baking sheet by spraying it lightly with cooking spray or lining with parchment. Thaw dough for 5 minutes at room temperature. Turn out of the cake pan onto a cutting board. Cut the dough into 10 equal wedges and place on baking sheet about 2 inches apart. Brush scones with milk and sprinkle with sugar. Bake scones until golden brown, 30-40 minutes. Cool on baking sheet for a few minutes and then transfer to cooling racks. Serve scones with clotted cream and preserves. They may be frozen up to four weeks. Cook clotted cream in top of a double boiler over simmering water until reduced by half. It should be the consistency of butter with a golden crust on top. Transfer, including crust, to a bowl. Cover and let stand 2 hours. Refrigerate 12 hours uncovered. Stir crust into cream before serving. Keeps up to 4 days.

*SERVES 10*

Our members complete over 100 philanthropic activities annually. These range from providing games and snacks with fun interaction with teenagers, providing a Pumpkin Patch for little ones, organizing and staffing a bazaar fundraiser for the elderly, baking and staffing a bake sale for an area historical site, creating fleece blankets for the elderly and the young, helping those less fortunate shop for the holiday season, etc. We also have collections at each meeting for items such as baby/toddler needs, clothing for those away from home, gifts for teenagers, and toys for all ages, coats, etc.

# Southern Biscuit Muffins

2½ cups all-purpose flour
¼ cup sugar
1½ tablespoons baking powder
¼ teaspoon salt

½ cup plus 2 tablespoons unsalted butter
1 cup cold milk

Preheat oven to 350°. In a bowl or food processor, combine the flour, sugar, baking powder and salt; mix well, breaking up any lumps. Work the butter in until mixture resembles coarse cornmeal. Gradually stir in milk, mix just until moistened. Do not overbeat. Grease and fill 12 muffin cups then bake until golden brown, about 35-40 minutes. The finished muffins should have a thick crust with a cake-like center.

*SERVES 12*

# Tiny Cinnamon Rolls

1 (8 ounce) can refrigerated crescent rolls
1½ teaspoons sugar
½ teaspoon cinnamon

⅓ cup sifted powdered sugar
1 teaspoon milk
¼ teaspoon vanilla extract

Preheat oven to 350°. Unroll crescent roll dough and separate into 4 rectangles, pinch seams to seal. Stir together sugar and cinnamon; sprinkle evenly over rectangles. Roll up, jellyroll fashion, starting with a long side; press edges to seal. Cut each log into 5 slices and place in a lightly greased 8 inch round cake pan. Bake for 12 minutes. Combine powdered sugar, milk and vanilla, stirring until smooth. Drizzle over warm cinnamon rolls.

*SERVES 20 ROLLS*

These are pretty placed in a Christmas tree shape on a shiny pizza pan and drizzled with tinted frosting and sprinkles. May need to double recipe to create tree shape with a trunk or can be arranged with a wreath form and decorated.

# Autumn Salad

2 tablespoons extra virgin olive oil
2 tablespoons red wine vinegar
½ teaspoon sugar
½ teaspoon garlic, minced
¼ teaspoon paprika
¼ teaspoon dry mustard
⅛ teaspoon salt
⅛ teaspoon dried basil

⅛ teaspoon ground red pepper
5 cups mixed salad greens
4 cups torn romaine lettuce
2½ cups cubed Asian pear
2 cups chopped Granny Smith apple
½ cup thinly sliced red onion
¼ cup (1 ounce) crumbled goat cheese

Combine extra virgin olive oil, red wine vinegar, sugar, minced garlic, paprika, dry mustard, salt, basil and red pepper in a bowl, stirring with a whisk. Combine salad greens, romaine lettuce, Asian pear, apple and red onion in a large bowl. Drizzle with vinaigrette and toss well to coat. Sprinkle with crumbled goat cheese.

*SERVES 12*

# Tortellini Soup

1 (9 ounce) package refrigerated
   cheese tortellini
2 (10.75 ounce) cans reduced sodium
   condensed tomato soup, undiluted
2 cups vegetable broth
2 cups 2% milk
2 cups half and half cream
½ cup oil-packed sun-dried tomatoes,
   chopped

1 teaspoon onion powder
1 teaspoon garlic powder
1 teaspoon dried basil
½ teaspoon salt
½ cup shredded Parmesan cheese
1 teaspoon sour cream for each
   serving bowl

Cook tortellini according to package directions. In Dutch oven, combine soup, broth, milk, cream, tomatoes, onion powder, garlic powder, basil and salt. Heat through, stirring frequently. Drain tortellini and carefully add to soup. Stir in cheese. Spoon into serving bowls and top with sour cream. Serve with French bread.

*SERVES 8*

# Roasted Corn Chowder

3 red bell peppers, halved and seeded

3 ears shucked corn

1½ pounds tomatoes, halved, seeded and peeled (about 4)

2 tablespoons extra virgin olive oil

4 cups chopped onions (about 2 medium)

3 (14 ounce) cans fat free, less sodium chicken broth

¼ teaspoon freshly ground black pepper

½ teaspoon salt

¼ cup (1 ounce) crumbled blue cheese

2 tablespoons chopped fresh chives

Prepare grill to medium-high heat. Arrange bell peppers, skin side down, and corn, in single layer on a grill rack. Grill 5 minutes, turning corn occasionally. Add tomatoes. Grill an additional 5 minutes or until vegetables are slightly charred. Remove from heat; cool 10 minutes. Coarsely chop tomatoes and bell peppers; place in medium bowl. Cut kernels from ears of corn; add to tomato mixture. Heat oil in large Dutch oven over medium heat. Add onions and cook 7 minutes until tender, stirring occasionally. Stir in tomato mixture and cook 3 minutes, stirring occasionally. Increase heat to high and stir in broth. Bring to boil. Reduce heat and simmer 30 minutes until vegetables are tender. Cool 20 minutes. Place ⅓ tomato mixture in blender and process until smooth. Place puréed mixture in large bowl and repeat procedure until all mixture has been puréed. Wipe pan clean with paper towel. Press tomato mixture through a sieve into cleaned pan. Discard solids. Place pan over medium heat and heat thoroughly. Stir in salt and black pepper. Ladle 1½ cups soup into each of 6 bowls. Top each with 2 teaspoons cheese and 1 teaspoon chives.

*SERVES 8*

# Five Hour Beef Stew

2 pounds stew beef

5 carrots, quartered

3 potatoes, cut in chunks

1 onion, chopped

6 tablespoons minute tapioca

3 teaspoons salt

1 tablespoon sugar

1 (12 ounce) can tomato-vegetable juice cocktail

1 (12 ounce) can spicy tomato-vegetable juice cocktail

Place stew beef, carrots, potatoes and onion in a Dutch oven. Sprinkle tapioca, salt and sugar over all. Pour in both tomato-vegetable juice cocktails. Cover Dutch oven with foil then with lid over it. Cook at 250° for 5 hours. No peeking! Serve with hot biscuits. Easy and good.

*SERVES 6*

# Savory Stew

4 to 5 pieces chicken
½ pound stew meat
¼ cup vegetable oil
1 onion, diced

SAUCE

2 cans beef broth
3 ounces tomato paste
½ cup smooth peanut butter

1 green pepper, chopped
1 small eggplant, peeled and cubed
4 ounces canned mushrooms

½ teaspoon salt
Pinch of ground cayenne pepper

Bake chicken in 350° oven for 45 minutes. Cool, remove skin and cut chicken into bite-sized pieces. Brown beef in oil. Remove and set aside. Sauté onion and green pepper in remaining oil and beef drippings until tender. Add eggplant and mushrooms and continue sautéing 10 minutes until eggplant is tender. In separate pot, combine all sauce ingredients: beef broth, tomato paste, peanut butter, salt and cayenne pepper. Whisk until smooth. Add sauce, chicken and beef to vegetables and simmer on stovetop 30 minutes. You may also cook this in your slow cooker, on low for 3-4 hours. Serve over rice or with crusty bread.

*SERVES 6-8*

# Plaza Steak Soup

½ cup butter
1 cup flour
½ gallon (8 cups) water
2 pounds ground beef
1 cup chopped onions
1 cup chopped carrots

1 cup chopped celery
2 cups frozen mixed vegetables
1 can tomatoes
1 tablespoon seasoned salt flavor
  enhancer
1 bottle browning sauce
1 teaspoon pepper

In a 4-5 quart pan, melt butter and mix in flour. Stir in water. Sauté ground beef (drain grease) and add to soup. Add frozen vegetables, onions, carrots, celery, tomatoes, seasoned salt flavor enhancer, browning sauce and pepper. Bring to boil. Reduce heat and simmer until vegetables are done.

*SERVES 8*

# Italian Sausage Soup

12 ounces Italian sausage

2 (14 ounce) cans artichoke hearts, drained or 2 (9 ounce) packages frozen artichoke hearts, thawed

3 (14 ounce) cans Italian plum, diced tomatoes

1 package onion soup mix

¾ cup water

1 to 2 tablespoons Italian seasoning

Parmesan cheese for garnish

Crumble sausage into pieces in a soup pot. Brown and drain off fat. Cut artichoke hearts into bite-sized pieces. Add artichoke hearts and diced tomatoes to sausage. Stir in onion soup mix, water and Italian seasoning. Heat through. Garnish as desired. Soup may be made several days in advance.

*SERVES 8*

# Bacon Tomato Soup

1 pound bacon

1 large green bell pepper, diced

1 large yellow onion, diced

3 (14.5 ounce) cans chopped tomatoes, undrained

1 tablespoon sugar

1 tablespoon dried basil

1 tablespoon minced garlic

2 chicken bouillon cubes

1 quart whipping cream

Fresh basil, optional

Dice bacon into ½ inch pieces. Sauté in skillet until crisp. Using a slotted spoon, remove bacon from pan and drain on paper towel. Reserve 2 tablespoons bacon grease and add to it the onions and peppers. Sauté 5 minutes until soft. Transfer onions, peppers and bacon to a stockpot. Add tomatoes, sugar, basil, garlic, bouillon cubes and cream. Bring to a boil. Reduce heat, cover and simmer for 15 minutes. Garnish with fresh basil and serve.

*SERVES 4-6*

# French Loaves

| | |
|---|---|
| 2 tablespoons active dry yeast | 1 teaspoon sugar |
| 2 cups warm water (110° to 115°) | 4½ to 5 cups bread flour |
| 2 teaspoons salt | 1 teaspoon cornmeal |

In large bowl, dissolve yeast in warm water. Add the salt, sugar and 2 cups bread flour. Beat until smooth. Stir in enough remaining flour to form soft dough. Turn dough onto floured surface and knead until smooth and elastic, 6-8 minutes. Place in greased bowl, turning once to grease the top. Cover and let rise in warm place until doubled, 1 hour. Punch dough down. Turn onto lightly floured surface. Divide in half. Shape into 12 inch long loaves. Place seam side down on greased baking sheet. Cover and let rise until doubled, 30 minutes. Sprinkle with cornmeal. With sharp knife, make 4 shallow slashes across top of each loaf. Bake at 450° for 15-20 minutes or until golden brown.

*SERVES 2 LOAVES*

# Herb Rolls

| | |
|---|---|
| 1 can butterflake biscuits | ½ teaspoon dill weed |
| ⅓ cup butter | 1 tablespoon onion flakes |
| 1½ teaspoons parsley flakes | 2 tablespoons Parmesan cheese |

Preheat oven to 425°. Melt butter and mix with parsley flakes, dill weed, onion flakes and Parmesan cheese. Place in pie pan. Cut biscuits in halves. Coat and dredge biscuits in herb mixture. Bake in same pan for 12 minutes.

*SERVES 16*

# Tippins Cornbread

| | |
|---|---|
| 1 (8.5 ounce) package cornbread mix | 1 (8.5 ounce) box yellow cake mix |

Prepare each mix according to instructions on the box. Combine both mixes and pour into a 9x13 inch greased pan. Bake according to cake mix directions. Time may have to be adjusted slightly. Any size mixes work well as long as weight of each one is similar.

# Cheddar Biscuits

1¾ cups all-purpose flour

1 tablespoon plus 2 teaspoons baking
  powder

2½ teaspoons sugar

¼ teaspoon salt

3 tablespoons vegetable shortening,
  at room temperature

4 tablespoons cold unsalted butter,
  cut into ½ inch pieces

6 ounces grated Cheddar cheese
  (1¾ cups)

¾ cup whole milk

Position rack in upper third of oven and preheat to 425°. Lightly mist large baking sheet with cooking spray. Pulse flour, baking powder, sugar and salt in food processor. Add shortening and pulse until combined. Add butter and pulse 4-5 times until butter is pea sized. Add cheese and pulse 2-3 times. Pour in milk and pulse just until the mixture is moistened and forms a sticky dough. Turn onto clean surface and gently knead until dough comes together. Do not overwork dough or the biscuits will be tough. Drop dough onto baking sheet in scant ¼ cup portions, 2 inches apart. Bake until golden, 15-20 minutes.

## GARLIC BUTTER

3 tablespoons unsalted butter

1 clove garlic, smashed

1 teaspoon chopped fresh parsley

Melt butter with garlic in small saucepan over medium heat. Cook 1 minute. Remove from heat and stir in parsley. Brush biscuits with garlic butter and serve warm.

*SERVES 12*

# Beer Muffins

2¾ cups self-rising flour

3 tablespoons sugar

1 (12 ounce) can beer, at room
  temperature

4 tablespoons butter

Preheat oven to 375°. Combine flour, sugar and beer and mix well. Let set 5 minutes. Spray muffin tins with vegetable spray. Fill tins ¾ full and top each biscuit with a pat of butter and tap a little. Bake for 25 minutes. Do not over-bake. Serve quickly.

*SERVES 12*

# Pumpkin Bread Pudding with Caramel Sauce

2 cups half and half
1 (15 ounce) can pure pumpkin
1 cup firmly packed plus 2 tablespoons dark brown sugar
2 eggs
1½ teaspoons pumpkin pie spice

1½ teaspoons ground cinnamon
1½ teaspoons vanilla extract
10 cups (½ inch cubes) egg bread (challah bread)
½ cup golden raisins

Preheat oven to 350°. In a large bowl, whisk half and half, pumpkin, sugar, eggs, pumpkin pie spice, cinnamon and vanilla. Fold in bread cubes. Stir in golden raisins. Transfer mixture to an 11x7 inch glass baking dish. Let stand 15 minutes. Bake 50 minutes or until tester inserted into center of pudding comes out clean. Serve warm with caramel sauce.

**CARAMEL SAUCE**

1¼ cups packed dark brown sugar
½ cup unsalted butter

½ cup whipping cream
Powdered sugar

In heavy, medium saucepan whisk brown sugar and butter over medium heat until butter melts. Whisk in cream and stir until sugar dissolves and sauce is smooth, about 3 minutes. Sift powdered sugar over bread pudding.

*SERVES 8*

# Apple Cake

1½ cups oil
2 cups sugar
3 eggs
3 cups flour
1 teaspoon salt
1 teaspoon cinnamon

1 teaspoon baking soda
1 teaspoon vanilla extract
3 cups peeled, thickly sliced apples
1 cup chopped walnuts
1 cup raisins

Preheat oven to 350°. Using a mixer, beat oil and sugar. Add eggs and beat until mixture is creamy. Mix flour, salt, cinnamon and soda. Add to batter gradually at medium speed. Add vanilla and mix briefly as it will rise quickly through the beaters. Add apples, nuts and raisins. Hand mix to blend. Turn mixture into a buttered, floured 10 inch tube pan. Bake 1 hour 15 minutes. Cool in pan before serving.

*SERVES 16*

# Crock-Pot Tortilla Soup

1 small onion, chopped
1 teaspoon minced garlic
1 small bunch cilantro, chopped
2 tablespoons butter
1 (15 ounce) can tomato sauce
20 ounces chicken broth
2 tablespoons taco seasoning
(or to taste)

1 (14.5 ounce) can diced tomatoes
2 cups frozen corn
3 to 4 frozen boneless, skinless chicken
breasts
1 tablespoon Worcestershire sauce
1 (14.5 ounce) can black beans, well
rinsed

Combine onion, garlic, cilantro, butter, tomato sauce, chicken broth, taco seasoning, diced tomatoes, corn, chicken and Worcestershire sauce in crock-pot. Cook 8-10 hours on low setting or 4-5 hours on high setting. Shred the chicken and return to crock-pot. Add the black beans 30 minutes prior to serving.

*SERVES 10*

Two cans tomatoes with green chilies may be substituted for the 1 can diced tomatoes. An additional can of black beans with jalapeños may be added if desired.

# Spicy Minestrone Soup

1 pound hot Italian sausage

1 teaspoon olive oil

1 onion, chopped

3 cloves garlic, minced

1 green pepper, chopped

1 white potato, peeled and cut into chunks

2 (14.5 ounce) cans diced tomatoes with chilies

¼ cup chopped parsley

1 teaspoon dried basil

1 teaspoon fennel seeds

2 teaspoons dried oregano

½ teaspoon red pepper flakes

Salt and pepper

2 (26 ounce) boxes beef stock

1 (16 ounce) can red kidney beans

1 cup large shell macaroni

1 zucchini, unpeeled, cut into chunks

½ cup Parmesan cheese

Cook sausage in olive oil. Remove from skillet and drain on paper towel. To skillet add onion, garlic, green pepper and potato. Cook 5 minutes. Add tomatoes with green chilies, parsley, basil, fennel, oregano, pepper flakes, salt, pepper, beef stock and cooked sausage. Bring to a boil. Reduce heat and simmer for 30 minutes. Add beans, pasta and zucchini. Cook another 20 minutes. Sprinkle Parmesan cheese on top and serve.

*SERVES 8*

# Roasted Vegetable Chicken Noodle Soup

1 cup peeled carrots, cut into 1 inch cubes (3 medium)

1 medium onion, cut into 1 inch cubes

1 cup celery (3 ribs), cut into 1 inch cubes

1 tablespoon olive oil

1 cup water

4 (14.5 ounce) cans fat-free chicken broth

2 cloves garlic, minced

½ teaspoon dried thyme

½ teaspoon pepper

¼ teaspoon salt

1 pound boneless, skinless chicken breasts, cut into bite size pieces

2 cups uncooked no-yolk noodles

Preheat oven to 400°. Spray a jelly roll pan with vegetable spray. Combine carrots, onions and celery. Drizzle with olive oil and toss well to coat. Arrange vegetables on prepared pan and bake 40 minutes or until browned. Stir to coat 2-3 times. Combine water, chicken broth, garlic, thyme, salt and pepper in a Dutch oven. Bring to boil and stir in uncooked chicken. Reduce heat to simmer and continue cooking 20 minutes. Pour broth through a sieve for a clear broth. Put chicken back into broth and add noodles. Continue cooking for 10 more minutes, stirring occasionally. Stir in vegetables and serve.

*SERVES 6*

# Mulled Cider and Wine

4 cups apple cider
4 cups orange-pineapple juice
½ cup sugar
6 cinnamon sticks
1 teaspoon whole allspice
1 teaspoon whole cloves

1 (2 inch) piece fresh ginger, peeled
   and sliced
1 lemon, sliced
1 orange, sliced
4 cups red wine

In large pan combine cider, orange-pineapple juice, sugar, cinnamon sticks, allspice, cloves, ginger, lemon and orange slices. Simmer 30 minutes. Add the red wine, stir well and heat thoroughly. Strain and serve warm.

*SERVES 12*

# Avoid the Tomatoes Bruschetta

1 loaf ciabatta bread
Extra virgin olive oil
Sea salt
Ground black pepper

¼ pound sliced goat cheese
¼ cup pistachios, toasted
½ cup sliced, pitted dates
Balsamic vinegar reduction

Light your charcoal or gas grill. Slice ciabatta bread into ½ inch slices. Brush each slice with olive oil and season with sea salt and freshly ground pepper. Grill slices on both sides until lightly browned. Top each slice with a thick layer of fresh goat cheese. Lightly press toasted pistachios into the cheese and top with sliced, pitted dates. Drizzle with olive oil and balsamic vinegar reduction. Cut into quarters, arrange on a platter and serve.

*SERVES 10*

Balsamic reduction can be purchased in stores or made with 1 cup balsamic vinegar in a small saucepan. Bring it to a boil. Reduce heat to lowest temperature and cook until thick, 30-40 minutes. Drizzle with your favorite honey.

# Sun-Dried Tomato and Spinach Torta

4 (8 ounce) packages cream cheese
1½ cups grated Parmesan cheese
¾ cup crumbled feta cheese
1 teaspoon garlic powder

1 cup frozen spinach, thawed and drained completely
1 cup chopped sun-dried tomatoes
1 cup toasted pine nuts
1 (3 ounce) jar prepared pesto

In a large mixing bowl combine cream cheese, Parmesan cheese and crumbled feta cheese with garlic powder. Beat with electric mixer until well combined. Divide cheese mixture into thirds. Combine ⅓ cheese mixture and spinach and set aside. Line an 8 inch round cake pan with plastic wrap. Spread ⅓ of cheese mixture in bottom of pan. Layer half of tomatoes on cheese. Spread spinach mixture over tomatoes. Layer remaining tomatoes on top of spinach mixture. Top with remaining cheese mixture. Refrigerate 1 hour. Invert onto serving dish and remove from pan. Carefully remove plastic wrap. Cover sides of torta with pine nuts. Spread pesto on top. Cover and refrigerate until ready to serve. Serve with crackers.

*SERVES 15-20*

# Chicken in a Hurry

2 frying chickens or 8 breast halves
1 (8 ounce) bottle Russian salad dressing

1 (18 ounce) jar apricot preserves
1 envelope dry onion soup mix

Skin chicken, if desired, and place pieces in single layer in large baking dish. Combine remaining ingredients, spread over chicken and marinate several hours or overnight. Preheat oven to 275°. Bake uncovered for 2 hours. Baste occasionally with sauce while baking. Serve with rice or mashed potatoes and drizzle with remaining sauce.

*SERVES 6*

Accompany with Baked Apricot Casserole

# Cheese Grits Soufflé

6 cups boiling water
2 teaspoons salt
1½ cups quick cooking grits
¾ cup butter

1 pound grated Cheddar cheese plus
   extra for topping
4 eggs, beaten

Preheat oven to 350°. Combine water, salt and grits and cook for 5 minutes. Remove from heat and in order add butter, eggs and cheese. Stir until smooth. Pour into buttered 2½ quart casserole and bake 1 hour. Sprinkle lightly with grated cheese as soon as you remove it from oven.

*SERVES 10*

This recipe makes a good luncheon dish as well as a substitute for starchy vegetable with meats. It can also be cut in half.

# Fennel and Red Onion Salad

¼ cup whole berry cranberry sauce
2 tablespoons aged balsamic vinegar
¼ cup extra virgin olive oil
Salt and freshly ground pepper
1 fennel bulb, thinly sliced by hand

1 small red onion, thinly sliced by hand
1 large heart of romaine lettuce,
   chopped
½ cup dried cranberries
1 cup walnuts, toasted

In a medium bowl combine cranberry sauce and vinegar. Whisk in olive oil and season with salt and pepper. Combine with the fennel, onion, romaine lettuce, cranberries and toasted walnuts and toss to coat.

*SERVES 4*

# Baked Apricot Casserole

1 (17 ounce) can apricot halves, drained
1 cup light brown sugar, firmly packed

1½ cups butter cracker crumbs
½ cup butter

Preheat oven to 350°. In a greased casserole dish arrange apricot halves cut side up. Sprinkle apricots with brown sugar and top with cracker crumbs. Dot crumbs with butter. Bake for 35 minutes or until the casserole has thickened and is crusty on top.

*SERVES 4-6*

# Apple-Pecan Pie Cobbler

6 large Granny Smith apples, peeled and sliced
½ cup firmly packed light brown sugar

2 tablespoons all-purpose flour
¼ cup butter
½ cup dark corn syrup

**PECAN MUFFIN BATTER**

1 cup firmly packed light brown sugar
1 cup chopped pecans
½ cup all-purpose flour
½ teaspoon baking powder

¼ teaspoon salt
½ cup butter, melted
2 eggs, lightly beaten
1 teaspoon vanilla extract

Preheat oven to 425°. Toss together apples, brown sugar and flour. In large skillet melt butter. Add apple mixture and corn syrup to skillet and bring to a boil, stirring often. Cook 10 minutes. Divide hot apple mixture evenly between 6 lightly greased, 6 ounce, ovenproof ramekins or custard cups. For the muffin batter, combine brown sugar, pecans, flour, baking powder and salt. Stir together butter, eggs and vanilla. Add to dry ingredients and stir just until moistened. Spoon pecan pie muffin batter evenly over hot apple mixture. Bake for 15-20 minutes or until golden brown.

*SERVES 6*

May also use 3 (12 ounce) frozen cooked apples, thawed.

# Sweet Potato Biscuits and Butter

1 cup mashed cooked sweet potatoes
   (may use canned) at room
   temperature, divided
2 tablespoons brown sugar
1¼ cups heavy cream
3 cups self-rising flour

½ cup unsalted butter, softened
2 tablespoons honey
1 teaspoon grated lemon zest
¼ teaspoon salt
¼ teaspoon black pepper
¼ teaspoon cayenne pepper

Preheat oven to 450°. Lightly grease large baking sheet. In small bowl whisk together ¾ cup sweet potato, brown sugar and heavy cream until blended. Add flour; stir with fork until dough begins to come together. With hands, gather dough into ball. On floured surface, knead lightly 10 times. Roll out and cut into 12 biscuits. Place 1 inch apart on prepared sheet. Bake 12 minutes until golden brown and remove to wire rack to cool slightly. In the meantime, in small bowl, combine remaining ¼ cup sweet potato, butter, honey, lemon zest, salt, pepper and cayenne. With electric mixer whip up and serve with biscuits.

*SERVES 12*

# Honey Gingered Pork Tenderloin

2 (¾ pound) pork tenderloins
¼ cup honey
¼ cup soy sauce
¼ cup oyster sauce
2 tablespoons brown sugar
1 tablespoon plus 1 teaspoon minced
   fresh gingerroot

1 tablespoon minced garlic
1 tablespoon ketchup
¼ teaspoon onion powder
¼ teaspoon ground red pepper
¼ teaspoon ground cinnamon

Place tenderloins in a zip-top plastic bag. Combine honey, soy sauce, oyster sauce, brown sugar, gingerroot, garlic, ketchup, onion powder, pepper and cinnamon. Stir well. Pour over the tenderloins in the bag, seal tightly and refrigerate 8 hours or overnight, turning occasionally. Remove tenderloins and reserve marinade. Grill tenderloins over medium-hot coals 25-35 minutes. Turn and baste often with marinade. Tenderloins may also be cooked in glass pan, in 350° oven, 40 minutes or until meat reaches 150°. Pour marinade over tenderloins before baking. Let rest 10 minutes and slice thinly to serve. If baked in oven, marinade may be served on the side as sauce.

*SERVES 6-8*

# Chocolate-Praline Pecan Cake

1½ cups semisweet chocolate morsels
½ cup butter, softened
1 (16 ounce) package light brown
   sugar
3 eggs
2 cups all-purpose flour

1 teaspoon baking soda
½ teaspoon salt
1 (8 ounce) container sour cream
1 cup hot water
4 teaspoons vanilla extract, divided

**TOPPING**

2 cups firmly packed brown sugar
⅔ cup whipping cream
½ cup butter

2 cups powdered sugar, sifted
2 cups chopped pecans, toasted

Preheat oven to 350°. Melt chocolate morsels in a microwave-safe bowl on high for 30 second intervals, stirring after each, until melted and smooth (about 1½ minutes total time). Beat softened butter and brown sugar at medium speed with an electric mixer about 5 minutes, until well blended. Add eggs, one at a time, just until blended after each addition. Add melted chocolate, beating until blended. Sift together flour, soda and salt. Gradually add dry ingredients to chocolate mixture alternately with sour cream, blending after each addition, beginning and ending with flour mixture. Beat at low speed just until blended. Gradually add hot water in a slow steady stream, beating at low speed just until blended. Stir in 2 teaspoons vanilla. Spoon batter evenly into 2 greased and floured aluminum foil lined 9x9 inch square pans. Bake for 40 minutes or until a toothpick inserted in center comes out clean. Cool in pans on wire racks. Bring 2 cups brown sugar, whipping cream and ½ cup butter to a boil in a 3 quart saucepan over medium heat. Stir often and boil 1 minute. Remove from heat, whisk in powdered sugar and remaining 2 teaspoons vanilla. Add pecans, stirring gently 3-5 minutes or until mixture begins to cool and thicken slightly. Pour immediately over cakes in pans. Cool completely and cut into squares.

*SERVES 18*

JCYM identified and filled a great need in Johnson County when we established Temporary Lodging for Children (now Kids TLC) in 1971. This emergency shelter provides help to young victims of abuse, neglect and family disruptions as well as support and education for those families and street outreach to youth who have left their family homes. We continue to support this agency both financially and through volunteer efforts.

# Indian Summer Gratin

1 tablespoon plus ½ teaspoon unsalted butter

4 slices bacon

1½ cups fresh bread crumbs

½ cup plus 2 tablespoons grated Parmigiano-Reggiano cheese

1 tablespoon extra virgin olive oil

1½ teaspoons chopped thyme, divided

1 large leek (white and light green parts only), halved and sliced ¼ inch thick, well rinsed and drained

2 teaspoons minced fresh garlic

1¾ to 2 cups fresh corn kernels (3-4 large ears)

⅔ cup heavy cream

¾ cup low sodium chicken broth

½ teaspoon lemon zest

2½ cups peeled and seeded butternut squash, cut into ½ inch dice

1½ cups Yukon gold potatoes, cut into ⅓ inch dice

Salt

Black pepper

Preheat oven to 400°. Position oven rack in the center of your oven. Grease 2 quart dish with ½ teaspoon butter. In 12 inch skillet, over medium heat, cook bacon until crisp. Transfer to paper towels. Reserve 2 tablespoons of bacon grease. When bacon is cool, crumble and place in bowl with bread crumbs, 2 tablespoons cheese, olive oil, half of the thyme and a large pinch of salt. Mix well. Set aside. Add remaining 1 tablespoon butter to the bacon grease in skillet and melt over medium heat. Add leeks and a pinch of salt and cook, stirring often, until softened and golden. Add garlic, stir well, and add corn, ¼ teaspoon salt and a pinch of pepper. Cook, stirring, until corn is slightly shrunken. Cool slightly. In a bowl combine cream, chicken broth, lemon zest, ½ teaspoon salt and ¼ teaspoon pepper. Mix well and set aside. In large bowl, combine bacon, corn-leek mixture, diced squash, diced potatoes and 1 teaspoon thyme. Toss to combine well. Spread mixture evenly in gratin dish. Sprinkle with remaining cheese over top. Stir cream mixture one more time and pour over all. Press down on vegetables with spatula so liquid is distributed evenly. Sprinkle bread crumb mixture over all. Cover with foil and bake 20 minutes. Remove foil and continue baking 25 minutes. Liquid should have bubbled below surface of vegetables, leaving browned bits around edge of pan. Cool 20 minutes before serving.

*SERVES 4 AS MAIN DISH OR 6 AS SIDE*

# Hot Mexican Cider

5 cups apple cider
¼ cup fresh lemon juice
½ teaspoon salt

1⅔ cups tequila
⅓ cup orange-flavored liqueur
8 lemon slices for garnish

In saucepan combine cider, lemon juice and salt. Bring mixture to a simmer. Add tequila and liqueur. Place over medium heat, stirring until hot. Divide mixture into 8 mugs. Garnish with lemon slices and serve.

*SERVES 8*

# Tangy Herb Cheese Spread

8 ounces sour cream
¼ cup chopped chives
¼ cup chopped parsley
¼ cup chopped shallots

2 teaspoons salt
1 tablespoon minced garlic
2 (8 ounce) packages cream cheese
4 ounce log goat cheese

In a food processor combine sour cream, chives, parsley, shallots, salt and garlic. Blend until smooth. Add cream cheese and goat cheese and blend until all ingredients are mixed well. Serve in medium bowl with water crackers. Garnish with chopped chives on top. May be made a day ahead.

*SERVES 24*

# Buffalo Chicken Dip

4 boneless, skinless chicken breast
   halves, boiled and shredded
   (about 2 pounds)
1 (12 ounce) bottle hot pepper sauce

2 (8 ounce) packages cream cheese
1 (16 ounce) bottle ranch dressing
8 ounces sharp Cheddar cheese, grated

Preheat oven to 375°. In 9x13 inch pan, combine chicken and hot sauce, spreading out in 1 layer. In saucepan, combine cream cheese and ranch dressing over medium heat, stirring until smooth. (You may also place cream cheese in microwave-safe bowl, on high, 1-2 minutes.) Stir in ranch dressing. Pour this mixture over the chicken, spreading evenly. Sprinkle with Cheddar cheese. Bake uncovered 30 minutes or until bubbly. Watch that it doesn't get too brown. Serve hot or warm with corn chips and/or celery.

*SERVES 4 CUPS*

# Crab and Artichoke Appetizer Pizza

1 (12 inch) prepared pizza crust

1 (14 ounce) can water-packed artichoke hearts, drained and chopped

1 (4 ounce) can lump or backfin crabmeat

⅔ cup grated Parmesan cheese

½ cup light mayonnaise

1 teaspoon minced garlic

¼ teaspoon salt

⅛ teaspoon black pepper

¼ cup pitted, sliced Kalamata olives, well drained

¼ cup finely chopped red bell pepper

Preheat oven according to pizza crust package directions. Crisp the crust until golden brown. Carefully remove crust from oven and set aside. Combine chopped artichoke hearts, crabmeat, cheese, mayonnaise, garlic, salt and pepper, stirring to mix well. Spread mixture over crust, out to edges. Top with olives. Return pizza to oven and bake 12-15 minutes or until top is slightly brown and bubbling along the edges. Remove and scatter red pepper over the crust. Cut into small squares and serve warm.

*SERVES 8*

# Tijuana Tidbits

4 cups tortilla chips, broken into 1½ inch pieces

3 cups crispy corn cereal

1 (3.5 ounce) bag microwave popcorn, popped

1 (12 ounce) can mixed cocktail nuts

½ cup light corn syrup

½ cup butter

1 cup firmly packed brown sugar

1 tablespoon chili powder

⅛ teaspoon cinnamon

⅛ to ⅓ teaspoon ground red pepper, optional

Preheat oven to 250°. Combine chips, cereal, popcorn and nuts in large roasting pan. In saucepan combine corn syrup, butter, brown sugar, chili powder, cinnamon and pepper. Heat to boiling. Pour over cereal mixture in pan, stirring to coat well. Bake 1 hour, stirring every 20 minutes. Remove from oven and turn onto sheet of waxed paper. Let cool. Store in airtight container up to 2 weeks.

*SERVES 18-20*

# Roasted Butternut Squash & Curry Soup

3 to 4 pounds butternut squash,
  peeled and seeded

2 yellow onions

2 McIntosh apples, peeled and cored

3 tablespoons olive oil

Kosher salt and pepper to taste

2-4 cups chicken stock

½ teaspoon curry

**CONDIMENTS**

1 bunch green onions (both green and
  white part) diced diagonally

1 cup flaked, sweetened coconut,
  lightly toasted

1 cup cashews, roasted and chopped

1 banana, diced

Preheat oven 425°. Cut butternut squash, onions and apples into 1 inch cubes. Place on sheet pan and toss with olive oil, salt and pepper. Divide the squash mixture into two sheet pans and spread in a single layer. Roast 35-45 minutes, tossing occasionally until very tender. Meanwhile, heat chicken stock to a simmer. When vegetables are done, place in food processor in batches and process using the steel blade. Add some chicken stock and coarsely purée. When all vegetables have been processed, place them in large pot and add enough chicken stock to make a thick soup. Add curry powder, 1 teaspoon salt and ½ teaspoon pepper. Taste to be sure you have a good curry flavor. Reheat and serve hot with condiments either on the side or on top of each serving.

*Acorn squash may be used instead of butternut squash.*

*SERVES 4-6*

# French Dip Sandwiches

3 to 4 pound beef pot roast

1 (14 ounce) can beef broth

1 (12 ounce) can beer

1 (10.5 ounce) can condensed French
  onion soup

1 large onion, sliced

8-10 hoagies or ciabatta rolls

Remove fat from beef. Cut roast to fit into 3½-6 quart slow-cooker. Add broth, beer, soup and onion. Cover and cook on low heat setting 8-10 hours or on high setting for 5 hours. Remove meat from cooker. Using two forks, shred the meat. Serve on rolls. Pour remaining juices into individual serving bowls to use for dipping.

*SERVES 8-10*

# Peanut Butter and Toffee Candy Bark

1 pound bittersweet chocolate chips
1 (⅔ ounce) Butterfinger candy bar, cut into 1 inch wedges
8 (.55 ounce) peanut butter cups, cut into 1 inch wedges
¼ cup honey roasted peanuts

3 ounces high quality white chocolate, chopped
3 ounces mini candy-coated peanut butter pieces, optional
3 ounces candy-coated chocolate pieces, optional

Line baking sheet with foil. Place chocolate chips in medium heavy saucepan and stir over low heat until melted. Pour onto foil lined pan and spread to ¼ inch thickness. Place white chocolate in small, heavy saucepan. Stir constantly over very low heat, until melted and warm, not hot. Remove from heat. Dip spoon into white chocolate and wave from side to side, in zigzag motion, over bark. Scatter candy pieces over making sure they touch melted chocolate. Chill 30 minutes or until firm. Slide foil with candy onto work surface. Peel off foil. Cut bark into irregular pieces.

*SERVES 30*

# Candy Corn Popcorn Balls

8 cups popped light butter microwave popcorn
1 cup candy corn
¼ cup butter

¼ teaspoon salt
1 (10 ounce) bag marshmallows
Cooking spray

Combine popcorn and candy corn in large bowl. Over medium heat, place ¼ cup butter in saucepan and melt. Stir in ¼ teaspoon salt and marshmallows. Reduce heat to low. Cook 7 minutes, stirring constantly or until marshmallows melt and mixture is smooth. Combine marshmallow mixture with the popcorn mixture. Spray hands with cooking spray. Shape popcorn mixture into 20 (2-inch balls).

*SERVES 20*

# Best Bloody Mary

1 quart clamato juice
½ cup fresh lime juice
2 tablespoons horseradish (or to taste)
4 to 5 dashes Worcestershire sauce

1 teaspoon celery seed
1½ cups vodka
Lime wedges for garnish

Combine clamato juice, lime juice, Worcestershire sauce, celery seed and vodka in large pitcher. Stir very well. Serve over ice garnished with lime wedges.

*SERVES 8*

# Divine Egg Casserole

18 hard-boiled eggs, sliced
½ pound bacon
¼ cup butter
½ cup flour
1 cup half and half
1 cup milk
1 pound grated sharp Cheddar cheese
½ teaspoon salt

¼ teaspoon white pepper
1 clove garlic, crushed
¼ teaspoon marjoram
¼ teaspoon thyme
¼ teaspoon basil
¼ cup parsley, freshly minced
1½ to 2 cups dried bread crumbs
2 tablespoons melted butter

Preheat oven to 350°. Fry bacon until crisp. Crumble and set aside. Make sauce of butter, flour, half and half and milk. Heat over low heat until thickened. Add cheese to sauce and stir until melted. Add salt, pepper, garlic, seasonings and parsley to sauce. Remove from heat. In greased 9x13 inch casserole, assemble egg casserole in layers. First, cover bottom of casserole dish with ½ of sliced eggs. Next, sprinkle with ½ of bacon and then cover with ½ of sauce, repeat layers; top with bread crumbs. Drizzle with melted butter. Bake for 20 minutes, uncovered. Allow to sit 10 minutes before serving. May make ahead (except for bread crumbs) and refrigerate. If refrigerated, bake for 45 minutes.

*SERVES 12*

# Crescent Rolls Bars

2 tubes crescent rolls
2 cups sugar, divided
1 (8 ounce) package cream cheese
1 teaspoon vanilla extract
⅓ cup butter, melted
1 tablespoon cinnamon

Preheat oven to 350°. Using vegetable spray, spray bottom only of a 9x13 inch pan. Unroll crescent rolls. Spread 1 roll in pan and press to cover bottom only. Mix cream cheese, 1 cup sugar and vanilla. Spread over crescent dough. Unroll second tube of crescent rolls. Spread over cheese mixture. Melt ⅓ cup butter and spread over crescent dough. Combine 1 cup sugar mixed with 1 tablespoon cinnamon and sprinkle over melted butter. Bake approximately 35 minutes or until toothpick inserted in center of crust comes out clean. Best when served warm or at room temperature.

*SERVES 24*

# Slow Cooker Pulled-Pork Sandwiches

1 large yellow onion, sliced
¾ cup tomato salsa (medium heat)
⅓ cup plus 2 tablespoons cider vinegar
⅓ cup firmly packed light brown sugar
1 tablespoon ground cumin
1 tablespoon chili powder
Kosher salt to taste
4 to 4½ pound bone-in pork shoulder, trimmed
3 tablespoons tomato paste
Toasted hamburger buns

In a 4-quart slow cooker, combine onion, salsa, ⅓ cup vinegar, brown sugar, cumin, chili powder and salt. Add pork shoulder and turn to coat well. Cover slow cooker and cook 5-6 hours on high or 7-8 hours on low. Transfer pork to cutting board. Using two forks, shred the pork. Discard bone and fat. Put 1 cup juice and onions from slow cooker in large bowl. Whisk in the tomato paste, 2 tablespoons vinegar and kosher salt. Add pulled pork and stir to combine well. If pork seems dry, add more juices from slow cooker as needed. Mound shredded pork on toasted hamburger buns.

*SERVES 12-16*

# Mexican Salsa

2 (14.5 ounce) cans stewed tomatoes

2 (8 ounce) cans mushrooms, drained
and chopped fine

2 (2.5 ounce) cans chopped ripe olives

2 (4 ounce) cans green chilies
(do not drain)

6 green onions, chopped

Garlic powder to taste

Seasoned salt to taste

Pepper to taste

4 tablespoons vinegar

5 tablespoons light olive oil

In a large bowl, combine stewed tomatoes, mushrooms, olives, chilies, onions, garlic powder, salt, pepper, vinegar and olive oil. Mix well, cover and refrigerate until well chilled. Serve with tortilla chips. Variation: May substitute one can Mexican style tomatoes for one can stewed tomatoes.

*SERVES 8-10*

# Meatloaf Sliders

8 ounces 97 percent fat-free ground
beef

¼ cup finely chopped onion

1 egg

¼ cup plain bread crumbs

2 tablespoons low-fat milk

¼ cup grated Parmesan cheese

2 teaspoons chopped fresh parsley,
optional

1½ teaspoons Worcestershire sauce

1½ teaspoons Dijon mustard

¼ teaspoon salt

⅛ teaspoon ground black pepper

2 teaspoons vegetable oil

¼ cup ketchup

6 whole-wheat slider buns

In medium bowl, combine ground beef, onion, egg, bread crumbs, low-fat milk, Parmesan cheese, parsley, Worcestershire sauce, Dijon mustard, salt and black pepper. Mix well and form into 6 (3 inch) patties. Heat oil in skillet over medium heat. Cook patties 4 minutes on each side, or until cooked to desired doneness. Top patties with ketchup. Serve on slider buns.

*SERVES 6*

# Red Bean Toss

1 (14.5 ounce) can red kidney beans
   (rinsed and drained)
1 cup chopped celery
⅓ cup chopped sweet pickle or relish
¼ cup chopped onion
1 cup sharp Cheddar cheese, diced

½ teaspoon salt
½ teaspoon chili powder
½ teaspoon Worcestershire sauce
Few drops hot pepper sauce
½ cup mayonnaise
1 cup crushed corn chips

Preheat oven to 425°. Combine kidney beans, celery, sweet pickle relish, onion and cheese. Blend salt, chili powder, Worcestershire sauce and hot pepper sauce with mayonnaise. Add to bean mixture and toss lightly. Turn into greased 1 quart baking dish; sprinkle with corn chips. Bake until it bubbles.

*SERVES 4*

Best to make the day ahead so the flavors blend. Add crushed chips and bake.

# Raspberry Black Bean Salsa

2 (14.5 ounce) cans black beans, rinsed
   and drained
1 (8 ounce) package cream cheese,
   softened

½ (16 ounce) jar raspberry salsa
1 (8 ounce) block hot pepper jack
   cheese, shredded

Preheat oven to 275°. Grease an 8x11 inch dish with vegetable spray. Cover bottom of pan with black beans. Dab cream cheese over beans. Pour salsa over cream cheese. Cover with hot pepper jack cheese. Bake for 35 minutes.

*SERVES 10-12*

# Apple Slaw

½ to 1 cup light sour cream
½ to 1 cup light mayonnaise
1½ to 2 tablespoons white vinegar
1 teaspoon sugar
½ teaspoon salt
½ teaspoon pepper

2 cups red apples, unpeeled and chopped
3 to 4 green onions, diced
¼ to ½ cup sliced almonds
½ to 1 cup dried cranberries
1 (16 ounce) package cabbage and carrot coleslaw

Combine sour cream, mayonnaise, vinegar, sugar, salt and pepper. Blend well. Add apples, green onions, almonds, cranberries, cabbage and carrot slaw. Stir well.

*SERVES 8*

May be made the night before. Let sit out 15-20 minutes before serving.

# Indoor Barbecue Beef Brisket

4 to 5 pound beef brisket
1 medium onion, diced
3 cloves garlic, minced
1 jalapeño pepper, stemmed, seeded, minced
Salt and pepper to taste

2 cups hickory or mesquite smoke-flavored barbecue sauce
¼ cup Worcestershire sauce
¼ cup white vinegar
2 tablespoons brown sugar
2 tablespoons liquid smoke flavoring
1 teaspoon salt

Season brisket with salt and pepper. In large Dutch oven, sear brisket on all sides over high heat. Reduce heat and add enough water to cover. Add onion, garlic and jalapeño pepper. Bring to boil, lower heat and simmer for 2 hours. Remove meat reserving liquid. Preheat oven to 250°. Return brisket to Dutch oven. Combine barbecue sauce, vinegar, Worcestershire sauce, brown sugar, liquid smoke and salt. Pour over brisket, cover and bake 4 hours. While brisket is cooking, place reserved liquid in saucepan and reduce by ⅔ over medium heat. Keep warm. Remove brisket from Dutch oven and allow to cool 15 minutes. Before serving, pour liquid over sliced brisket.

*SERVES 6-8*

# White Chocolate Chunk Cookies

⅔ cup butter, softened
⅔ cup brown sugar
2 eggs
1½ cups old-fashioned oats
1½ cups flour

1 teaspoon baking soda
½ teaspoon salt
1 (6 ounce) package dried cranberries
⅔ cup white chocolate chunks or chips

Preheat oven to 375°. Using electric mixer, beat butter and sugar until light and fluffy. Add eggs, mixing well. Combine oatmeal, flour, baking soda and salt in separate bowl. Add to butter mixture in several additions, mixing well after each addition. Stir in dried cranberries and chocolate chunks. Drop by rounded teaspoonfuls onto ungreased cookie sheets. Bake 10-12 minutes or until golden brown. Cool on wire rack.

*SERVES 30*

# Symphony Brownies

1 package brownie mix for 9x13 pan

3 (8 ounce) chocolate bars with almonds and toffee chips

Prepare brownie mix according to package directions. Spoon half of the brownie mix into greased 9x13 pan. Place 3 chocolate bars side by side on the batter. Cover with remaining batter. Bake according to package directions. Cool completely before cutting.

*SERVES 24*

# Cornucopia Mix

1 (14.5 ounce) package cone-shaped corn chips
1 (12 ounce) can mixed nuts with cashews
2 egg whites

2 tablespoons orange juice
1⅓ cups sugar
2 teaspoons cinnamon
1 cup dried cranberries (or dried cherries)

Preheat oven to 275°. Grease jelly roll pan. Mix corn chips and nuts. Beat egg whites, orange juice, sugar and cinnamon with whisk until foamy. Toss with chip mix. Bake 15 minutes. Stir mix, add cranberries and bake another 15 minutes, stirring once.

*SERVES 15-20*

# Blood Orange Martinis

4 cups blood orange juice
2 cups orange-flavored vodka
1 cup orange liqueur

Coarse sugar, optional
Blood orange slices, optional

Combine orange juice, vodka and orange liqueur in large pitcher. Cover and chill until ready to serve. Pour into sugar-rimmed glasses and garnish, if desired, with thinly sliced blood oranges.

*SERVES 14*

For sugared rims, dip rims of stemmed glasses in thin coating of light corn syrup or water and then dip rims in plateful of coarse sugar.

# Honey Wheat Casserole Bread

1½ cups bread flour or all-purpose flour, divided
1 cup whole wheat flour
3 tablespoons non-fat dry milk
1 package regular active yeast

1 teaspoon salt
2 tablespoons honey
2 tablespoons oil
1 cup hot water
1 tablespoon wheat germ

In large mixing bowl, mix ½ cup bread flour, 1 cup wheat flour, dry milk, yeast, salt, honey and oil. Mix at low speed until blended. With mixer still going, add hot water and continue mixing at high speed for 3 minutes until dough is smooth. Gradually add remaining 1 cup flour, mixing at high speed until smooth. Turn dough into a greased 2 quart casserole. Sprinkle wheat germ on top. Let rise in a warm place until almost doubled, about 45 minutes. Bake at 375° for 20-30 minutes or until wooden skewer inserted in center comes out clean. Cool 10 minutes before removing from casserole.

*SERVES 8-10*

# Crabby Dip

1 (3 ounce) package cream cheese, at room temperature

¼ cup sour cream (not reduced fat)

3 tablespoons mayonnaise

1 small onion (for ½ teaspoon juice)

1½ teaspoons fresh lemon juice

¾ teaspoon seafood seasoning

½ teaspoon Worcestershire sauce

8 ounces pasteurized, refrigerated crabmeat

Thick cocktail bread slices, for serving

Preheat oven to 350°. Spray a ceramic or glass 1 quart baking dish with cooking spray and set aside. In medium bowl, combine cream cheese, sour cream and mayonnaise. Peel onion and grate over waxed paper, using smallest holes of grater; juice will puddle at the bottom of the grater. Scoop up ½ teaspoon juice and add to cream cheese mixture. Reserve remaining onion for another use. Stir in lemon juice, seafood seasoning and Worcestershire sauce. Drain crab and pick over carefully to remove pieces of shell. Add crabmeat to cream cheese mixture and fold well. Spread mixture in prepared pan. Cover and refrigerate up to 24 hours or may bake right away in preheated oven 20 minutes or until lightly browned and bubbly. Serve hot with cocktail bread slices.

*SERVES 8*

Bake slightly longer if refrigerated.

# Fall Fling Salad

8 cups mixed salad greens

½ cup cooked couscous

2 Granny Smith apples, sliced

½ cup baby beets, peeled and cooked as desired

½ cup Mandarin oranges, segmented

½ cup dried cranberries

3 to 4 slices red onion

¼ cup candied walnuts

¼ cup crumbled feta cheese, optional

Poppy seed dressing (your favorite)

In large bowl layer mixed greens, couscous, apples, beets, oranges, cranberries, onion, walnuts and feta cheese. Top with your favorite poppy seed salad dressing.

*SERVES 4*

# Pumpkin Cheese Ball

2 (8 ounce) blocks extra-sharp Cheddar cheese, shredded

1 (8 ounce) package cream cheese, softened

1 (8 ounce) container chive-onion cream cheese

2 teaspoons paprika

½ teaspoon ground red pepper

1 broccoli stalk

Red and green apple wedges

Combine Cheddar cheese, cream cheese, chive-onion cream cheese, paprika and red pepper. Cover and chill 4 hours or until mixture is firm enough to be shaped. Shape mixture into a ball, resembling a pumpkin. Smooth entire outer surface with a frosting spatula or butter knife. Using fingertips, make vertical grooves in ball. Cut florets from broccoli stalk to resemble a pumpkin stem. Press into top of cheese ball. Serve cheese ball with apple wedges.

*SERVES 16*

To make ahead, wrap cheese ball in plastic wrap, without stalk, and store in refrigerator up to 2 days. Attach stalk before serving.

# Brandied Mushrooms

3 pounds fresh mushrooms

8 tablespoons butter

Seasoning salt

¼ cup Worcestershire sauce

½ cup brandy

Slice mushrooms lengthwise. In skillet, sauté mushrooms in butter until browned. Sprinkle with seasoning salt to taste. Add Worcestershire sauce and simmer until most of the sauce is absorbed by the mushrooms. Add brandy and continue simmering until mushrooms are tender.

*SERVES 4-6*

# Stuffed Turkey Roll

1 (8 ounce) package sliced fresh mushrooms

1 large onion, chopped

2 garlic cloves, minced

1 tablespoon melted butter

1 (10 ounce) box frozen spinach, thawed and well drained

1 cup Italian bread crumbs

½ cup grated Parmesan cheese

1 egg, beaten

½ teaspoon dried thyme

½ teaspoon dried oregano

1½ teaspoons salt, divided

1 teaspoon ground black pepper, divided

3 to 3½ pound boneless turkey breast

1 teaspoon rubbed sage

¼ teaspoon paprika

1 tablespoon butter, softened

Cooking string (for tying)

Preheat oven to 350°. Sauté mushrooms, onion and garlic in melted butter over medium heat until onions are tender. Set aside. Combine spinach, bread crumbs, Parmesan cheese, egg, thyme, oregano, ½ teaspoon salt and ½ teaspoon ground pepper. Stir in sautéed vegetables. Remove turkey breast from wrapper; place on plastic wrap. Pound breast to flatten to ½ inch thickness. Spread spinach filling over turkey. Roll up, tying securely with heavy string. Place seam side down in lightly greased roasting pan. Combine sage, 1 teaspoon salt, ½ teaspoon pepper and paprika. Rub softened butter over turkey roll; rub with seasonings. Bake uncovered for 1 hour 10 minutes or until meat thermometer reads 170°. Cover with aluminum foil and let rest for 15 minutes. Remove string and slice.

*SERVES 8*

# Cranberry Walnut Salad

16 cups mixed greens

1 cup sweetened, dried cranberries

1 cup walnuts, toasted

11 ounces goat cheese, crumbled

1 tablespoon Dijon mustard

¼ cup fresh lemon juice

2 tablespoons maple syrup

1 cup extra virgin olive oil

½ teaspoon salt

⅛ teaspoon fresh ground black pepper

Combine mustard, lemon juice, syrup, oil, salt and pepper and mix well. Cover and chill. Pour over greens, cranberries and walnuts. Top with goat cheese crumbles and serve.

*SERVES 8-10*

# Sweet Potato Crème Brûlée

1 large sweet potato, baked, skinned
and mashed (about 1¼ cups)
¼ cup firmly packed brown sugar
1 tablespoon fresh lemon juice
2 cups whipping cream

¼ cup sugar
7 egg yolks, lightly beaten
1 tablespoon vanilla extract
⅓ cup firmly packed brown sugar

Preheat oven to 325°. Combine mashed sweet potato, brown sugar and lemon juice. Spoon potato mixture into a buttered 10x2 inch quiche pan, to form a ¼ inch thick layer. Stir together cream, sugar, egg yolks and vanilla in medium saucepan. Cook over medium heat, stirring constantly, until hot. Do not boil. Pour over sweet potato mixture, place dish in a shallow pan. Add hot water to shallow pan, about halfway up the quiche pan. Bake for 1 hour or until knife inserted in center comes out almost clean. Carefully remove dish from water, cool on wire rack. Cover and chill for 8 hours. Sprinkle custard with ⅓ cup brown sugar. Place on cookie sheet and broil until sugar melts, 3-5 minutes. Let stand until sugar hardens.

*SERVES 8-10*

Can also be made in a glass pie pan or individual ramekins.

The annual Homes for the Holidays Tour held the third Wednesday in November has become a Kansas City tradition. Between 3,000 to 4,000 tour guests have the opportunity to explore five distinctive Johnson County homes lovingly decorated for the upcoming holiday seasons.

# European Chocolate Truffle Cake

8 ounces good quality semisweet
  chocolate

1 cup unsalted butter

**CHOCOLATE GANACHE ICING**

1 cup heavy whipping cream

10 ounces semisweet chocolate chips

1 cup sugar

4 eggs, well beaten

Whipped cream, optional

Preheat oven to 350°. Grease and line with foil an 8-inch springform pan. Melt butter in medium-sized glass bowl for 1-2 minutes. Add chocolate and microwave 30 seconds longer. Let sit about 3-4 minutes, add sugar and stir. When cool stir in beaten eggs. Pour batter into prepared pan and bake 30-35 minutes, or until crust forms on top. Cool to room temperature, then refrigerate overnight in pan. Remove from pan. Make ganache by putting whipping cream in large saucepan. Heat to almost boiling. Remove from burner, add chocolate chips and let sit for 4-5 minutes. Then stir to blend. Pour ganache over cake and spread over the top. It will be glossy. Carefully transfer iced cake onto serving plate. Serve each slice with a dollop of whipped cream if desired.

*SERVES 8-10*

May decorate with chocolate hearts for Valentine's; Easter eggs for Easter and any other decorations you prefer.

Heavy cream, bowl and beaters should be very cold before whipping. If you overwhip cream (it separates into solids and liquids), gently fold in a few tablespoons of milk or more cream.

# Fresh Pear Pie Streusel with Dried Cherries

## STREUSEL

1 cup unbleached all-purpose flour
½ cup old-fashioned rolled oats
½ cup firmly packed light brown sugar

¼ teaspoon salt
4 ounces unsalted butter, melted

## FILLING

3 pounds Anjou or Bartlett pears
   (5-6 medium), peeled, cored and
   cut lengthwise into 8 wedges, then
   crosswise into ½-inch thick slices
   (about 7 cups)
1½ tablespoons fresh lemon juice
⅔ cup sugar
¼ cup unbleached all-purpose flour

¼ teaspoon salt
¼ teaspoon ground cinnamon
⅛ teaspoon freshly grated nutmeg
¾ cup dried tart cherries, coarsely
   chopped
1 pie crust

Preheat oven to 425°. Prebake fork-pricked pie crust for 20 minutes. Remove from oven. Position rack in center of oven. Set heavy-duty rimmed baking sheet on the rack, and set oven to 350°. In medium bowl combine flour, oats, sugar and salt. Using your fingers, blend butter into flour mixture. The mixture will be moist. Set aside. In large bowl, toss pears with lemon juice. In small bowl, whisk sugar, flour, salt, cinnamon and nutmeg. Add sugar mixture to pears and toss well. Stir in cherries. Mound filling into pie crust. Sprinkle streusel topping over pear mixture, pressing streusel between your fingers into small lumps as you sprinkle them. Put pie on heated baking sheet and bake 55-60 minutes or until pastry is golden-brown, and the filling is bubbly and thickened around the edges. Transfer onto rack and cool completely before serving. Pie may be stored at room temperature for up to 2 days.

*SERVES 8*

We honor our founders by supporting philanthropies that serve from the youngest to the oldest members of our community. We provide historical educational opportunities to our school youth and guided tours for all ages. We help those who are abused and frightened. We help those who deal with physical and/or mental challenges daily. We better our community.

# Grand Marnier®-Glazed Carrots

3 tablespoons butter
1 pound baby carrots
3 tablespoons orange marmalade

⅓ cup Grand Marnier® liqueur
2 tablespoons chopped fresh parsley

Melt butter in large skillet over medium-high heat. Add carrots and toss to coat. Stir in marmalade and heat until melted. Add liqueur and bring to a boil. Lower heat and simmer, uncovered, 5 minutes. Uncover carrots and continue cooking, about 5 minutes, until tender and the liquid has been reduced to a glaze. Sprinkle with parsley and serve.

*SERVES 4*

If you do not have a bottle of Grand Marnier® on hand, you can always purchase small trial size bottles.

# Pumpkin-Pie Parfaits

13 gingersnaps, chocolate wafers or
graham crackers, divided
1 tablespoon unsalted butter, melted
¾ cup plus 1 tablespoon powdered
sugar

½ cup canned pure pumpkin
2½ teaspoons bourbon, divided
Pinch of freshly grated nutmeg
½ cup white chocolate chips
2 cups cold whipping cream, divided

Crush 7 cookies into crumbs. Brush bottoms and nearly 1 inch up the sides of 6 parfaits glasses with melted butter. Add a spoonful of crumbs in each glass and roll around to coat insides of glasses. Pour out excess crumbs and reserve for topping. Refrigerate prepared glasses. Put ¾ cup powdered sugar, pumpkin, 1½ teaspoons bourbon and the nutmeg in a food processor. Pulse 1 minute until smooth. Set aside. Place white chocolate chips in microwave-safe bowl and microwave on 50% power until chips are melted, about 1 minute, stirring halfway through. Add to pumpkin mixture and process until combined and then transfer to large bowl. Beat 1½ cups cream in a bowl until soft peaks form. Fold into the pumpkin mixture until smooth. Divide among prepared glasses and refrigerate until ready to serve. Before serving beat remaining cream with a mixer until foamy. Add remaining 1 tablespoon powdered sugar and 1 teaspoon bourbon and continue beating until soft peaks form. Top the parfaits with the whipped cream, reserved cookie crumbs and the remaining 6 cookies.

*SERVES 6*

# Red Wine Sangría

¾ cup simple syrup
 (½ cup each sugar and water)
2 bottles Spanish red wine
¾ cup brandy
½ cup triple sec

¾ cup orange juice
2 oranges, thinly sliced
2 Granny Smith apples, cored and
 thinly sliced
2 lemons, thinly sliced

To make simple syrup combine water and sugar in saucepan. Bring to boil. Reduce heat to simmer and continue simmering 5 minutes, stirring occasionally. Cool. Combine simple syrup, wine, brandy, triple sec, orange juice, oranges, apples and lemons in large pitcher. Refrigerate, covered, 2 hours or up to 2 days. Serve over ice. Can be frozen.

*SERVES 8*

# Salsa Cheesecake

1 (8 ounce) package cream cheese,
 softened
1 (8 ounce) package reduced fat
 cream cheese, softened
6 ounces shredded Monterey Jack
 cheese
½ cup Parmesan cheese
3 (8 ounce) containers light sour
 cream, divided

1 tablespoon flour
3 eggs
2 tablespoons sliced green onions
1 cup mild salsa
1 (4.25 ounce) can chopped green
 chilies
2 tablespoons diced red bell pepper
1 tablespoon fresh parsley
1 cup guacamole

Preheat oven to 350°. Beat cheeses at medium speed, with electric mixer, until light and fluffy. Add 1 container sour cream, flour and eggs. Beat until blended. Stir in green onions, salsa, chilies, bell pepper and parsley. Pour into 9 inch springform pan and bake for 45 minutes. Remove to wire rack to cool. Gently run knife around edges of pan before removing from pan. Cover and chill 6 hours or overnight. Spread guacamole over cheesecake. Garnish as desired.

*SERVES 20*

# Cowboy Caviar

1 (14.5 ounce) can shoe peg corn
1 (14.5 ounce) can black-eyed peas
2 tomatoes, chopped
½ bunch green onions, chopped
1 bunch cilantro or Italian parsley, chopped
1 (2.5 ounce) can diced green chilies

¼ cup red wine vinegar or balsamic vinegar
¼ cup olive oil
2 cloves garlic, minced
1 teaspoon cumin
Salt and pepper to taste

In a large bowl, combine corn, peas, tomatoes, onions, parsley, chilies, wine vinegar, olive oil, minced garlic, cumin, salt and pepper. Toss well and refrigerate, covered, a few hours. Serve with scoop corn chips.

*SERVES 6-8*

If your chips are stale pop them in the microwave for 30-60 seconds. Let stand for two minutes to crisp.

# Southwest Sweet Potato Hash

2 medium sweet potatoes
1 tablespoon vegetable oil
1 (11 ounce) can Southwestern-style corn with black beans and peppers, drained
½ cup sour cream

2 tablespoons chipotle salsa
3 medium avocados, sliced
Fresh cilantro and chili powder to taste
Salt to taste

Peel and quarter sweet potatoes. Place in microwave safe dish; cover and cook on high 5-8 minutes until tender. Cool slightly and cut into chunks. Sprinkle lightly with salt. In large skillet, heat oil over medium heat. Add potatoes, cook until browned and crisp, about 3 minutes. Add corn, cook about 3 minutes. Meanwhile, stir together sour cream and chipotle salsa. Transfer potato mixture to large bowl. Top with sliced avocados, cilantro leaves and chili powder. Serve with chipotle sour cream sauce.

*SERVES 4*

# Taco Chicken Soup

1 pre-cooked rotisserie chicken
4 (15 ounce) cans plain chicken broth
4 (15 ounce) cans chicken broth with Italian seasonings
1 (14.5 ounce) can tomatoes with chilies
1 (16 ounce) jar pizza sauce

1 small onion, chopped
1 cup grated carrots
1 cup celery, chopped
2 cups regular rice
1 pound shredded processed cheese loaf

Debone chicken and cut into bite-size pieces. In large Dutch oven, combine cut up chicken, all broth, tomatoes with chilies, pizza sauce, onion, carrots, celery and rice. Simmer until rice is cooked. Add shredded cheese and keep stirring until it melts. Soup might require more broth, depending on desired consistency.

*SERVES 12-16*

# Bourbon Panna Cotta

1½ cups sugar, divided
½ teaspoon fresh lemon juice
2 tablespoons water
4 cups whipping cream

½ cup pecans, toasted and chopped
3 tablespoons bourbon
2 cups whole milk
2 envelopes unflavored gelatin

Set out 8 (8 ounce) custard cups or ramekins. Combine ½ cup sugar, lemon juice and water in small heavy saucepan and bring to boil over high heat. Boil until the sugar dissolves. Reduce heat to medium, brush down the sides of saucepan with wet pastry brush to remove any sugar crystals. Cook, shaking the pan to swirl the caramel (do not stir) until it is mahogany in color, approximately 20 minutes. If the caramel is not dark enough, the flavor will be weak. If it's cooked too long, it will be bitter. Quickly spoon a little caramel into each custard cup, swirling it around to coat the bottom. Set aside. In medium saucepan, combine the cream, 1 cup sugar, pecans and bourbon and bring to a simmer over medium heat, 10 minutes. Remove from heat and set to cool a few moments. Meanwhile, put milk in medium bowl and sprinkle gelatin over the surface. Do not stir. Let gelatin soak 5 minutes, allowing a skin to form on the milk. Pour cream over gelatin mixture, whisking to dissolve. Strain and pour into the caramel-lined cups. Refrigerate at least 6 hours or overnight. Unmold by running a knife around the edge of each cup. Carefully flip panna cotta onto serving plate.

*SERVES 8*

# Green Onion Cornbread

5 tablespoons unsalted butter, divided  
1⅓ cups yellow stone-ground cornmeal  
¾ cup all-purpose flour  
3 tablespoons sugar  
1 teaspoon salt  
1 tablespoon plus 1 teaspoon baking powder

½ teaspoon baking soda  
1 cup milk  
1 egg  
½ cup chopped green onions  
1 tablespoon cracked black pepper

Preheat oven to 425°. In small saucepan melt 4 tablespoons butter. Remove from heat. Put remaining 1 tablespoon butter in 9 inch round cake pan or cast iron skillet. Heat the pan in oven while preparing the cornbread batter. In medium bowl, sift together cornmeal, flour, sugar, salt, baking powder and baking soda. In separate bowl, whisk together egg, milk, onions and pepper. Combine with dry ingredients and mix thoroughly. Pour into prepared cake pan or skillet and bake 35-40 minutes or until toothpick inserted in center of bread comes out clean. Cool in pan 15 minutes before serving.

*SERVES 6-8*

# Kahlúa Cake

1 box yellow cake mix  
1 (4 ounce) box vanilla pudding mix  
4 eggs  
1¼ cups strong coffee, divided  
½ cup vegetable oil

1 cup Kahlúa liqueur, divided  
½ cup butter  
½ cup sugar  
Vanilla ice cream, optional

Preheat oven to 350°. Combine cake mix, vanilla pudding, eggs, ¾ cup coffee, oil and ¾ cup Kahlúa. Mix well. Pour into greased Bundt pan (may also use a tube pan). Bake 45 minutes. Let cool 15 minutes; remove from pan. Meanwhile, prepare glaze by combining butter, coffee, sugar and Kahlúa in a saucepan. Bring to a boil over medium heat. Reduce heat and allow to simmer 5 minutes. Poke holes in cake using a toothpick. Spoon glaze over cake, using it all up. Cover and let sit 6 hours or overnight. Serve with small scoop of vanilla ice cream.

*SERVES 8-10*

# Peanut Butter Fudge Bars

1 cup creamy peanut butter
1 box yellow cake mix
½ cup melted butter plus
   2 tablespoons melted butter
2 eggs
1 (14 ounce) can sweetened condensed
   milk

2 teaspoons vanilla extract
½ teaspoon salt
1 (12 ounce) bag semisweet chocolate
   chips
1 cup coconut
1 cup finely chopped walnuts

Preheat oven to 350°. Combine cake mix, peanut butter, ½ cup melted butter and eggs. Stir until blended. Press ⅔ mixture into a 9x13 inch ungreased, pan. In separate bowl, combine condensed milk, 2 tablespoons melted butter, vanilla and salt. Stir in chocolate chips, coconut and walnuts. Spread over cake mix layer. Crumble reserved dough over all. Bake 25-30 minutes until golden. Cool overnight and cut into squares.

*SERVES 15-18*

# Famous French Onion Soup

3 pounds onions
½ cup butter
1½ teaspoons ground black pepper
2 tablespoons paprika
1 bay leaf
¾ cup all-purpose flour

3 quarts canned beef broth
1 cup white wine, optional
2 teaspoons salt, or to taste
Browning sauce, optional
6-8 slices French bread
6-8 slices Swiss cheese

Peel and slice onions ⅛ inch thick. Melt butter and sauté onions on low heat 1½ hours in large soup pot. Add pepper, paprika, bay leaf, flour, broth, wine and salt. Simmer 2 hours. Adjust color to rich brown, by using browning sauce. Season with salt to taste. Serve in ovenproof bowls, and top with ½ inch slice of French bread. Top bread with sliced Swiss cheese. Brown in broiler 3-5 minutes.

*SERVES 6-8*

# Autumn Soup

2 tablespoons olive oil
3 carrots, cut into medium chunks
1 large yellow onion, medium diced
2 cloves garlic, minced
2 cups butternut squash, peeled and
  cut into ½ inch cubes
¼ teaspoon ground allspice
Cayenne pepper to taste
Kosher salt to taste
1 quart low-salt chicken broth
1 (14.5 ounce) can no salt diced
  tomatoes
4 sprigs fresh thyme
2 cups, lightly packed, chopped kale
1 cup low-salt canned chickpeas

Heat oil in large soup pot over medium heat. Add carrots and onion and cook stirring occasionally until soft. Add garlic and continue cooking 1 minute. Add squash, allspice, cayenne and 1 teaspoon salt and stir well. Add broth, tomatoes with juice and thyme and bring to a boil. Reduce heat to medium. Cover and simmer 10 minutes. Add kale and chickpeas and cook uncovered until squash is tender and the kale has wilted, about 10 minutes. Discard thyme leaves before serving. Season to taste with additional salt and cayenne. May be refrigerated 3 days or frozen up to 2 months.

*SERVES 6-8*

Thyme leaves may be wrapped and tied in a bundle for easy removal.

# Amazing Margaritas

4 parts sweet and sour mix
1 part orange juice
⅛ part lime juice

2 parts tequila
¾ part Grand Marnier®

This recipe is designed to make as much as you need. Can substitute cups for parts and it would make almost 8 cups. Have plenty of supplies because guests will love this drink.

# Homemade Kahlúa

1 pound regular grind coffee
2 quarts water plus 6 cups
6 cups sugar

1 ounce vanilla extract
2 tablespoons chocolate syrup

In a large saucepan, bring 2 quarts (8 cups) of water and coffee to a boil for 6 minutes. Cool and strain. To make the simple syrup, bring the 6 cups of water and sugar to a boil for 10 minutes. Cool. Add sugar mixture, vanilla, coffee mixture and chocolate syrup together. Bottle in glass jars and age 4 weeks. If you can't wait, it is good right off the stove.

*MAKES 3½ TO 4 QUARTS*

# Passion Fruit Rum Punch

1 (12 ounce) can frozen passion fruit
    juice concentrate, thawed
1½ cups white rum
1 cup cold water

½ cup fresh lime juice
Crushed ice
1 lime, cut into 6 wedges (garnish)

Mix passion fruit concentrate, rum, water and lime juice in a large pitcher. Fill 6 glasses with ice and pour rum punch over it. Garnish each with a lime wedge and serve.

*SERVES 6*

# Chopped Mexican Salad with Veggies and Avocado

2 large orange or red bell peppers cored and seeded

2 ears fresh corn, husked

1 tablespoon extra virgin olive oil

¼ teaspoon Kosher salt

¼ teaspoon black pepper, ground

2 large avocados, peeled

2 large firm-ripe tomatoes, cored, seeded and cut into ¼ inch dice (about 1¾ cups)

1 small jicama, peeled and cut into ¼ inch dice (about 2½ cups)

1 (15 ounce) can black beans, drained and rinsed

¼ cup coarsely chopped fresh cilantro

**HONEY-LIME CUMIN VINAIGRETTE**

1 small clove garlic

¼ teaspoon Kosher salt

3 tablespoons fresh lime juice

3 tablespoons fresh orange juice

2 teaspoons chopped shallot

1 tablespoon honey, more to taste

¾ teaspoon cumin seeds, toasted and finely ground

¼ cup extra virgin olive oil

¼ teaspoon ground black pepper, to taste

Preheat oven to 425°. Cut peppers in half lengthwise, place on baking sheet place cut side down, along with the corn. Drizzle oil over the peppers and corn, coat thoroughly, and sprinkle with salt and pepper. Roast in oven about 20 minutes or until the peppers are soft, brown and slightly shriveled. The corn should be lightly brown in spots. Remove from oven, cool and scrape away the skin from the peppers, cut the kernels from the corn, set aside and let cool. Artfully arrange the corn, tomatoes, pepper, jicama, avocado and black beans in stripes or piles on a small platter or serving dish. Sprinkle with the chopped cilantro. Serve the vinaigrette in a pitcher or drizzle over the salad platter just before serving. For the vinaigrette: Mince and mash the garlic to a paste with ¼ teaspoon kosher salt. In a medium bowl, whisk the garlic paste with the lime and orange juices, shallot, honey and toasted ground cumin. Slowly add the oil in a thin stream, whisking until well blended. Season to taste with black pepper and add more salt and honey if needed.

*SERVES 8*

# Baby Romaine Salad with Spicy Chicken

8 cups loosely packed baby romaine lettuce

2 cups iceberg lettuce, thinly sliced, washed and dried

½ cup fresh cilantro leaves, loosely packed

1 chipotle chili (from a can of chipotle in adobo sauce) thinly chopped, plus 2 tablespoons adobo sauce

3 oil-packed sun-dried tomatoes, drained and chopped

2 tablespoons balsamic vinegar

2 teaspoons firmly packed light brown sugar

1 teaspoon Dijon mustard

½ cup plus 3 tablespoons extra virgin olive oil

Kosher salt and freshly ground black pepper

2 tablespoons all-purpose flour

2 tablespoons fine cornmeal (preferably white)

1 tablespoon chili powder

1 teaspoon ground cumin

1¼ pounds boneless, skinless chicken breast (about 3 small) cut crosswise into 1 inch strips

½ small red onion, thinly sliced, cut in half

1 ripe avocado, cut into ¾ inch pieces

1½ cups cooked fresh corn kernels

1 lime, cut into quarters

Toss the romaine, iceberg and half of the cilantro in a large bowl. In a blender or food processor purée the chipotle chili and adobo sauce, sun-dried tomatoes, vinegar, brown sugar and mustard. With the machine running, slowly pour in ½ cup of the oil. Transfer to a measuring cup; season to taste with salt and pepper. In a shallow dish, mix the flour, cornmeal, chili powder and cumin with 1½ teaspoons salt and ½ teaspoon pepper. Season the chicken with 1 teaspoon salt and dredge in the flour mixture. Heat 2 tablespoons of the remaining oil in a heavy nonstick skillet over medium heat until it simmers, about 1 minute. Add half the chicken strips, evenly spaced, cook without touching for 2 minutes. Transfer to a large plate, drain on paper towels and sprinkle with salt. Reduce the heat to medium, add the remaining 1 tablespoon of oil and cook the rest of the chicken. Put the vinaigrette in a medium skillet and cook, stirring until warm, about 1 minute. Pour vinaigrette in small bowl and whisk to combine. Gently toss the greens with ½ cup of vinaigrette or enough to lightly coat. Arrange 4 plates with greens, top with chicken, onion, avocado, corn and the remaining ¼ cup of cilantro. Drizzle with remaining vinaigrette; serve with lime wedges on the side.

*SERVES 4*

# White Enchiladas

1 pound hamburger, browned and
    seasoned
2 cans cream of mushroom soup
½ soup can water
1 (4 ounce) can green chilies, cut fine,
    undrained

1 tablespoon instant onion
½ pound longhorn cheese, shredded
12 to 15 tortillas, corn or flour
Oil for frying tortillas

Preheat oven to 350°. Mix hamburger, soup, water and chilies. Add onion and cheese. Heat slowly until cheese is melted, stirring occasionally. Dip 12-15 tortillas in hot oil until soft, draining well. Layer tortillas and sauce in a sprayed 9x13 inch casserole dish. Bake for 20-30 minutes. This is excellent reheated.

*SERVES 6*

# Chili-Rubbed Rib-Eye Steak with Corn and Green Chili Ragoût

1 teaspoon chili powder
1 teaspoon ground coriander
1 teaspoon kosher salt, more to taste
2 (8 ounce) boneless beef rib-eye
    steaks (about ¾ inch thick)
2 teaspoons canola or vegetable oil
1 small poblano, Anaheim or mildly
    hot fresh pepper, seeded and cut
    into ¼ inch dice

½ teaspoon freshly ground black
    pepper
1 generous cup fresh corn kernels
    (about 2 medium ears)
½ cup whipping cream
1 tablespoon minced oil-packed
    sun-dried tomatoes
1 tablespoon fresh lime juice

In a small bowl, mix the chili powder, coriander and salt. Rub the mixture on the steaks. Heat the oil in a 10-11 inch skillet over high heat until very hot. Add the steaks, reduce the heat to medium high, and cook until they are well browned and done to your liking, about 3 minutes per side for medium rare. Transfer to a plate and cover loosely to keep warm. Add the chili to the pan, season with salt and pepper and cook over medium high heat, stirring frequently, until softened and starting to brown, about 2 minutes. Add the corn and continue to cook until slightly brown, 1-2 minutes. Add the cream and boil until it has reduced and the mixture is thick, 1-2 minutes. Remove from the heat, stir in the sun-dried tomato, lime juice and the accumulated juices from the steak. Salt and pepper to taste. Serve the rib-eyes whole or sliced arranged on plates with corn ragoût on top or alongside.

*SERVES 2*

# South of the Border Veggie-Chili and Fixins

¼ cup olive oil, divided

1 poblano pepper, stemmed, seeded and chopped

1 medium onion, chopped

¾ cup diced red bell pepper

½ cup diced yellow bell pepper

1 large jalapeño pepper, seeded and minced

2 tablespoons minced cilantro stems

1½ tablespoons minced garlic

2 tablespoons chili powder

1 tablespoon Southwest seasoning

1 teaspoon ground cumin

½ teaspoon Mexican oregano, crumbled

2 teaspoons salt, divided

2 cans diced tomatoes with juice

6 cups low sodium vegetable or chicken stock

2 cups cooked kidney beans, drained

4 cups diced zucchini

4 cups diced yellow squash

1 tablespoon yellow cornmeal

2 tablespoons freshly chopped cilantro leaves

Sour cream, grated Cheddar cheese, chopped green onions, tortilla strips for garnish

In a large Dutch oven over medium heat, put 2 tablespoons of the oil and sauté the onions, poblano, red and yellow bell peppers until soft and lightly caramelized, about 6 minutes. Add the jalapeño, cilantro stems, garlic, chili powder, seasoning, cumin, oregano and 1½ teaspoons of salt and cook, stirring until fragrant, about 2 minutes. Add the tomatoes and stock and bring to a boil, reduce heat to a simmer and cook 10 minutes. Add the beans and continue to cook at a simmer until the flavors come together, 30-40 minutes. Preheat oven to broil. Toss the zucchini with 1 tablespoon of the remaining oil and ¼ teaspoon of the remaining salt and place on a large baking sheet. Broil until caramelized around the edges, 5-7 minutes. Remove from oven and repeat with the squash, remaining tablespoon of oil and ¼ teaspoon of salt. Set the zucchini and squash aside to cool. Once the chili has simmered about 40 minutes, add zucchini, squash, cornmeal, cilantro and cook for 10 minutes. Serve with bowls of sour cream, cheese, green onions and tortilla strips as garnish.

*SERVES 4-6*

Best if made a day ahead.

# Rice with Green Chilies

3 cups sour cream (24 ounces)

2 (4 ounce) cans chopped mild green chilies

4 cups cooked rice

2½ cups Monterey Jack cheese (8 ounces)

2½ cups grated Cheddar cheese (8 ounces)

Salt and pepper to taste

Preheat oven to 375°. Mix together sour cream and chilies and set aside. Toss cheeses together. Butter a 1½ quart casserole dish. Put half of the rice in the casserole dish, spread half of the sour cream mixture on the rice, top with half the cheeses and sprinkle with salt and pepper. Repeat these layers a second time. Cover casserole and bake for 25 minutes. Remove cover and bake an additional 10 minutes or until bubbly.

*SERVES 6-8*

This may be easily halved or doubled, and may be assembled early in the day, refrigerated and baked later. Allow more baking time if casserole is chilled.

Cooked rice can be stored covered in the refrigerator for up to one week or in the freezer for 2-3 months. To reheat, thaw and place in a saucepan with 2-3 tablespoons water. Simmer covered, until hot, 5-10 minutes. To reheat in microwave, put in bowl and cook on high for 3 minutes.

# Southwestern-Style Potato Salad

**DRESSING**

⅓ cup sour cream
⅓ cup mayonnaise
¼ cup extra virgin olive oil
3 tablespoons fresh lime juice
1 clove garlic, mashed to a paste

2 tablespoons freshly chopped oregano
1½ teaspoons cumin seeds, lightly toasted and ground
1 teaspoon kosher salt
½ teaspoon ground black pepper

**SALAD**

¼ cup plain rice vinegar
2 tablespoons kosher salt plus 2 teaspoons, divided
3½ pounds medium potatoes, such as Yukon Gold or red, scrubbed clean
1¼ cups fresh sweet corn kernels, blanched

1¼ cups diced red bell pepper
⅓ cup grated Cheddar cheese
½ cup thinly sliced green onions
¼ cup chopped cilantro

For the dressing, whisk sour cream, mayonnaise, olive oil, lime juice, garlic, oregano, cumin, salt and pepper together in a small bowl, set aside. To make the salad, combine the vinegar and 2 teaspoons salt in a large bowl. Let sit to dissolve the salt. Put the potatoes and 2 tablespoons salt in a 6 quart pot add enough cold water to cover by 1 inch. Bring to a boil over high heat and reduce the heat to maintain a simmer. Cook the potatoes until tender about 20-25 minutes. If the potatoes aren't the same size, remove them as they are cooked. Drain and set aside. When cool, peel the potatoes and cut into ¾ inch pieces. Add potatoes to the bowl with the vinegar and gently stir to coat. When the potatoes are completely cooled, gently fold the corn, peppers, cheese and onions into the potatoes. Generously coat the potatoes with the dressing, salt and pepper to taste. Garnish with chopped cilantro. Serve at room temperature or cool.

*SERVES 8*

JCYM partnered with the Kansas City Zoo in 1970 to develop their docent program, which is ongoing. Docents serve as tour guides at the Zoo for a variety of groups and also provide programs (taking some animals with them) to organizations outside of the Zoo.

# Grilled Fish Tacos

## LIME CILANTRO SOUR CREAM SAUCE

| | |
|---|---|
| 1 cup sour cream | Grated zest of 1 lime |
| ½ cup mayonnaise | 1 tablespoon lime juice |
| 3 tablespoons fresh cilantro, minced | |

Combine all ingredients, and whisk until smooth. Refrigerate up to 4 hours or until ready to serve.

## TACOS

| | |
|---|---|
| 2 teaspoons ancho chile powder, ground | 3 pounds firm whitefish (halibut, tilapia, or cod) |
| ½ teaspoon cumin, ground | 2 dozen 6 inch corn tortillas |
| 3 cloves garlic, minced | 2½ cups green cabbage, shredded |
| ½ teaspoon Kosher salt | 2½ cups red cabbage, shredded |
| ¼ teaspoon freshly ground black pepper | Pico de Gallo, prepared |
| 2 tablespoons olive oil | 4 limes, quartered |

In a small bowl, combine the ancho chile powder, cumin, garlic, salt and pepper, stir to mix. Add the oil and whisk until a loose paste is formed. Rub the fish with the spice paste and let marinate in the refrigerator for at least 30 minutes or up to 4 hours. Light a charcoal fire or preheat your gas grill on high. Oil the grill's cooking surface. Let the coals burn down to a medium high or adjust the gas grill burners to medium high. Grill the fish until just cooked through, 3-4 minutes per side. Transfer to a cutting board and coarsely chop. Divide the tortillas into 2 stacks and wrap each in aluminum foil. Place on the grill until heated through, about 5 minutes. In a large bowl, combine the green and red cabbage. To assemble the tacos, top 2 tortillas with the chunks of fish, a dollop of the sauce, a spoonful of the Pico de Gallo and some of the cabbage. Squeeze a wedge of lime over the filling, fold the tortilla, and serve.

*SERVES 6 TO 8 (YIELDS 12 TACOS)*

Eliminate "fish" odors by boiling a saucepan of water with a few whole cloves, stick of cinnamon and a slice of lemon.

# Winter Wonders

# Hanging of The Greens Brunch

Peach Sangría, page 70
Brunch Casserole, page 70
Canadian Bacon and Brie Quiche, page 71
Fabulous Eggs, page 71
Grits Cheese Casserole, page 72
Apple Puff, page 72
Hot Fruit Compote, page 73
Fluffy Fruit Salad, page 74
Deep Dish Gooey Butter Cake, page 74

## Substitutions

Petite Cheese Cake Tarts, page 74
Blueberry Oatmeal Crisp, page 73

# Holiday Open House

Wassail, page 75
Pomegranate and Cranberry Bellini, page 76
Prosciutto, Fig and Goat Cheese Pastry Rounds, page 75
Tequila Shrimp, page 76
Smothered Meatballs, page 77
Mini Muffulettas, page 77
Double Cheese Tartlets, page 78
Chicken Tenders with Blue Cheese, page 80
Sweet Spiced Nuts, page 79
Chocolate Truffle Bites, page 78
Cranberry Lime Squares, page 79

## Substitutions

Pepper Bowl Dip, page 81
Chutney Chicken Spread, page 81
Deviled Pecans, page 80

# An Elegant Holiday Dinner

Moose Milk, page 82
Brie and Artichoke Dip, page 82
Blue Cheese Bacon Dip, page 83
Salmon Party Ball, page 86
Cranberry, Feta and Pecan Salad, page 83
Spinach and Cheese Soufflé, page 85
Scalloped Potatoes with Crème Fraîche, page 84
Holiday Prime Rib Roast with Horseradish Sauce, page 84
Bourbon Chocolate Pecan Pie, page 85
Spinach and Mushroom Panade, page 86

# Ring in the New Year

Pop the Cork Champagne Punch, page 87
Baked Honey Raisin Brie, page 87
Mixed Greens with Pear and Gorgonzola, page 88
Roast Pork Tenderloin Stuffed with Honeyed Apples and Pecans, page 87
Almond Pear Cream Cheese Torte, page 88

## Substitutions

Connoisseur's Casserole, page 89
Chocolate-Covered Cherry Cookies, page 89

# A Taste of The Big Easy

Whiskey Slush, page 90
Crab Louis, page 91
Toasted Rice, page 92
Creole Fried Rice, page 90
Grits with Greens and Shrimp, page 92
Gumbo, page 94
Jambalaya, page 93
Praline-Apple Bread, page 96
Brûléed Key Lime Tarts, page 95

## Substitutions
Okra and Butter Bean Stew, page 97
Bourbon Praline Cake, page 98
Shrimp and Chicken Étouffée, page 99
Quick Shrimp Gumbo, page 97
Ruby Grapefruit, page 99

# Cozy Fireside Supper

Scalloped Cabbage, page 100
Italian Bean Soup, page 101
Creamy Farfalle, page 101
Smothered Pork Chops, page 100
Squash Apple Bake, page 102
Savory Bread Pudding, page 103
Creamy Spinach and Parsnips, page 104
Nutty Caramel Cookie Tart, page 105
Baked Pears with Almonds, page 106

## Substitutions
Quick Meat Loaf, page 105
Artichoke Lasagna, page 107
Pineapple Carrots, page 106

# A Little Thai with My Chai

Shrimp and Lime Soup, page 108
Hot and Sour Soup, page 108
Shrimp and Mushroom Wontons, page 109
Spicy Thai-Style Chicken in Lettuce Cups, page 110
Vietnamese-Style Chicken Salad, page 111
Thai Dipping Sauce, page 112
Thai-Style Pineapple Snack, page 112
Brown Rice Salad with Citrus-Thai Basil Vinaigrette, page 113
Thai Iced Tea, page 113

# Goodbye Winter

Cranberry Tea, page 114
Asparagus Soup, page 114
Green Salad with Pears, Prosciutto and Avocado, page 115
Soda Bread, page 115
Crock-Pot Corned Beef and Cabbage, page 116
Spinach Casserole, page 116
Balsamic Roasted Brussels Sprouts, page 117
O'Henry Bars, page 118
Cheesecake with Chocolate Crust and Cherries, page 118

## Substitutions

Vegetable Sauté with Orange and Balsamic Sauce, page 119
Pork Tenderloin with Mushrooms and Olives, page 119
Macaroni and Cheese, page 117
The Best Bread Pudding, page 120

# Peach Sangría

2 bottles peach chardonnay
1 cup orange juice
1 cup peach schnapps

2 tablespoons grenadine syrup
½ cup simple syrup
16 ounces frozen, unsweetened sliced peaches, thawed

Combine wine, orange juice, schnapps and grenadine in large container. Make simple syrup by boiling ¾ cup sugar and ¾ cup water until sugar is dissolved. Place syrup in blender with thawed peaches and purée. Add purée to wine mixture and stir to mix well. Refrigerate 2 hours until well chilled. Serve over crushed ice in balloon-shaped wine glasses. Thread wedges of lime, lemon and orange onto wooden skewers and place one across top of each glass.

*SERVES 8-10*

# Brunch Casserole

1 pound bulk pork sausage
1 tube refrigerated crescent rolls
4 eggs

2 tablespoons milk
⅛ teaspoon black pepper
¾ cup shredded Cheddar cheese

Preheat oven to 400°. Brown and drain sausage. Pat rolls lightly, in greased 9x13 inch pan. Pat up on sides to create rim. Seal all seams. Sprinkle browned sausage over crust. Top with shredded cheese. (Up to this point, it can be done and refrigerated the night before.) Mix eggs, milk and pepper and beat lightly. Pour over sausage and mixture. Bake for 15 minutes.

*SERVES 12*

Additions such as mushrooms, green chilies, ham or bacon may be included. To double this recipe, bake in jelly roll pan 20-30 minutes.

# Canadian Bacon and Brie Quiche

16 Canadian bacon slices
8 ounces Brie cheese
8 eggs
½ cup mayonnaise (may be low fat)

½ teaspoon white pepper
¼ cup grated Parmesan cheese
½ teaspoon Italian seasoning
Fresh rosemary sprigs for garnish

Preheat oven to 375°. Arrange bacon slices in bottom and up sides of lightly greased 9½ inch pie plate, slightly overlapping each slice. Remove rind from cheese and cut into cubes. Whisk eggs, mayonnaise, pepper and Italian seasoning together. Fold in Brie and Parmesan cheese. Pour mixture in prepared pie plate and bake 35 minutes or until knife inserted in center comes out clean. Let stand 5 minutes before serving. Garnish if desired.

*SERVES 8*

# Fabulous Eggs

4 slices bacon
½ pound dried beef
1 (4 ounce) jar sliced mushrooms, drained
¼ cup butter
½ cup flour
1 quart milk

Dash of black pepper
16 eggs
¼ teaspoon salt
1 cup evaporated milk
¼ cup butter
2 cups grated Cheddar cheese

Preheat oven to 275°. Chop bacon and fry until almost done. Add dried beef, mushrooms, butter and flour and stir well. Cook for 3-5 minutes. Add milk, stirring quickly. Add pepper. Cook to the consistency of pudding (add cornstarch if necessary). Lightly beat eggs with ¼ teaspoon salt and evaporated milk. Melt butter in large pan and scramble egg mixture in it until soft. Butter casserole dish, layer sauce, eggs and repeat until all ingredients are used up. End with sauce on top. Cover with grated cheese. Cover with foil and bake for 35-40 minutes. This may also be prepared the day before and refrigerated. Simply bake and serve.

*SERVES 12*

# Grits Cheese Casserole

| | |
|---|---|
| 4 cups milk | 2 cups shredded sharp Cheddar cheese |
| ¼ cup butter | 1 teaspoon salt |
| 1 cup uncooked quick-cooking grits | ½ teaspoon black pepper |
| 1 egg, slightly beaten | ¼ cup grated Parmesan cheese |

Preheat oven to 350°. In large saucepan over medium heat, bring milk to light boil. Gradually whisk in butter and grits. Reduce heat to simmer, whisking constantly, 5-7 minutes or until grits are done. Remove from heat. Stir in egg, shredded Cheddar cheese and salt. Pour into lightly greased 11x7 inch baking pan. Sprinkle with Parmesan. Bake, covered, 35-40 minutes or until its set. Serve immediately.

*SERVES 6*

# Apple Puff

| | |
|---|---|
| 8 eggs | ¾ teaspoon cinnamon |
| 1½ cups milk | ½ teaspoon salt |
| 1 cup flour | ½ cup butter |
| 3 tablespoons sugar | 3 Granny Smith apples |
| 1½ teaspoons vanilla extract | ¼ cup firmly packed brown sugar |

Preheat oven to 425°. Heat butter to melt in a 9x13 inch pan. Combine egg, milk, flour, sugar, vanilla, cinnamon and salt in a blender. Blend until smooth. Peel and thinly slice apples. Stir apples into melted butter. Bake until butter sizzles. Process egg mixture briefly and pour over apple mixture. Top with brown sugar. Bake 20 minutes or until knife inserted in center comes out clean and pancake is browned and puffed. Serve immediately, plain or with warm maple syrup or honey.

*SERVES 12-14*

Keep brown sugar in the freezer. It won't harden like it will if kept in the pantry so you can easily measure the sugar when you need it.

# Hot Fruit Compote

1 (17 ounce) can apricot halves, drained

1 (16 ounce) can pear halves, drained

1 (16 ounce) can peach halves, drained

1 (15 ounce) can pineapple chunks, drained

⅓ cup maraschino cherries, cut in half

1 (15 ounce) jar applesauce

½ cup sugar

⅓ cup cream sherry

1 teaspoon ground cinnamon

¼ teaspoon ground nutmeg

2 tablespoons butter

Preheat oven to 325°. Arrange apricots, pears, peaches and pineapple in layers in ungreased 3 quart baking dish. Set aside. Pour applesauce in small saucepan and cook uncovered 5 minutes. Stir in sherry, sugar, cinnamon and nutmeg. Stir in cherries. Pour over fruit mixture. Dot with butter and bake for 1 hour.

*SERVES 8-10*

# Blueberry Oatmeal Crisp

3 pints blueberries

½ cup sugar

Juice and zest of 1 lemon

3 tablespoons flour

1 cup all-purpose flour

1 cup firmly packed light brown sugar

⅔ cup rolled oats

½ teaspoon cinnamon

¼ teaspoon salt

½ cup plus 2 tablespoons cold, unsalted butter, cut into small cubes

Preheat oven to 400°. Mix berries, sugar, lemon juice, zest and 3 tablespoons flour. Butter a 9x13 inch glass pan. In blender, combine flour, brown sugar, oats, cinnamon and salt. Add butter and pulse in 2 to 3 second bursts until mixture is clumpy. Transfer berry mixture to prepared pan. Spread crumbs evenly over fruit. Bake for 30 minutes until bubbly. Let cool 15 minutes and serve. Tastes great at any temperature.

*SERVES 10*

73

# Fluffy Fruit Salad

1 (8 ounce) package cream cheese, softened

1 (12 ounce) container frozen whipped topping, thawed

¾ cup sugar

10 ounces frozen strawberries with juice

1 (15 ounce) can pineapple, drained

2 bananas, sliced

1 to 2 cups pecans

Combine sugar and cream cheese, then fold in whipped topping. Add strawberries, pineapple, bananas and pecans. Place in serving bowl and refrigerate until ready to serve.

*SERVES 6-8*

# Deep Dish Gooey Butter Cake

1 (18 ounce) box yellow cake mix

½ cup melted butter

4 eggs, divided

1 pound powdered sugar

1 (8 ounce) package cream cheese, at room temperature

Preheat oven to 350°. Combine yellow cake mix with butter and eggs and mix well. Pat into greased and floured 9x13 inch pan. Top with mixture of powdered sugar, cream cheese and eggs. Bake for 40-45 minutes. Top should be golden brown. Center will remain soft. Do not overbake. Can be frozen.

*SERVES 15*

# Petite Cheese Cake Tarts

1 (8 ounce) package cream cheese, softened

¾ cup sugar

2 eggs

1 teaspoon vanilla extract

12 vanilla wafers

1 can cherry pie filling

12 foil cupcake holders

Preheat oven to 375°. Combine cheese, sugar and eggs and beat well. Add vanilla last. Place vanilla wafers in foil cupcake holders and then Into cupcake tins. Fill with cheese mixture ½ to ¾ full. Bake for 10-12 minutes. Top with cherry pie filling and refrigerate.

*SERVES 12*

# Wassail

1 cup sugar

3 cups water

3 to 4 cinnamon sticks, 2 inches long

1 tablespoon whole cloves

1 tablespoon whole allspice

1 gallon apple cider

1 (12 ounce) can frozen lemonade

1 (12 ounce) can frozen orange juice

6 cups water

Simmer sugar, 3 cups water, cinnamon sticks, cloves and allspice 2-3 hours. Add apple cider, lemonade, orange juice and 6 cups water. Mix well. Refrigerate. Heat when ready to serve.

*SERVES 20-24*

# Prosciutto, Fig and Goat Cheese Pastry Rounds

½ (17.3 ounce) package frozen puff pastry

3 tablespoons fig preserves

1 egg

3 ounces thinly sliced prosciutto

3 (2 to 2½ inch diameter) goat cheese logs

½ cup fig preserves

Preheat oven to 400°. Line baking sheet with foil. Grease foil and set aside. Unfold thawed pastry on lightly floured surface. Roll out to 12 inch square and cut into 4 (6 inch) squares. Place 1 tablespoon fig preserves in center of each square. Place prosciutto and goat cheese on top of preserves. Bring pastry edges up and over cheese rounds, pleating and pinching edges to cover. Seal and trim excess pastry. Invert each one on prepared baking sheet, smooth side up. Brush pastry with beaten egg. Cut small slits In each pastry to allow steam to escape. Cut remaining pastry square into decorative leaves and place on brushed pastry. Brush with additional egg. Bake 20-22 minutes or until golden brown. Let stand 15 minutes before serving. If desired, serve with ⅓ cup fig preserves for dipping.

*SERVES 12*

# Pomegranate and Cranberry Bellini

1½ cups simple syrup

1 cup ice

1¼ cups pomegranate juice, chilled

1 cup cranberry juice, chilled

2 limes, thinly sliced

1 bunch, fresh mint

Pomegranate seeds, optional

1 (750 milliliter) bottle Prosecco, chilled

To make simple syrup: Combine 1 cup water and 1 cup sugar in a saucepan. Boil 1 minute. Reduce heat and simmer 5 minutes until sugar is dissolved. Allow to cool 10 minutes. Place ice in a pitcher, add simple syrup, pomegranate juice and cranberry juice. Stir well. Serve in cups or champagne flutes with slice of lime, mint sprig and seeds in each glass. Slowly add Prosecco.

*SERVES 12*

# Tequila Shrimp

12 large shrimp

Oil for sautéing

1 large poblano pepper

1 tomato, seeded and diced

4 tablespoons tequila

2 tablespoons lime juice

6 tablespoons butter

Salt, pepper and cayenne pepper to taste

Peel and devein shrimp. Heat skillet and add enough oil to cover bottom. Sauté shrimp 30 seconds on each side or until pink. Add seeded and julienned pepper and tomato. Cook 30 seconds longer. Add tequila and flame it. Once flame has died down, add lime juice and simmer 1 minute. Stir in butter, salt and peppers. Once butter has melted, remove from heat and serve over rice.

*SERVES 4-6 AS APPETIZER*

Chicken may be substituted in place of shrimp.

# Smothered Meatballs

2 pounds lean ground beef
⅓ cup finely chopped green bell pepper
⅓ cup finely chopped onion
2 eggs
1½ cups Italian bread crumbs
½ teaspoon salt
¼ teaspoon ground black pepper

2 (10.75 ounce) cans condensed golden mushroom soup
1 cup sliced fresh mushrooms
1 cup sour cream
½ cup milk
2 tablespoons browning sauce
Salt and pepper to taste

Preheat oven to 375°. In large mixing bowl, combine beef, green pepper, onion, eggs, seasoned bread crumbs, salt and pepper. Mix thoroughly. Shape mixture into 2 inch meatballs. Place 1 inch apart on large cookie sheet. Bake 30 minutes. While they are baking, make the sauce. In a 9x13 inch pan, combine soup, mushrooms, sour cream, milk, browning sauce, salt and pepper to taste. Blend well. Add cooked meatballs to pan and toss to coat well. Return to oven and bake 20-30 minutes, or until sauce is bubbling.

*SERVES 8, OR 16-20 AS APPETIZERS*

Can make meatballs much smaller and bake in shorter period. Put in crock-pot with sauce and heat 2-3 hours on low.

# Mini Muffulettas

28 (1.1 ounce) crusty, bakery rolls
1 jar premade olive tapenade
¾ pound Genoa salami, 28 thin slices

¾ pound thinly sliced, deli ham
28 thinly sliced, provolone cheese
Pimiento-stuffed olives for garnish

Arrange bottom halves of rolls on work surface. For each sandwich, spoon 1 tablespoon olive tapenade on each roll bottom. Layer salami, ham and cheese over tapenade. Spoon 1 more tablespoon tapenade over cheese and cover with top of roll. Cut in half and secure with wooden picks. Garnish with olives if desired. Store in airtight container in refrigerator up to 2 days before serving.

*SERVES 28*

# Double Cheese Tartlets

2 (1.9 ounce) frozen, mini-phyllo
pastry shells
Parchment paper
¼ cup crumbled blue cheese
¼ cup whipping cream

2 teaspoons brandy, optional
2 eggs
½ cup (2 ounces) finely shredded
Gouda cheese

Preheat oven to 425°. Place pastry shells on large baking sheet lined with parchment paper. Mash blue cheese and cream until almost smooth. Stir in brandy until smooth. Stir in eggs until well blended. Stir in cheese. Spoon mixture into tart shells and bake 18 minutes or until set.

*SERVES 30*

# Chocolate Truffle Bites

1½ (15 ounce) packages refrigerated
pie crusts
2 (4 ounce) semisweet chocolate
baking bars, chopped
1 cup whipping cream

1½ teaspoons vanilla extract
Pinch of salt
Sweetened whipped cream
Garnish: chocolate shavings

Preheat oven to 425°. Unroll 3 pie crusts and stack on top of each other. Cut pie crust stack 10 times, using a 4-inch round cutter, making 30 rounds. Press rounds into bottoms of ungreased muffin tins. (Dough will come halfway up the sides, forming a cup.) Flute edges with fork, if desired. Bake rounds 8-10 minutes or until golden. Let cool 10 minutes. Remove from tins to wire racks to continue cooling (20 minutes). Meanwhile, stir together chocolate and cream in a 3½ quart heavy saucepan over low heat. Cook, stirring constantly, 4-5 minutes or until chocolate is melted and mixture is smooth. Remove from heat, stir in vanilla and salt. Let cool 30 minutes. Pour 1 tablespoon chocolate mixture into each pie crust. Cover and chill 1-24 hours. Top each with dollop of sweetened whipped cream. Garnish if desired.

*SERVES 30*

May use mini-phyllo pastry shells if desired.

# Sweet Spiced Nuts

1 egg white
1 tablespoon water
⅔ cup sugar
Kosher salt

1 teaspoon pumpkin pie spice or
  chai spice blend
¼ teaspoon cayenne pepper
3 cups mixed nuts
2 dashes Worcestershire sauce

Preheat oven to 275°. Line a large baking sheet with parchment paper. Whisk egg white with 1 tablespoon water until frothy. In small bowl, combine sugar, a pinch of salt, pumpkin spice and cayenne pepper. Toss the nuts in egg white mixture then stir in the spice mixture and Worcestershire sauce. Spoon mixture onto prepared cookie sheet in small clusters and bake 30-35 minutes or until golden. Cool completely and break into pieces. Store in airtight container.

*SERVES 3 CUPS*

# Cranberry Lime Squares

2¼ cups flour, divided
½ cup powdered sugar
1 tablespoon plus 1 teaspoon grated
  lime peel, divided
¼ teaspoon salt
1 cup butter

2 cups sugar
1 teaspoon baking powder
4 eggs
¼ cup lime juice
1 cup dried cranberries
Additional powdered sugar

Preheat oven to 350°. Spray 9x13 inch pan with cooking spray. Combine 2 cups flour, ½ cup powdered sugar, 1 tablespoon lime peel and salt in a large bowl. Add the butter, cut with pastry blender until mix forms coarse crumbs. Press mixture evenly into baking pan. Bake 20 minutes or until golden. Meanwhile, combine ¼ cup flour, sugar and baking powder in bowl and mix well. In separate bowl, combine eggs and lime juice. Add flour mixture to egg mixture and beat with electric mixer at medium speed, until mixture is well blended. Stir in 1 teaspoon lime peel and cranberries. Pour over warm crust. Bake 20 minutes until golden. Cool completely in pan on wire rack. Sprinkle with powdered sugar and chill 2 hours. Cut into squares and serve chilled.

*SERVES 24-26*

# Chicken Tenders with Blue Cheese

2½ cups panko bread crumbs
Kosher salt and black pepper to taste
1½ pounds chicken tenders
¾ cup mayonnaise, divided
1 tablespoon hot pepper sauce

¼ teaspoon cayenne
¾ cup crumbled blue cheese
½ cup sour cream
3 tablespoons milk

Pour panko bread crumbs into pie plate, and toss with salt and pepper. Trim off any exposed tendon ends from the wide tips of the chicken tenders. In medium bowl, whisk ¼ cup mayonnaise with the hot sauce, cayenne and ⅛ teaspoon salt. Add the chicken and toss with your hands to coat well. Coat each chicken tender in the panko crumbs and arrange in single layer on a heavy duty rimmed baking sheet. Refrigerate while you heat the broiler and make the sauce. Position rack 6 inches from the broiler element and heat the broiler on high for at least 10 minutes. Meanwhile, combine the remaining ½ cup mayonnaise with the blue cheese, sour cream, milk, ½ teaspoon salt and a few grinds of pepper in a medium bowl. Whisk until well combined and only small bits of cheese remain intact. Broil tenders, turning once, until they are crisp and golden brown in spots on the outside and cooked through, 4-6 minutes per side. Rotate pan if necessary for even browning. Transfer to a platter and serve with dipping sauce.

*SERVES 4*

# Deviled Pecans

1 pound shelled pecans
⅓ cup melted butter
1 tablespoon Worcestershire sauce

½ teaspoon hot pepper sauce
¼ teaspoon pepper
1 teaspoon salt

Preheat oven to 300°. Place nuts in shallow baking pan. Combine butter, Worcestershire sauce, hot pepper sauce, pepper and salt. Toss with nuts to mix well. Bake 20 minutes, stirring several times. Let cool on thick paper towels.

# Pepper Bowl Dip

1 green pepper, finely chopped
1 tomato, finely chopped
1 bunch green onions, thinly sliced
1 (8 ounce) package cream cheese, softened
½ cup sour cream
1 teaspoon dry mustard
1 teaspoon salt
½ teaspoon pepper
Assorted vegetables for dipping

In large bowl, combine pepper, tomato, green onions, softened cream cheese, sour cream, dry mustard, salt and black pepper. Mix well, cover and refrigerate. Serve with assorted vegetables.

Dip looks especially attractive when served in scooped out green, red or yellow pepper bowls.

# Chutney Chicken Spread

8 ounces cooked chicken
1 (8 ounce) package cream cheese, softened
2 tablespoons mango chutney
1 teaspoon curry powder
2 tablespoons grated onion
¼ cup mayonnaise
Dash pepper
¼ cup toasted slivered almonds

Process chicken in food processor 5 second. Add bite size chicken pieces, softened cream cheese, chutney, curry powder, grated onion, mayonnaise and pepper. Process together until well blended. Place in an au gratin dish. Sprinkle with almonds. Bake at 350° for 15 minutes. Serve with crackers, crisped bread or garlic rounds.

*SERVES 4-6 AS APPETIZER*

# Moose Milk

| | |
|---|---|
| 6 eggs | 2 cups sugar |
| 1 cup brandy | 1½ quarts milk |
| 1 cup rum | 1 pint cream, whipped |
| 2 cups bourbon | |

With electric beaters, beat eggs until well mixed. Add brandy, rum, bourbon, sugar and milk. Pour into punch bowl and float whipped cream on top. Serve in small cups.

*SERVES 24*

Place a bowl of ice under the punch bowl and garnish around the edges.

# Brie and Artichoke Dip

| | |
|---|---|
| 2 tablespoons butter | 1 (6 ounce) jar marinated artichoke hearts, drained and chopped |
| 2 tablespoons all-purpose flour | |
| 1 tablespoon dry mustard | ¼ cup roasted red sweet peppers, chopped |
| 1 cup milk | |
| 3 (4.5 ounce) rounds Brie cheese, rind removed cut into 1-inch cubes | Belgian endive leaves |
| | Toasted baguette slices |
| | Red pepper strips |

In medium saucepan, melt butter over medium heat. Stir in flour and mustard. Add milk and whisk until smooth. Cook and stir over medium heat until mixture is thick and bubbly. Gradually add Brie. Whisk until smooth. Stir in artichoke hearts and sweet peppers. Heat through. Transfer to serving bowl. Serve with endive leaves, sliced baguette and red pepper strips.

*SERVES 3 CUPS*

# Blue Cheese Bacon Dip

7 bacon slices, chopped

2 garlic cloves, minced

2 (8 ounce) packages cream cheese, softened

⅓ cup half and half

4 ounces crumbled blue cheese

2 tablespoons chopped fresh chives

3 tablespoons chopped walnuts

Grape clusters

Flatbread or assorted crackers

Preheat oven to 350°. In a skillet, cook cut up bacon over medium heat until crisp. Drain bacon and set aside. Add garlic to skillet and sauté 1 minute. Beat cream cheese with electric mixer until smooth. Add half and half and continue beating. Add bacon, garlic, blue cheese and chives. Spoon into 4 (1 cup) individual baking dishes. Bake for 15 minutes or until golden. Sprinkle evenly with toasted, chopped walnuts and serve with flatbread or assorted crackers.

*SERVES 12*

# Cranberry, Feta and Pecan Salad

4 cups romaine lettuce

4 cups fresh spinach

1 cup dried cranberries

½ cup crumbled feta cheese

1 medium red onion, thinly sliced

1 cup pecan halves, toasted

1 cup olive oil

¾ cup sugar

½ cup red wine vinegar

2 cloves garlic, minced

½ teaspoon salt

½ teaspoon paprika

½ teaspoon ground black pepper

¼ teaspoon cayenne pepper

In large salad bowl, combine lettuce and spinach. Add cranberries and cheese. Top with sliced onions. In separate bowl combine olive oil, sugar, vinegar, garlic, salt, paprika, pepper and cayenne pepper. Whisk well and drizzle over salad mixture. Top with toasted pecans and serve.

*SERVES 6-8*

Dressing will last up to 1 month if refrigerated.

# Scalloped Potatoes with Crème Fraîche

2 cloves garlic, mashed

3 tablespoons unsalted butter

3 pounds Yukon gold potatoes

3 cups half and half

½ cup crème fraîche

2 tablespoons all-purpose flour

2 teaspoons fresh thyme

⅛-¼ teaspoon ground mace

Kosher salt

Ground black pepper

¼ cup chopped chives

Preheat oven to 350°. Rub smashed garlic all over inside 3-quart baking dish then mince it. Grease dish with ½ tablespoon butter. Slice potatoes ⅛ inch thick. Combine in a large saucepan with minced garlic, 2½ tablespoons butter, half and half, crème fraîche, flour, thyme, mace, 2½ teaspoons salt and pepper to taste. Bring to boil over medium heat and cook 1-2 minutes, stirring until mixture thickens slightly. Stir in chives and transfer to prepared baking dish, shaking it to distribute potatoes evenly. Bake uncovered until potatoes are fork-tender, about an hour, occasionally spooning some of the liquid over the top. Let cool 10 minutes before serving.

*SERVES 8*

# Holiday Prime Rib Roast with Horseradish Sauce

4 pounds prime rib

2 cloves garlic, crushed

1 teaspoon salt

1 teaspoon cracked black pepper

1 teaspoon dried thyme leaves

Preheat oven to 350°. Combine garlic, salt, pepper and thyme and press evenly over roast. Place roast on rack in shallow roasting pan. Insert meat thermometer so bulb is inserted in thickest part. Do not add water or cover. Roast 18-20 minutes per pound for rare to medium. Remove roast from oven when meat thermometer registers 135° for medium. Let stand 15 minutes before carving.

**HORSERADISH SAUCE**

1 cup whipping cream

¼ cup horseradish

2 tablespoons chopped fresh parsley

¼ teaspoon salt

Beat whipping cream at medium speed with a heavy-duty electric mixer for 1 minute or until soft peaks form. Fold in horseradish, parsley and salt. Serve immediately or cover and refrigerate up to 8 hours.

*SERVES 8-10*

# Spinach and Cheese Soufflé

20 ounces frozen chopped spinach, thawed

2 eggs, separated

1 (12 ounce) container cottage cheese

1½ cups freshly grated Parmesan cheese

¼ cup butter, melted

2 tablespoons minced onion

1 garlic clove, pressed

2 tablespoons all-purpose flour

½ teaspoon baking powder

½ teaspoon lemon pepper

Preheat oven to 350°. Grease bottom of 1 quart soufflé dish. Set aside. Drain spinach well, pressing between paper towels. Process spinach, egg yolks, cottage cheese, Parmesan cheese, melted butter, minced onion and pressed garlic in food processor until smooth, stopping to scrape down the sides. Combine flour, baking powder and lemon pepper and gradually add to spinach mixture, processing until well blended. In separate bowl, beat egg whites at high speed with electric mixer until stiff peaks form. Fold into spinach mixture. Pour into soufflé dish. Bake for 45-50 minutes or until puffed and set in center. Serve immediately.

*SERVES 4-6*

# Bourbon Chocolate Pecan Pie

1 (9 inch) pie crust

4 eggs

1 cup dark corn syrup

6 tablespoons butter

½ cup sugar

¼ cup firmly packed light brown sugar

3 tablespoons bourbon, optional

1 tablespoon flour

1 tablespoon vanilla extract

1 cup pecans, coarsely chopped

1 cup semisweet chocolate morsels, melted

Preheat oven to 350°. Place pie crust into lightly greased 9-inch pie pan. In medium bowl, whisk together eggs, corn syrup, melted butter, sugar, brown sugar, bourbon, flour and vanilla. Stir in chopped pecans and melted chocolate. Pour filling into pie crust and bake on lowest oven rack 1 hour or until set. Cover pie with aluminum foil, loosely, after 20 minutes of baking. Cool completely before serving.

*SERVES 8*

# Salmon Party Ball

1 (16 ounce) can salmon
1 (8 ounce) package cream cheese,
  softened
1 tablespoon lemon juice
2 teaspoons grated onion

1 teaspoon horseradish
¼ teaspoon salt
¼ teaspoon liquid smoke
½ cup chopped pecans

Drain and flake salmon. Combine with softened cream cheese, lemon juice, onion, horseradish, salt and liquid smoke. Chill at least 1 hour. Shape in ball and roll in nuts. Cover and chill again until ready to serve. Serve with crackers.

# Spinach and Mushroom Panade

10 (½ inch) slices sourdough bread
1 tablespoon extra virgin olive oil
1 tablespoon butter
2 large yellow onions, chopped
1 pound button mushrooms, sliced
2 cloves garlic, minced
¼ cup dry white wine
1 tablespoon minced fresh thyme or
  1 teaspoon dried thyme

1½ teaspoons salt
Coarsely ground black pepper
1 (16 ounce) package frozen chopped
  spinach, thawed and well drained
1½ cups Gruyère or Swiss cheese,
  divided
3 to 4 cups homemade or canned, low
  sodium chicken or vegetable broth

Preheat oven to 350°. Tear bread into 1 inch pieces and toast until lightly browned, 12-15 minutes, stirring once. Heat oil and butter over medium heat in 12 inch sauté pan or skillet. When butter melts add chopped onions and cook 10 minutes. Increase heat to medium-high, add rinsed and sliced (¼ inch thick) mushrooms, minced garlic, wine, thyme, salt and pepper. Cook until liquid evaporates and mushrooms shrink, 10-15 minutes. Stir in well drained spinach. Coat 9x13 inch pan with cooking spray. Place half the bread in pan. Drizzle half the onion mixture over bread and sprinkle on half the cheese. Repeat layers. Slowly pour 2 cups broth over top, allowing bread to soak up broth and pressing with the back of a spoon. Add remaining broth until it reaches 1 inch below the pan's rim. Increase oven temperature to 375°. Cover pan with aluminum foil and place on a baking sheet to catch drips. Bake covered for 30 minutes. Remove foil and bake 35-45 minutes until bubbling, puffed and deep golden brown. Let stand 5 minutes before serving.

*SERVES 12*

# Pop the Cork Champagne Punch

4 (6 ounce) cans frozen lemonade, undiluted

4 (6 ounce) cans frozen pineapple juice, undiluted

6 cups water

2 (33.8 ounce) bottles ginger ale

1 (33.8 ounce) bottle tonic water

1 (25.4 ounce) bottle champagne

Ice ring

Combine thawed and undiluted lemonade, pineapple juice and water and chill. Pour chilled juice mixture in punch bowl. Stir in tonic water, ginger ale and champagne. Add ice ring.

*SERVES 30*

# Baked Honey Raisin Brie

¼ cup orange liqueur

1 cup golden raisins

2 (8 ounce) Brie rounds

3 tablespoons honey

Apple slices and crackers for serving

Preheat oven to 350°. Microwave liqueur on high for 1 minute. Pour over raisins and let stand 5 minutes. Trim rind off top of Brie, leaving ½ inch margin. Place Brie on oven proof pie plate. Spoon raisin mixture over top, drizzle with honey. Bake for 12-15 minutes. Serve immediately with assorted crackers and apple slices.

# Roast Pork Tenderloin Stuffed with Honeyed Apples and Pecans

2 Granny Smith apples, peeled and finely chopped

½ cup finely chopped pecans

2 green onions, including tops, finely chopped

3 tablespoons honey

Salt and pepper to taste

2 (1 pound) pork tenderloins

3 tablespoons peanut oil

Preheat oven to 375°. In small bowl combine apples, pecans, green onions, salt and pepper to taste. Stir until well blended and set aside. Rub tenderloins well with oil and place on work surface. Using a sharp knife, cut pocket lengthwise in each tenderloin to within ½ inch of the other side. Fill pockets with equal amounts of apple and pecan mixture, tie tenderloins with cooking twine to secure pockets. Season with salt and pepper. Transfer to large, heavy rimmed baking pan and roast 30 minutes until tender. Remove from oven, discard twine and let tenderloins rest 10 minutes before carving and serving.

*SERVES 6*

# Mixed Greens with Pear and Gorgonzola

**BALSAMIC SYRUP**

2 shallots, minced

½ cup balsamic vinegar

**DRESSING**

½ cup extra virgin olive oil

2 tablespoons sherry

1 tablespoon honey

⅓ cup balsamic vinegar

Salt and pepper to taste

**SALAD**

3 pears

Juice of 1 lemon

½ cup English walnuts

3 tablespoons powdered sugar

4 ounces Gorgonzola cheese

6 cups mixed greens

Prepare balsamic syrup by cooking shallots in olive oil until tender. Add balsamic vinegar and reduce over medium heat, until syrupy. For the dressing, place balsamic syrup, olive oil, sherry, honey and vinegar in blender and blend to smooth consistency. Season with salt and pepper to taste. Chill until ready to dress the salad.

*SERVES 6*

# Almond Pear Cream Cheese Torte

½ cup butter

1 cup sugar, divided

1 cup flour

1 (8 ounce) package cream cheese, softened

1 egg

½ teaspoon vanilla extract

½ teaspoon cinnamon

¼ cup sliced almonds

4 cups sliced pears (about 4 medium)

Preheat oven to 425°. Beat butter and ⅓ cup sugar in small bowl, with electric mixer on medium speed, until light and fluffy. Add flour and mix well. Spread firmly onto bottom and 1 inch up sides of a 9 inch springform pan. Beat cream cheese and ⅓ cup of the remaining sugar in same bowl until well blended. Add egg and vanilla and mix well. Spread evenly over crust. Combine remaining ⅓ cup sugar and cinnamon. Add to pears in large bowl. Toss to coat well. Arrange over cream cheese layer. Sprinkle with almonds. Bake 10 minutes. Reduce temperature to 375° and continue baking 25 minutes or until center is set. Cool on wire rack. Loosen torte from rim of pan. Cover and refrigerate 3 hours prior to serving. Store leftover torte in refrigerator.

*SERVES 8-10*

# Connoisseur's Casserole

1 (12 ounce) can white shoe peg corn, drained

1 (16 ounce) can French green beans, drained

½ cup celery, chopped

½ cup onion, chopped

1 (2 ounce) jar chopped pimiento

½ cup sour cream

½ cup grated sharp Cheddar cheese

1 (10 ounce) can cream of celery soup

½ teaspoon salt

½ teaspoon pepper

**TOPPING**

1 cup butter-flavored cracker crumbs

¼ cup butter

½ cup slivered almonds

Preheat oven to 350°. In large bowl, combine corn, beans, celery, onion, pimiento, sour cream, Cheddar cheese, celery soup, salt and pepper. Place in 2 quart casserole. Combine cracker crumbs with butter and almonds and sprinkle over casserole. Bake for 45 minutes.

*SERVES 6*

Yellow corn may be used in place of the white shoe peg corn. This may also be frozen.

# Chocolate-Covered Cherry Cookies

⅓ cup butter, softened

⅓ cup shortening

1 egg

1 (17.5 ounce) package chocolate chip cookie mix

½ cup unsweetened cocoa

42 assorted chocolate-covered cherries

½ cup powdered sugar

4 to 5 teaspoons cherry liqueur or maraschino cherry juice

Preheat oven to 375°. Beat butter and shortening in large bowl, until fluffy. Add egg and continue beating until well blended. Combine cookie mix and cocoa; gradually add to butter mixture, beating well. Shape dough into 1-inch balls. Place balls 2 inches apart on ungreased baking sheets. Bake 8-10 minutes. Cool 2 minutes. Gently press 1 cherry in center of each cookie. Cool completely on baking sheets and transfer to wire racks. Combine powdered sugar and liqueur in small bowl. Stir well until smooth. Glaze must be smooth and thick yet easy to drizzle. Place glaze in small zip-top plastic bag. Snip a tiny hole in one corner of bag. Drizzle glaze over cookies and let stand until set.

*SERVES 3½ DOZEN*

# Whiskey Slush

2 cups unsweetened brewed black tea
5 cups water
2 cups good whiskey
¼ cup sugar
1 (12 ounce) can frozen lemonade concentrate, thawed
1 (6 ounce) can frozen orange juice concentrate, thawed
Chilled ginger ale, as needed

Combine the tea, water, whiskey, sugar and the two juice concentrates in a 9x13 inch pan. Put the pan in the freezer. Stir the mixture with a fork about every 45 minutes. Continue this for a couple of hours until the mixture has the consistency of a granita; icy, slushy and granular. To serve, use an ice-cream scoop or large, heavy spoon and fill a glass two-thirds full with the frozen tea. Top with a bit of ginger ale but don't stir. Let the ginger ale blend with the frozen tea and serve.

*SERVES 6-8*

# Creole Fried Rice

1 cup uncooked long-grain rice
2 cups chicken broth
1 pound skinned and boned chicken thighs
1½ teaspoons Creole seasoning, divided
2 tablespoons vegetable oil
½ pound andouille or smoked sausage, sliced
½ small onion, chopped
½ small green bell pepper, chopped
2 garlic cloves, chopped
1 cup frozen sliced okra, thawed
3 plum tomatoes, chopped
2 green onions, sliced (green part only)

Cook rice according to package directions, substituting chicken broth for water. Spread cooked rice in a thin layer on a baking sheet. Let cool for 30 minutes or until completely cooled. Cut chicken thighs into 1 inch pieces and toss with 1 teaspoon Creole seasoning. Cook chicken in hot oil in a large skillet over medium heat for 3 minutes, add sausage and cook for 3-4 minutes, until lightly browned. Add onion, bell pepper and garlic; cook 5 minutes or until onion is tender. Stir in okra and remaining ½ teaspoon Creole seasoning. Increase heat to high; add rice, and cook, stirring constantly for 4 minutes or until thoroughly heated. Stir in tomatoes. Sprinkle with sliced green onions and serve immediately.

*SERVES 6-8*

# Crab Louis

**DRESSING**

1 cup mayonnaise

2 tablespoons lemon juice

1 tablespoon chives

1 tablespoon finely chopped green onion,

1 tablespoon minced green bell pepper

½ cup chili sauce

¼ teaspoon hot pepper sauce

1 teaspoon Worcestershire sauce

⅛ teaspoon cayenne pepper

Salt

**SALAD**

4 (6 ounce) cans lump crabmeat or 1 (16 ounce) can, drained

Lettuce

6 tomatoes, cut into wedges

6 hard-boiled eggs, cut into wedges

To make dressing, combine mayonnaise, lemon juice, chives, onion, green pepper, chili sauce, hot sauce, Worcestershire and pepper. Mix well. Add salt to taste and chill. Pick through crabmeat, removing any bits of shell. For each serving, arrange a bed of lettuce on a plate and place a generous serving of crabmeat in center. Surround with tomato wedges and egg wedges. Drizzle generously with chilled dressing.

*SERVES 6*

Make salad dressing ahead of time and chill to allow seasonings to meld properly. Dressing keeps well in refrigerator.

The first philanthropy we adopted on a continuing basis was the Crippled Children's Nursery School. We supported the American Cancer Society for over 35 years and have worked with the Johnson County Christmas Bureau for almost 30 years.

# Toasted Rice

4 tablespoons butter

2 cups converted long-grain rice

1 teaspoon salt

½ teaspoon black pepper

2 cups chicken broth

2 cups water

¼ cup chopped green onions

¼ cup chopped parsley

Melt butter in a pot over medium-high heat. Stir in rice, salt and pepper. Cook stirring until the rice is golden, about 5 minutes. Add chicken broth and water, bring to a simmer, then cover and cook over low heat, 15 minutes. Remove from the heat and let stand 5 minutes. Fluff with a fork and stir in chopped green onions and parsley.

*SERVES 4-6*

# Grits with Greens and Shrimp

2 cups milk

2 cups water

1 cup uncooked grits

1 clove garlic, chopped

1 cup whipping cream

¼ to ½ cup butter

1 to 2 cups freshly grated Parmigiano-Reggiano cheese

1 pound shrimp, peeled and deveined

⅓ pound baby spinach, baby turnip greens or arugula, washed and dried

Salt and pepper

Bring milk and water to simmer in heavy-bottomed non-stick saucepan over medium heat. Add grits and garlic and bring just to boil. Cook until soft and creamy, adding whipping cream as needed to make loose but not runny mixture. Add as much butter and cheese as desired, stirring to make sure cheese doesn't stick. Add shrimp and cook a few minutes until shrimp turn pink. Fold in greens and remove from heat. Greens will cook in hot grits. Season with salt and pepper. Serve in chafing dish for a party or individually as an appetizer or main course.

*SERVES 4-6*

To make a dip, add enough cream to grits to make consistency of a dip. Chop shrimp and greens before adding to hot grits. Serve with tortilla chips.

# Jambalaya

3 tablespoons olive oil
1 small onion, chopped
1 clove garlic, minced
1 bay leaf
3 cups water
1½ cups uncooked rice
½ teaspoon thyme
1½ teaspoons salt
1 tablespoon chopped jalapeño pepper

1 (14.5 ounce) can Italian tomatoes
⅛ teaspoon cayenne pepper
¼ pound smoked sausage, sliced
½ pound cooked shrimp, peeled and deveined
¼ pound scallops
(may omit and double shrimp)
1 tablespoon coriander
Hot pepper sauce to taste

Heat olive oil, add onion and garlic; sauté until tender. Add rice and cook 1 minute. Add 3 cups water, thyme, salt, jalapeño pepper, coriander, cayenne pepper and bay leaf. Bring to a boil, then cover and reduce heat. Simmer rice for 15 minutes, then take out the bay leaf. Add tomatoes, smoked sausage, shrimp and scallops and cook for 5 minutes.

*SERVES 8*

May substitute chicken for the shrimp or scallops.

If you have a head of garlic that is sprouting, do not throw it away! Separate the cloves and plant them close together in a pot or in your garden. The young shoots that appear are garlic chives. They are mild with a faint garlic taste-perfect for eggs, salads and sandwiches.

# Gumbo

## STOCK

3 tablespoons vegetable oil

3 pounds medium shrimp, shelled,
  deveined and shells reserved

2 tablespoons tomato paste

1 gallon plus 2 cups clam juice

1 medium onion, finely chopped

2 celery ribs, chopped

1 large carrot, chopped

8 bay leaves

## ROUX

1½ cups all-purpose flour

1 cup vegetable oil

## GUMBO

¼ cup vegetable oil

4 large garlic cloves, minced

1 large onion, finely chopped

2 celery ribs, finely chopped

2 cups canned crushed tomatoes

1 large green bell pepper, finely
  chopped

1 pound okra, sliced into
  ½ inch rounds

1 tablespoon chili powder

1 tablespoon paprika

1½ tablespoons filé powder, see note

1 tablespoon dried oregano

1 teaspoon dried thyme

1 teaspoon cayenne pepper

1 teaspoon ground white pepper

Salt

Shelled and deveined shrimp,
  from the stock

1 pound lump crabmeat, picked over

Steamed rice, sliced green onions and
  Hot pepper sauce, for serving

Make the stock by heating oil in a stockpot. Add the shrimp shells and cook over high heat, until starting to brown, 5 minutes. Add the tomato paste and cook until it begins to stick to the pot, 2 minutes. Add the clam juice, onion, celery, carrot and bay leaves and bring to a boil. Simmer over moderately low heat for 25 minutes. Strain the stock into a heatproof bowl. Meanwhile, make the roux by whisking the flour with the oil in a saucepan to make a paste. Cook over moderate heat, stirring often, until the roux turns golden brown, 30 minutes. Increase the heat to moderately high and cook, stirring, until the roux is dark brown, 10 minutes longer. Scrape the roux into a bowl and reserve. Make the gumbo in a stockpot, heat 2 tablespoons of the oil. Add the garlic, onion and celery; cook over moderate heat, stirring until softened. Add the roux and cook until bubbling. Stir in the stock and tomatoes and bring to boil. Reduce the heat to moderately low. Simmer for 1½ hours until no floury taste remains. Skim off the fat. In a skillet, heat the remaining 2 tablespoons of oil. Add the green pepper, okra, chili powder, paprika, file, oregano, thyme, cayenne and white pepper. Season with salt and cook over moderately low heat, stirring until fragrant, 5 minutes. Stir in a ladleful of the liquid in the stockpot, scrape up the browned bits and transfer to the

## Gumbo, continued

gumbo in the pot. Simmer, stirring, for 1 hour. Add the shrimp to the pot and cook, just until pink throughout, 2 minutes. Stir in the crab; season with salt. Serve with steamed rice, green onions and hot pepper sauce.

*SERVES 15*

Filé powder is made from ground, dried sassafras leaves.

# Brûléed Key Lime Tarts

10 chocolate sandwich cream cookies
2 tablespoons butter, melted
5 egg yolks
1 (14 ounce) can sweetened condensed milk
⅔ cup Key lime juice, divided

Zest of 1 lime
3 tablespoons sugar, plus 8 teaspoons for sprinkling
3 kaffir lime leaves, optional
Pinch of salt
Whipped cream for garnish

Preheat oven to 350°. In a food processor, finely grind the cookies. Pulse in the butter. Lightly spray 4 (4½ inch) fluted tartlet pans with removable bottoms; press the ground cookie mixture into the bottoms. Set the pans on a baking sheet and bake for 8 minutes or until the edges look dry. Let cool. In a bowl whisk the yolks, condensed milk, ⅓ cup of the Key lime juice and lime zest. Pour the filling into the pans and bake for 15 minutes until the edges are just firm. Let cool for 30 minutes then freeze until very cool about 2 hours. In a small saucepan combine the 3 tablespoons sugar with 3 tablespoons water, the lime leaves and salt. Cook until the sugar has dissolved then cool. Discard the lime leaves. Stir in the remaining ⅓ cup lime juice and refrigerate. Sprinkle 2 teaspoons of the sugar over each tart and caramelize with a blow torch. Unmold the tarts and place in a shallow bowl. Pour in the Key lime sauce. Serve with whipped cream.

*SERVES 4*

# Praline-Apple Bread

1½ cups chopped pecans, divided
1 (8 ounce) container sour cream
1 cup sugar
2 eggs
1 tablespoons vanilla extract
2 cups all-purpose flour
2 teaspoons baking powder

½ teaspoon baking soda
½ teaspoon salt
1½ cups finely chopped, peeled
    Granny Smith apples
    (about ¾ pound)
½ cup butter
½ cup firmly packed light brown sugar

Preheat oven to 350°. Bake ½ cup pecans in a single layer in a shallow pan 6-8 minutes or until toasted and fragrant, stirring after 4 minutes. Beat sour cream, sugar, eggs and vanilla at low speed for 2 minutes. Stir together the flour, baking powder, baking soda and salt. Add to sour cream mixture, beating just until blended. Stir in apples and ½ cup toasted pecans. Spoon batter into a greased and floured 9x5 inch loaf pan. Sprinkle with remaining 1 cup chopped pecans; lightly press pecans into batter. Bake for 1 hour to 1 hour 5 minutes or until a wooden pick inserted into center comes out clean. Shield with aluminum foil after 50 minutes to prevent excessive browning. Cool in pan on a wire rack 10 minutes; remove from pan to wire rack. Bring butter and brown sugar to a boil in a 1 quart heavy saucepan over medium heat, stirring constantly, boil 1 minute. Remove from heat and spoon over top of bread which is on a serving platter. Let cool completely (about 1 hour).

*MAKES 1 LOAF*

To freeze, cool bread completely; wrap in plastic wrap, then in aluminum foil. Freeze up to 3 months. Thaw at room temperature.

JCYM founded the Story Hour for the Johnson County Library system.

Johnson County Young Matrons

# Okra and Butter Bean Stew

7 bacon strips, chopped
1 pound smoked sausage, halved and
   thinly sliced
1 large onion, chopped
2 small green peppers, chopped
3 cups water
2 (16 ounce) cans butter beans, rinsed
   and drained

1 (14.5 ounce) can diced tomatoes,
   undrained
1 (12 ounce) can tomato paste
1 teaspoon black pepper
¼ teaspoon salt
1 (16 ounce) package frozen sliced
   okra
Hot cooked rice, optional

In a Dutch oven, cook bacon and sausage over medium heat until bacon is crisp. Remove to paper towels. Drain pan, reserving 2 tablespoons drippings. Cook onion and green peppers in drippings until tender. Stir in water, beans, tomatoes, tomato paste, pepper and salt. Bring to a boil. Reduce heat; simmer uncovered, 10 minutes. Add bacon and sausage, cook 10 minutes longer. Add okra, cover and cook 8-10 minutes or until tender. Serve with rice if desired.

*SERVES 12*

# Quick Shrimp Gumbo

¼ cup all-purpose flour
¼ cup canola oil
3 celery ribs, chopped
1 medium green pepper, chopped
1 medium onion, chopped
1 (32 ounce) carton chicken broth
3 garlic cloves, minced
1 teaspoon salt
1 teaspoon pepper

½ teaspoon cayenne pepper
2 pounds uncooked large shrimp,
   peeled and deveined
1 (16 ounce) package frozen sliced
   okra
4 green onions, sliced
1 medium tomato, chopped
1½ teaspoons gumbo filé powder
Hot cooked rice

In a Dutch oven over medium heat, cook and stir flour and oil until caramel-colored, about 12 minutes (do not burn). Add the celery, green pepper and onions; cook and stir for 5-6 minutes or until tender. Stir in the broth, garlic, salt, pepper and cayenne; bring to a boil. Reduce heat, cover and simmer for 30 minutes. Stir in the shrimp, okra, green onions and tomato. Return to a boil. Reduce heat, cover and simmer for 10 minutes or until shrimp turns pink. Stir in the filé powder. Serve with rice.

*SERVES 10-12*

# Bourbon Praline Cake

**PRALINE LAYER**

4 tablespoons unsalted butter, plus more for greasing

⅓ cup firmly packed brown sugar

⅓ cup light corn syrup

¼ teaspoon kosher salt

1½ teaspoons vanilla extract

2¼ cups pecans, toasted

**CAKE**

1½ cups cake flour

1 teaspoon baking soda

¼ teaspoon freshly grated nutmeg

¼ teaspoon salt

⅓ cup buttermilk, at room temperature

2 tablespoons bourbon

¾ cup unsalted butter, at room temperature

1¼ cups sugar

3 eggs, at room temperature

½ cup pecans, toasted and chopped

Vanilla ice cream for serving

Preheat oven to 350°. Butter a 9 inch springform pan, then line the bottom and sides with parchment paper and butter the paper. Wrap the outside of the pan with foil. Make the praline layer by melting the butter in a saucepan over medium heat. Whisk in the brown sugar, corn syrup, kosher salt and vanilla. Spread in the prepared pan and scatter the pecans on top; set aside. Make the cake by whisking the flour, baking soda, nutmeg and salt in a large bowl. Whisk the buttermilk and bourbon in another bowl. Beat the butter and sugar with a mixer on medium-high speed until fluffy, about 10 minutes. With the mixer on low, beat in the eggs one at a time. Add the flour mixture in three parts, alternating with the buttermilk mixture. Fold in the pecans. Pour the batter into the pan and bake until a toothpick inserted into the center comes out clean, about 1 hour. Cool on a rack, 30 minutes. Remove the springform ring, invert the cake onto a plate and remove the paper. Serve with ice cream.

*SERVES 8*

When a cake recipe calls for flouring the baking pan, use a bit of the dry cake mix instead-no white mess on the outside of the cake.

# Shrimp and Chicken Étouffée

2 tablespoons vegetable oil
1 pound andouille sausage, diced
3 pounds skin-on, bone-in chicken
thighs
Kosher salt
½ cup plus 2 tablespoons all-purpose
flour
4 stalks celery, diced
1 large onion, diced

1 green bell pepper, chopped
4 cloves garlic, minced
¼ teaspoon cayenne pepper
4 cups chicken broth
1 pound medium shrimp, peeled and
deveined
2 tablespoons dry sherry
Freshly ground black pepper

Heat a large pot over medium-high heat; add oil and andouille and cook stirring until crisp, 4-5 minutes. Transfer to a plate. Season the chicken with salt, then add to the pot in batches to brown, 5 minutes per side. Transfer to the plate with the sausage. Make the roux by adding the flour to about ¼ cup of the drippings and stir scraping up the browned bits from the pan. Continue to cook, stirring until the mixture smells nutty and turns brown, 10-12 minutes. Add the celery, onion, bell pepper, garlic, cayenne and salt to taste. Cook, stirring, until the vegetables are tender, 6-8 minutes. Whisk in the broth. Return the chicken and sausage to the pot and simmer until the chicken is cooked through, about 25 minutes. Transfer the chicken to a plate and let cool slightly while the stew simmers; remove the skin and shred the meat. Return the meat to the pot. Stir in the shrimp and sherry and cook until the shrimp turn pink, 2-3 minutes. Season with salt and pepper.

*SERVES 8*

# Ruby Grapefruit

4 pink grapefruit
1 (10 ounce) package frozen
raspberries with syrup

2 to 4 tablespoons sugar

Peel and section grapefruit, saving all juices. Squeeze membrane for remaining juice. Put sections and juice in serving bowls. Heat raspberries and add sugar to taste. Remove from heat; cool a bit and purée in blender. Strain, if needed, and pour over grapefruit. This is a good sweet yet tart brunch accompaniment.

*SERVES 6*

# Scalloped Cabbage

3 to 4 cups sliced, cooked cabbage         1 tablespoon butter
½ cup buttered bread crumbs

**WHITE SAUCE**
2 tablespoons flour                        ¼ teaspoon salt
2 tablespoons butter                       1 cup milk

Preheat oven to 400°. To make white sauce, melt butter, stir in flour and salt. Whisk in milk and cook until thickened. Set aside. Boil cabbage until tender and drain well. Melt butter and stir in bread crumbs. Combine sauce with cooked cabbage in small casserole. Top with bread crumbs and bake for 20 minutes.

*SERVES 4-6*

# Smothered Pork Chops

1½ teaspoons salt                          ½ cup onion, chopped
1 teaspoon black pepper                    ½ green pepper, chopped
1 teaspoon dried basil                     4 pork chops (1 inch thick)
1 teaspoon oregano                         ½ cup flour
½ teaspoon dried rosemary, crushed         ½ cup vegetable oil
½ teaspoon dried thyme                     1 (14.5 ounce) can chicken broth
2 teaspoons garlic powder

Combine salt, pepper, basil, oregano, rosemary, thyme and garlic powder. Mix well and rub both sides of each pork chop. Set in refrigerator at least 20 minutes or overnight. When ready to cook, spread ½ cup flour onto wax paper. Dredge pork chops in flour until well coated. Save leftover flour for gravy. Heat ½ cup oil in large heavy skillet on high. Add pork chops and cook 6-8 minutes on each side until browned. Remove from skillet. Discard ⅔ of the oil and add ½ cup each onion and green pepper, cooking them until onion is transparent. Add 2 tablespoons of the leftover flour. Stir in 1½ cups water and the chicken broth, and stir until smooth. Return chops to skillet and bring to boil. Cover skillet, reduce heat and simmer 45 minutes. Serve chops with gravy over whipped potatoes or rice.

*SERVES 4*

# Italian Bean Soup

1 medium onion, thinly sliced
1 small potato, peeled and finely chopped
1 celery rib, chopped
3 garlic cloves, minced
2 tablespoons olive oil
3 (14.5 ounce) cans reduced sodium chicken broth

1 (15 ounce) can white kidney beans
1 (14.5 ounce) can Italian stewed tomatoes
¼ cup minced fresh parsley
1 tablespoon prepared pesto
¼ cup uncooked orzo pasta
1 cup fresh baby spinach
¼ cup grated Romano cheese

In a Dutch oven, sauté onion, potato, celery and garlic in oil until tender. Stir in broth, beans, tomatoes, parsley and pesto. Bring to boil. Stir in orzo. Reduce heat; cover and simmer 10-15 minutes or until pasta is tender. Add spinach and cook just until it is wilted. Sprinkle each serving with cheese before serving.

*SERVES 6*

# Creamy Farfalle

2 to 3 garlic cloves, minced
12 mushrooms, thinly sliced
1 (10 ounce) bag frozen peas
½ cup basil leaves, shredded or torn
5 slices center cut bacon
1 medium onion, chopped

1 bay leaf
1 (32 ounce) can Italian tomatoes
¼ cup mascarpone cheese
Salt and pepper to taste
1 pound Farfalle bow tie pasta

Heat a large pot of water to boil. Salt water, add pasta and cook al dente, 6-7 minutes. Heat a deep large skillet with 1 tablespoon olive oil over medium heat. Add bacon and fry crisp for 3-4 minutes. Remove bacon from skillet and crumble. Set aside. Add onions, garlic, bay leaf and mushrooms. Season with salt and pepper and cook until tender but not browned. Crush tomatoes then add to mixture and simmer 15 minutes on low heat. Stir peas into the sauce. Return to bubbling and stir in bacon, cheese and basil. Adjust seasoning as needed. Drain pasta, toss with sauce.

*SERVES 4*

# Squash Apple Bake

2 pounds sweet potatoes, peeled and cubed

1½ pounds butternut squash, peeled and cubed

½ cup firmly packed light brown sugar, divided

3 eggs, beaten

1 tablespoon butter, divided

2 teaspoons vanilla extract

2 teaspoons cinnamon, divided

½ teaspoon nutmeg

½ teaspoon salt

1 cup chopped pecans

2 Golden Delicious apples, peeled and thinly sliced

Cook sweet potatoes in water for 20 minutes or until tender. Drain. Meanwhile, cook squash in a separate pan of water for 10 minutes; drain. Preheat oven to 350°. Mix ¼ cup brown sugar, eggs, 1½ teaspoons butter, vanilla, 1½ teaspoons cinnamon, nutmeg and salt. Reserve ¼ cup of this mixture for squash. Purée cooked sweet potatoes with remaining egg mixture in food processor until smooth. Grease a 9x13 inch pan with cooking spray. Spread puréed mixture in pan. Sprinkle evenly with chopped pecans. Purée squash with reserved ¼ cup egg mixture until smooth. Spread over pecan layer. Arrange peeled apple slices over squash. Mix remaining brown sugar and cinnamon. Sprinkle over apples. Drizzle with remaining butter and bake 40-50 minutes or until center is set. Let stand 10 minutes before serving.

*SERVES 12*

Can use frozen butternut squash (thawed).

# Savory Bread Pudding

¼ cup butter

2 large yellow onions, sliced ⅛ inch thick

16 ounces sliced baby Portobello mushrooms

2 tablespoons balsamic vinegar

1½ teaspoons salt, divided

¼ teaspoon pepper, divided

1 pound loaf day old French bread, cut into 1 inch pieces

½ cup melted butter

1 pound package hickory smoked bacon, cooked and crumbled

2 cups whole milk

2 cups whipping cream

¼ teaspoon ground nutmeg

8 eggs, beaten

In large Dutch oven, melt butter over medium-low heat. Add onions and mushrooms, cover and cook 30 minutes, stirring occasionally. Remove cover and increase heat to medium-high. Cook for 10-12 minutes, stirring frequently. Add vinegar, ½ teaspoon salt and ¼ teaspoon pepper. Cook, stirring constantly, 1-2 minutes, or until vinegar evaporates. Set aside. In large bowl, toss cubed bread with melted butter, onion mixture and cooked and crumbled bacon. Toss to combine. Preheat oven to 325°. Lightly grease 9x13 inch pan with vegetable spray. In large saucepan, combine milk, cream, nutmeg, and remaining salt and pepper. Heat over medium-low heat until milk mixture barely begins to simmer, stirring frequently. Remove from heat. Whisking constantly, slowly add eggs until smooth. Pour custard mixture over bread; let stand 10 minutes. Spoon mixture into prepared pan. Place pan into larger pan. Add to this pan enough hot water to reach half way up sides of baking dish. Bake 1 hour or until custard is set and bread is golden brown.

*SERVES 12*

All is not work in our organization-we like to have fun as well. We tour local and area museums and galleries, enjoy social groups such as cards and bridge, discuss a range of books in our book club, challenge our wits with games such as mah jongg, enjoy local restaurants, use our busy hands to create handmade gifts and we're always open to suggestions for other activities that would be enjoyed by a few or many.

# Creamy Spinach and Parsnips

4 tablespoons unsalted butter, divided

2 tablespoons vegetable oil

2 pounds small parsnips, cut into ¾ inch pieces

2 large shallots, thinly sliced

1 cup turkey stock or canned low-sodium broth

1 teaspoon chopped thyme

Salt and freshly ground black pepper

1¼ pounds baby spinach (20 cups)

2 tablespoons all-purpose flour

2 cups half and half (or whole milk)

¼ teaspoon freshly grated nutmeg

In a large, deep skillet, melt 2 tablespoons of butter in the oil. Add the parsnips and cook over moderately high heat, stirring occasionally, until lightly browned, about 6 minutes. Add the shallots and cook, stirring until softened, about 2 minutes. Add the stock and thyme; bring to a boil. Season with salt and pepper, cover and simmer over low heat until the parsnips are tender, about 8 minutes. Meanwhile, fill a large deep pot with 2 inches of water and bring to a boil. Add the spinach in large handfuls and blanch, stirring just until wilted, about 10 seconds. Drain and cool under running water. Squeeze the spinach dry and coarsely chop it. Stir the spinach into the parsnips. In a medium saucepan, melt the remaining 2 tablespoons of butter and cook over moderately high heat until lightly browned, about 4 minutes. Whisk in the flour and cook, whisking for 1 minute. Whisk in the half and half and nutmeg, season with salt and pepper and bring the sauce to a boil, whisking until thickened, about 2 minutes. Stir the sauce into the spinach and parsnips and bring to a simmer. Transfer to a bowl and serve.

*SERVES 12*

The creamed vegetables can be refrigerated for up to 3 days and re-warmed over low heat. Stir in a little stock if the sauce is too thick.

# Nutty Caramel Cookie Tart

1 (16.5 ounce) roll refrigerated sugar
   cookies
⅓ cup dry roasted peanuts
⅓ cup caramel ice cream topping

¼ cup creamy peanut butter
½ teaspoon ground cinnamon
½ cup peanut butter chips
¼ cup vanilla baking chips

Heat oven to 350°. Press cookie dough evenly in bottom of ungreased 9 inch springform pan. If dough is sticky, use floured fingers. Bake 17-22 minutes or until golden. Meanwhile, place peanuts in zip-top plastic bag and seal. Crush peanuts with rolling pin and set aside. In medium microwavable bowl, cook caramel topping, peanut butter and cinnamon, uncovered, on high 30-60 seconds. Stir well. Drizzle mixture evenly over partially baked crust. Sprinkle with peanut butter chips, vanilla chips and crushed peanuts. Bake 12-18 minutes or longer until edges are golden brown. Cool completely for 1 hour 30 minutes. Run sharp knife around edge of tart to loosen. Remove side of pan. To serve, cut tart into wedges. Store tightly in covered container at room temperature.

*SERVES 16*


# Quick Meat Loaf

⅓ cup chopped green onions
3 tablespoons dry bread crumbs
2 teaspoons garlic, minced
½ teaspoon salt
½ teaspoon dry mustard
¼ teaspoon black pepper

¼ teaspoon crushed red pepper
1 pound ground sirloin
1 egg, lightly beaten
6 tablespoons ketchup, divided
Cooking spray

Preheat oven to 400°. Combine green onions, bread crumbs, garlic, salt, mustard, pepper, crushed red pepper, sirloin and egg. Add ¼ cup ketchup. Mix well with hands until combined. Shape into 9x4 inch loaf on a broiler pan coated with vegetable spray. Bake 20 minutes. Brush top with remaining 2 tablespoons ketchup. Bake 7 additional minutes or until done. Slice loaf into 8 equal pieces.

*SERVES 4*

# Baked Pears with Almonds

| | |
|---|---|
| 4 Bartlett pears, medium ripe | ¼ cup honey |
| ½ cup white wine | ½ teaspoon ground cinnamon |
| 1 tablespoon lemon juice | ¼ teaspoon ground cloves |
| ½ teaspoon lemon zest | 1 teaspoon vanilla extract |
| ¼ cup sugar | |

**ALMOND FILLING**

| | |
|---|---|
| ½ cup whole raw almonds | ¼ teaspoon cinnamon |
| 3 tablespoons sugar | 1 egg white |
| ¼ teaspoon grated lemon zest | |

Preheat oven to 375°. Combine wine, lemon juice, lemon zest, sugar, honey, cinnamon, cloves and vanilla in a 9x13 inch baking dish. Peel, halve and core 4 pears. Then place cut-side down in the baking dish. Bake 15-25 minutes. While pears bake, make almond filling by blending almonds, sugar, lemon peel, cinnamon and egg white in a food processor or blender until almonds are finely chopped. Invert baked pears in baking dish and fill with almond mixture. Bake 10 minutes. Place under broiler to lightly brown topping. Place pears on serving plates. Spoon syrup over pears and serve with light vanilla ice cream or frozen yogurt.

*SERVES 8*

# Pineapple Carrots

| | |
|---|---|
| 2 cups carrots, thinly sliced | ⅛ teaspoon nutmeg |
| ¾ cup unsweetened pineapple juice | Fresh ground black pepper to taste |
| ¾ teaspoon cinnamon | |

In medium saucepan, combine pineapple juice, cinnamon, nutmeg and pepper. Bring mixture to boil. Reduce heat and add carrots. Cover and simmer 6 minutes or until carrots are tender-crisp.

*SERVES 3-4*

# Artichoke Lasagna

**BÉCHAMEL SAUCE**

½ cup butter

2 tablespoons onion, grated

½ cup all-purpose flour

1 teaspoon salt

⅛ teaspoon white pepper

1½ teaspoons instant chicken bouillon (or 2 cubes, crushed)

1 cup light cream or half and half

1 cup milk

**FILLING**

2 cups cottage cheese

2 eggs, slightly beaten

½ cup Parmesan cheese, divided

1½ cups shredded Cheddar cheese, divided

8 ounces lasagna noodles, cooked and drained

2 (9 ounce) packages frozen artichoke hearts, cooked and drained

Preheat oven to 350°. For béchamel sauce, melt butter over low heat; add onion and sauté until tender. Blend flour, salt, pepper and bouillon. Cool, stirring constantly, until roux bubbles for 2 minutes. Add cream and milk, stirring vigorously to blend well. Bring to a boil over medium heat, stirring constantly then boil for 1 minute. Cover and set aside. Make the filling by beating cottage cheese on high speed of mixer for 5 minutes. Stir in eggs and ¼ cup Parmesan cheese. Combine with sauce. Assemble by placing ⅓ of cooked noodles in bottom of buttered 9x13 inch baking dish. Spread with ⅓ of sauce mixture and 1 package of cooked and drained artichoke hearts. Sprinkle with ½ of the Cheddar cheese. Repeat for the second layer. For the top layer, place noodles, remaining sauce, and remaining Parmesan cheese. Bake 35-40 minutes; let rest 10 minutes before serving.

*SERVES 12*

May be made the night before. Let sit out 15-20 minutes before serving.

# Shrimp and Lime Soup

1½ pounds raw shrimp, peeled and deveined

8 cups water

¼ teaspoon grated lime rind

1 tablespoon chopped lemon grass or ¼ teaspoon grated lemon rind

2 teaspoons fish sauce

⅓ cup lime juice

4 tablespoons chopped cilantro leaves

3 tablespoons sliced green onions

1 red chili, seeded, julienned and cut into 1 inch pieces

Salt and pepper to taste

Slivers of green onions for garnish

Wash shrimp in cold water, drain and dry on paper towels, set aside. Pour the water into a large saucepan, bring to a boil. Add the lime rind and lemon grass, reduce the heat, simmer for 10 minutes. Add the fish sauce and continue cooking for 5 minutes. Add the shrimp and lime juice, cook gently over low heat for a few minutes until shrimp become firm and turn a pale pink color. Add the chopped cilantro leaves, green onions and red chili strips to the soup. Add salt and pepper. Serve hot garnished with slivers of green onion.

*SERVES 6*

# Hot and Sour Soup

2 tablespoons peanut or canola oil

2 garlic cloves, minced

1 tablespoon grated fresh ginger

8 ounces fresh shiitake mushrooms, stemmed and sliced

8 cups chicken broth

1 (8 ounce) can sliced bamboo shoots, cut into slivers

¾ cup soy sauce, may use low sodium

½ cup seasoned rice vinegar

1 teaspoon sesame oil

½ to 1 teaspoon black pepper

1½ teaspoons chili paste or 1 red chili, seeded and sliced, optional

1½ pounds large shrimp, peeled and deveined

1 cup snow peas

2 tablespoons cornstarch mixed with 2 tablespoons water

1 egg, lightly beaten

Heat oil in a Dutch oven over medium heat. Add garlic and ginger; sauté 30 seconds or until fragrant. Add mushrooms; sauté 1 minute. Stir in broth, bamboo shoots, soy sauce, rice vinegar, sesame oil, pepper and (chili paste, if desired) bring to a boil. Stir in shrimp and snow peas, cook 2-3 minutes or until shrimp turn pink. Add cornstarch mixture and simmer 1-2 minutes or until slightly thickened. Remove from heat. Pour in egg, stirring slowly in one direction. Serve immediately.

*SERVES 10 TO 12*

# Shrimp and Mushroom Wontons

2 tablespoons butter
2 cloves garlic, chopped
1 cup chopped fresh mushrooms
½ cup chopped green onions
2 teaspoons soy sauce
2 teaspoons toasted sesame oil

¼ teaspoon salt
¼ teaspoon black pepper
1 pound fresh shrimp, peeled, deveined, and chopped
60 wonton or pot sticker wrappers
Vegetable oil or peanut oil

**SOY-SESAME DIPPING SAUCE**

⅔ cup soy sauce
½ cup rice vinegar
4 teaspoons toasted sesame oil
4 teaspoons sugar

2 tablespoons fresh lemon juice
4 teaspoons Thai garlic chili pepper sauce, optional
Sesame seeds and chopped green onions for garnish

For the dipping sauce: combine soy sauce, vinegar, oil, sugar and lemon juice. If desired, add Thai garlic chili pepper sauce. Whisk to combine. Garnish with sesame seeds and green onions. Set aside. In a large skillet, melt butter over medium heat; add garlic and cook 1 minute. Add mushrooms and cook 4-5 minutes or until all liquid evaporates. Add green onions and cook 2 minutes. Stir in soy sauce, sesame oil, salt and pepper. Stir in shrimp and cook until pink. Spoon 2 teaspoons shrimp mixture onto center of each wonton wrapper. Moisten wrapper edges with water and bring corners together, pressing edges to seal. In a Dutch oven pour oil to a depth of 6 inches, heat to 350°. Fry wontons, in batches, 2 minutes on each side or until golden brown. Drain on paper towels. Serve warm with dipping sauce.

*SERVES 30*

Baked Won chips are a unique alternative to crackers and tortilla chips for dips and they are low in calories! Cut wonton skins in half diagonally. Arrange in a single layer on ungreased baking sheets. Spray lightly with water. Bake at 375 degrees for 8 minutes, or until light brown. Serve warm or cold. They can also be seasoned, sprayed with water and baked. Try sprinkling evenly with 2 teaspoons grated Parmesan cheese, 2 teaspoons salt-free lemon and herb spice blend, 1½ teaspoons garlic power, or ¼ teaspoon cinnamon and 1½ teaspoons sugar. Or mold into mini-muffin tins and bake until light golden. These create delightful "bowls" for all types of fillings.

# Spicy Thai-Style Chicken in Lettuce Cups

3 tablespoons uncooked Jasmine rice

3 tablespoons fish sauce

1 stalk lemongrass, trimmed, outer layer removed and inner core minced (1 tablespoon)

1 teaspoon crushed red pepper flakes

½ teaspoon firmly packed light brown sugar

½ cup water

1¼ pounds ground chicken, preferably dark meat

1 medium shallot, minced (⅓ cup)

3 tablespoons fresh lime juice

3 medium green onions, thinly sliced on the diagonal

2 tablespoons fresh cilantro, coarsely chopped

2 tablespoons fresh mint, chopped

1 medium head butter lettuce, for serving

Toast the rice in a 8 inch skillet over medium-low heat, stirring frequently until golden, 4-5 minutes (the rice will begin to smoke after a few minutes). Let the rice cool slightly. Place in a food processor and process until the largest pieces resemble very coarse cornmeal; the mixture should not be completely powdery. Combine the fish sauce, lemongrass, pepper flakes, brown sugar and ½ cup water in a 12 inch nonstick skillet and bring to a simmer over high heat. Separate chicken into large clumps and add to the pan. Cook the chicken, breaking into small pieces with a wooden spoon until meat is no longer pink. Sprinkle 1 tablespoon of the ground rice over the chicken and continue to cook, stirring frequently until the liquid in the pan has thickened, about 2 minutes. Remove from heat, stir in the shallot. Sprinkle with the lime juice, green onions, cilantro and mint and stir gently to combine. Transfer to a serving dish and sprinkle with 1 teaspoon of the remaining ground rice. Serve with the lettuce leaves on the side to use as cups for the chicken.

*SERVES 4*

To keep lettuce fresh longer, wrap it in paper towels and place in a dry plastic bag before storing in the refrigerator.

# Vietnamese-Style Chicken Salad

3 small shallots, coarsely chopped (½ cup)

1 jalapeño pepper, chopped (seed first if you want less heat)

1 tablespoon sugar

Freshly ground black pepper

¼ cup rice vinegar

3 tablespoons fish sauce

1 pound, boneless, skinless, thin-sliced chicken breast cutlets

Kosher salt

6 ounce package coleslaw mix

1 cup fresh mint leaves, torn

¼ cup fresh cilantro leaves

¼ cup salted peanuts, coarsely chopped

Prepare a medium grill fire. With a mortar and pestle, pound the shallots, jalapeño pepper, sugar and ⅛ teaspoon pepper until the shallots are very soft (but not puréed) and liquid is released. Transfer to a large serving bowl and stir in the vinegar and fish sauce. Season the chicken with ¼ teaspoon salt and ⅛ teaspoon pepper and grill, turning once, until just cooked through, about 2 minutes per side. Let cool and then shred the chicken with your fingers into long thin strips, pulling the meat along its natural grain. Toss the coleslaw mix into the vinegar mixture. Add the chicken, mint and the cilantro and combine well. Top with the peanuts and serve at room temperature.

*SERVES 4*

If you don't have a grill, you can cook the chicken indoors on a ridged grill pan over medium heat for the same amount of time.

Our members founded and continue to serve as docents for the Shawnee Indian Mission, a historical site of great value to our community.

# Thai Dipping Sauce

¼ cup fresh lime juice

2½ tablespoons sugar

2 tablespoons fish sauce

1½ teaspoons rice vinegar

1½ teaspoons fresh cilantro, coarsely chopped

1 teaspoon garlic, minced,

½ teaspoon minced fresh hot or green chili (such as cayenne, Thai bird or Serrano)

Combine all the ingredients in a small bowl and stir until the sugar is dissolved. Let stand at least 30 minutes before serving to let the flavors develop and blend.

*SERVES 2*

Fantastic with grilled fish or pork.

# Thai-Style Pineapple Snack

Half of a ripe pineapple, peeled and cored

Kosher salt

Cayenne pepper

2 tablespoons fresh mint leaves, chopped

2 tablespoons fresh cilantro leaves, chopped

Lime wedges

Cut the pineapple into bite size wedges or slices. Put the salt, cayenne pepper, mint and cilantro into small bowls. Squeeze a bit of lime wedge onto the fruit. Then lightly dip the pineapple into a little salt and as much cayenne as you like and finish with the mint and cilantro.

*SERVES 6*

For true Southeast Asian taste, add a little bowl of fish sauce to your options of dippers.

# Brown Rice Salad with Citrus-Thai Basil Vinaigrette

2 cups cooked brown rice
2 carrots, grated
1 cup pea pods, thinly sliced on an angle
1 small red onion, halved and minced

6 green onions, thinly sliced on an angle
Garnish: Chopped fresh cilantro, Thai basil and/or mint leaves

**CITRUS-THAI BASIL VINAIGRETTE**

¾ cup orange juice
¼ cup lime juice
½ cup fresh Thai basil leaves, chopped (Substitute regular basil or mint leaves if needed)
1 cup fresh cilantro leaves

1 teaspoon kosher salt
¼ teaspoon freshly ground black pepper
1 heaping tablespoon honey
½ cup canola oil

To make the vinaigrette, combine all ingredients in a blender and blend for 1 minute, set aside. Combine the rice and vegetables in a large bowl. Add the vinaigrette and stir to combine. Let the salad sit at room temperature for 30 minutes before serving. Garnish with desired herbs.

*SERVES 4*

# Thai Iced Tea

8 cups water
6 tablespoons Thai tea leaves

½ cup sweetened condensed milk or more to taste
Crushed ice

Bring the water to a boil in a medium saucepan. Place tea in a tea strainer, add to the boiling water, remove from the heat and let steep for 5-10 minutes depending on how strong you like your tea. Strain the tea into a pitcher and stir in the condensed milk. Fill 4 highball glasses with crushed ice, pour in the tea and stir to chill. Add more sweetened condensed milk if desired.

*SERVES 4*

# Cranberry Tea

3½ cups sugar
½ cup cinnamon candies
6 to 12 whole cloves
1 quart cranberry cocktail juice

1 (6 ounce) can frozen lemonade, thawed, undiluted
1 (6 ounce) can frozen orange juice, thawed, undiluted

To sugar add candies and cloves, add 1 quart water. Cook until sugar is dissolved. Add cranberry juice, lemonade, orange juice and 3 quarts of water. Refrigerate, remove cloves and reheat. Serve hot.

*SERVES 6 QUARTS*

May omit the orange juice and cut down on the sugar.

# Asparagus Soup

45 asparagus spears, 8-10 inches long
2 cups carrots, grated
2 cups broccoli, chopped
2 cloves garlic, minced

½ cup onions, minced
1 cup sodium-free chicken broth, or 1 packet Herb Ox Sodium free chicken bouillon

Chop asparagus and broccoli, you may use frozen florets. Put all vegetables in a large pan. Add enough water to just cover the vegetables. Once the water is boiling, add the chicken bouillon packet. If you are using a liquid broth, add it before you add the water. Once the soup is boiling turn down the heat and simmer until the soup becomes thick.

*SERVE 6 (1 CUP) BOWLS*

# Green Salad with Pears, Prosciutto and Avocado

1 tablespoon fresh lemon juice
¼ teaspoon finely grated lemon zest
Pinch of sugar
3 tablespoons extra virgin olive oil
Kosher salt and freshly ground black pepper
3 cups baby arugula, spinach, or mesclun mix

2 thin slices prosciutto, cut crosswise into thin ribbons
1 small firm-ripe pear, cored and cut into thin wedges
½ small ripe avocado, pitted and cut into small cubes

In a small bowl, whisk the lemon juice, zest and sugar until the sugar is dissolved. Slowly whisk in the oil. Season the vinaigrette to taste with salt and pepper. In a large salad or mixing bowl, gently toss the arugula, prosciutto, avocado and pears with half of the dressing. Divide among 2 plates, drizzle with a little of the remaining dressing and serve immediately.

*SERVES 2*

# Soda Bread

3 cups all-purpose flour
⅓ cup sugar
1 tablespoon baking powder
1 teaspoon salt

1 teaspoon baking soda
1 egg, slightly beaten
2 cups buttermilk
¼ cup melted butter

Preheat oven to 325°. In a large bowl combine flour, sugar, baking powder, salt and soda. Stir to mix well. Blend the egg and buttermilk and add all at once to the flour mixture. Mix until everything is moist. Stir in the melted butter and mix well. Pour into a greased 9x5 inch loaf pan and bake for 1 hour to 1 hour 15 minutes or until a toothpick inserted in center is clean. Don't underbake. Remove from pan and cool on a rack. Place in a zip-top plastic bag and store for at least 8 hours before serving.

*SERVES 1 LOAF*

# Crock-Pot Corned Beef and Cabbage

6 to 8 medium potatoes, peeled and
cut into ½ inch thick slices

3 medium carrots, thinly sliced

2 ribs celery, thinly sliced

1 corned beef brisket, about 3 pounds

1 cabbage, about 2 pounds, cut into
wedges

½ teaspoon black pepper

1½ cups water

Lightly butter or spray a 5-6 quart crock-pot; layer potato slices over bottom of the pot with carrots and celery. Place corned beef on vegetables and place cabbage wedges around the meat. Sprinkle with the pepper and add water. Cover and cook on LOW setting for 7-8 hours, or until tender. Remove meat to a platter; cover with foil and let rest for 10-15 minutes before slicing.

*SERVES 8*

If not fixed in a crock-pot, boil beef according to the package directions. Remove from the pot and place in an oiled baking pan, bake for 30 minutes at 350° with a glaze of yellow mustard and brown sugar spread on the top of the meat. Serve with cooked vegetables.

# Spinach Casserole

½ cup butter

1 (8 ounce) package cream cheese,
softened

1 large bag frozen spinach

1 (8 ounce) can water chestnuts,
drained and chopped

1 (14.5 ounce) can artichoke hearts

½ teaspoon garlic powder

½ teaspoon onion powder

½ teaspoon salt

½ teaspoon black pepper

1 cup bread crumbs

1 cup Parmesan cheese

Preheat oven to 350°. Cream butter and cream cheese. Microwave spinach enough to separate, squeeze water out of spinach. Add spinach and water chestnuts to cream cheese mixture. Season to taste. Spray a 1½ quart casserole dish with non-stick spray. Layer artichoke hearts on bottom of the dish, spread spinach mixture over artichokes. Top with mixed bread crumbs and Parmesan cheese. Bake for 30 minutes.

*SERVES 8*

# Balsamic Roasted Brussels Sprouts

1 (16 ounce) package frozen Brussels sprouts, thawed, or equivalent amount of fresh sprouts
Olive oil cooking spray
1 thinly sliced (scant ½ ounce) prosciutto slice, diced into small pieces

2 tablespoons pecan pieces
2 tablespoons dried cranberries
1 tablespoon red wine vinegar
2 tablespoons balsamic vinegar
1 teaspoon Dijon mustard
1 teaspoon olive oil

Preheat oven to 400°. Line a 15x10 inch baking sheet with aluminum foil. Pat Brussels sprouts completely dry and place in a single layer on baking sheet. Sprinkle with prosciutto. Spray generously with olive oil spray. Roast for 30 minutes. Stir and sprinkle with pecans and cranberries. Spray again with olive oil spray and bake an additional 5-10 minutes or until tender and pecans are slightly toasted. Whisk together red wine vinegar, balsamic vinegar, Dijon and olive oil. Place Brussels sprouts in medium bowl and drizzle with vinaigrette. Toss gently to coat.

*SERVES 4*

# Macaroni and Cheese

6 tablespoons butter
½ cup all-purpose flour
4 cups milk, warmed
1 teaspoon dry mustard
¼ teaspoon nutmeg
¼ teaspoon cayenne pepper
Dash of salt and black pepper
Dash of hot sauce

Dash of Worcestershire sauce
3 cups shredded Cheddar cheese
1 pound cavatappi pasta, cooked al dente
1 cup crushed potato chips
5 slices bacon, cooked and crumbled
½ cup Parmesan cheese (for topping)

Preheat oven to 350°. Melt 6 tablespoons butter in a large saucepan over medium heat. Add flour; cook, stirring for 1 minutes. Whisk in the warmed milk and bring to a boil. Continue to whisk constantly. The mixture will thicken as the heat increases. Continue to stir while adding the dry mustard, nutmeg, cayenne, salt, pepper, hot sauce and Worcestershire. Stir in Cheddar cheese until it melts. Pour the cheese sauce over the pasta. Place in a 3 quart casserole dish. Sprinkle with chips, bacon, and Parmesan cheese. Bake for 35 minutes.

*SERVES 8*

# O'Henry Bars

⅔ cup butter
4 cups uncooked oatmeal
1 cup firmly packed brown sugar
½ cup light corn syrup

3 teaspoons vanilla extract
1 (6 ounce) package semisweet
  chocolate chips
⅔ cup peanut butter

Preheat oven to 350° Cream butter; stir in oats, sugar, corn syrup and vanilla. Spread mixture in a 9x13 inch greased pan. Bake for 15 minutes. (Don't bake any longer even though bars may not look cooked.) Cool. In a saucepan, melt chocolate chips and peanut butter. Spread over cooled bars and chill for several hours before cutting into bars.

*SERVES 2 DOZEN COOKIES*

# Cheesecake with Chocolate Crust and Cherries

2 cups chocolate graham cracker
  crumbs
¼ cup butter, melted
2 tablespoons sugar
4 (8 ounce) packages cream cheese,
  softened

⅔ cup sugar
½ cup sour cream
1 tablespoon grated orange zest
4 eggs
3 cans cherry pie filling
½ teaspoon almond extract

Heat oven to 325°. Mix cookie crumbs, butter and 2 tablespoons sugar. Press on bottom and slightly up side of ungreased 9 inch springform pan. Place cream cheese, sugar, sour cream and orange peel in food processor. Cover and process until smooth. Add eggs. Cover and process until well blended. Spread over crust. Bake about 1 hour 20 minutes or until center is set. Cool on wire rack 15 minutes. Run metal spatula along side of cheesecake to loosen; remove side of pan. Refrigerate uncovered 3 hours, cover and continue refrigerating at least 4 hours. Rinse and drain 2 cans of the cherries and add to the third can. Add almond extract and spread mixture evenly over cheesecake.

*SERVES 16*

# Vegetable Sauté with Orange and Balsamic Sauce

½ pound thin green beans, trimmed

2 tablespoons olive oil

2 medium shallots, halved and thinly sliced (about ½ cup)

1 teaspoon chopped fresh rosemary

1 medium yellow bell pepper, cored and sliced ¼ inch thick

3 tablespoons fresh orange juice

½ tablespoon balsamic vinegar

1 teaspoon finely grated orange zest

3 cups lightly packed fresh baby spinach leaves

Sea salt and freshly ground black pepper

In a pot fitted with a steamer basket, bring 1-2 inches of water to a boil. Put the green beans in the steamer basket, cover and steam until bright green and just beginning to soften, 2 minutes. Transfer beans to a bowl and set aside. Heat the oil in a 12 inch skillet over medium-high heat. Add the shallots and rosemary and cook, stirring until the shallots begin to brown, 1-2 minutes. Reduce the heat to medium, add the beans and bell pepper and cook stirring until the pepper begins to soften, about 2 minutes. Stir in the orange juice, balsamic vinegar and orange zest. Add the spinach and cook stirring until just wilted about 20 seconds. Remove from heat, season to taste with salt and pepper and serve.

*SERVES 4*

# Pork Tenderloin with Mushrooms and Olives

1 pork tenderloin, about 2 to 3 pounds

½ cup flour, seasoned with salt and pepper

2 tablespoons butter

1 onion, sliced

½ cup dry white wine, optional

½ pound mushrooms, sliced

⅛ tablespoon fresh rosemary

6 green olives, sliced

½ cup sliced almonds

2 tablespoons lemon juice

Cut pork tenderloin into 1 inch thick medallions, then roll each in seasoned flour. Sauté meat and sliced onion in 2 tablespoons butter until golden brown or approximately 10 minutes. Add white wine, or ½ cup water, mushrooms and rosemary. Cover skillet and simmer for 30 minutes. Add olives, almonds and lemon juice. Remove to serving plate.

*SERVES 6-8*

# The Best Bread Pudding

2 cups sugar
5 beaten eggs
2 cups milk
2 teaspoons vanilla extract

3 cups cubed Italian bread, placed in large bowl and set overnight to stale
1 cup firmly packed brown sugar
¼ cup butter, softened
1 cup chopped pecans

**SAUCE**

1 cup sugar
½ cup butter, melted
1 egg, beaten

2 teaspoons vanilla extract
¼ cup brandy

Preheat oven to 350°. Grease a 9x13 inch pan. Mix together the sugar, eggs and milk in a bowl; add vanilla. Pour over cubed bread and let sit for 10 minutes. In another bowl, mix and crumble together the brown sugar, butter and pecans. Pour bread mixture into prepared pan. Sprinkle brown sugar mixture over the top and bake for 35-45 minutes, or until set. Remove from oven. For the sauce; mix together the sugar, butter, egg and vanilla in a saucepan over medium heat. Stir together until the sugar is melted. Add the brandy, stirring well. Pour over the bread pudding. Serve warm or cold.

*SERVES 12*

Toasting nuts adds crispness and intensifies the flavor. Spread in a single layer on a baking sheet or pan. Preheat oven to 350°; place pan in oven and bake 5-10 minutes, or until nuts release their aroma, being careful not to burn. A smaller portion of nuts will toast much quicker than a larger amount. Toast a larger amount than needed and freeze extras up to 1 year in a tightly sealed container. Four ounces of nuts equals about 1 cup. Alternately, in a small skillet over low heat cook nuts in a small amount of butter until they are light brown. Stir constantly. Drain on paper towels. Or, you may place up to one cup of nuts on a paper plate and cook in the microwave (full power) for 1 minute 30 seconds or until hot.

# Spring Temptations

# After The Egg Hunt

Citrus Sunrise, page 126
Crab and Artichoke Stuffed Mushrooms, page 127
Triangle Treasures, page 127
Strawberry Avocado Walnut Salad, page 126
Green Asparagus with Black Olive Tapenade, page 128
Rosemary and Cheese Breadsticks, page 129
Tuscan Potato Bake, page 132
Baked Ham with Mango Chutney Glaze, page 128
Lime Tart with Blackberries and Blueberries, page 130
Coconut Macaroons, page 129

## Substitution

Berry Berry Cool Pie, page 131

# The Brunch Bunch

Champagne Punch, page 133
Cantaloupe Balls à la Orange, page 133
Antipasto Squares, page 134
South of the Border Breakfast, page 134
Very Fancy Brunch Bacon, page 133
Spinach and Bacon Quiche, page 135
BLT Salad, page 136
Fruit Casserole, page 135
Lemon Curd Pie, page 137
Coconut Cake, page 137

## Substitutions

Tomato Basil Squares, page 136
Berry Pizza Pie, page 138
Delicious Cucumber Dip, page 138

# Pomp and Circumstance

Piña Colada Punch (Non-Alcoholic), page 139
Chili Cheesecake, page 139
Watermelon Fire and Ice Salsa, page 140
Bacon Wrapped Jalapeños, page 140
Southwestern Cornbread Salad, page 142
Chicken Enchiladas, page 141
Marinated Asparagus, page 140
Pistachio Cake, page 142
Toffee Pecan Cookies, page 143

## Substitutions

Monterey Shrimp Dip, page 143
Fruit Trifle, page 144

# TGIF

Beer with a Punch, page 145
Chunky Gazpacho Salad, page 146
Shrimp Quesadillas, page 147
Fiery Beef Burgers, page 145
Oven Fries with Herbs and Pecorino, page 146
Roasted Cherry Tomatoes, page 148
Shoe Peg Corn, page 145
Thumbprint Cookies, page 148
Frozen Lemon Pie, page 147

# Catch of the Day

Salty Dog, page 149
Pesto Cheesecake, page 151
Blue Crab and Avocado Cocktail, page 150
Spinach Salad with Grapes and Shrimp, page 151
Roasted Salmon with Shallot and Grapefruit Sauce, page 152
Hot Onion Soufflé, page 150
Roasted Pencil Asparagus, page 152
Saffron Rice Pilaf, page 149
Raspberry Orange Trifle, page 153

## Substitution

Mini Chocolate Chip Angel Cakes, page 154

# That's Amore

Zucchini Squares, page 155
Mamma's Caponata, page 156
Caprese Salad, page 155
Italian Breadsticks, page 157
Penne with Sausage, Artichokes and Sun-Dried Tomatoes, page 158
Beef, Pork and Mushroom Lasagna, page 156
Rich and Cheesy Vegetable Lasagna, page 159
Seafood Lasagna, page 160
Lemon Pound Cake, page 161
White Chocolate Raspberry Bars, page 162

## Substitutions

Bowtie Pasta with Asparagus, page 163
Tiramisu Brownie Squares, page 162
Chicken Spaghetti Casserole, page 163
Mac's Meatballs, page 164

# Bridge Bites

Baked Jalapeño Matchsticks, page 165
Crab Rangoon Dip, page 165
Tangy Orange Ball, page 166
Hot Swiss Cheese and Onion Dip, page 167
Creamy Bacon Dip, page 166
Artichoke Hummus, page 167
Spinach and Chèvre Dip, page 167
Cajun Shrimp and Artichoke Dip, page 168
Avocado-Goat Cheese Spread, page 168
True Tapenade, page 169
Quick and Easy Tapenade, page 169
Baked Brie Parcels, page 170
Smoked Salmon Bites, page 171
Chicken Enchilada Dip, page 170
Artichoke Dip, page 171
Louisiana Crab Dip with Crudités, page 171

# Comfort Foods for Friends in Need

King Ranch Casserole, page 172
Cheesy Herb Coins, page 173
Quick Broccoli Salad, page 174
Green Bean Salad with Feta, page 174
Blueberry Oatmeal Crisp, page 173
Peanut Butter Fudge Bars, page 174
Zesty Ham Roll-Ups, page 172

# Citrus Sunrise

Crushed ice

½ cup cranberry juice

½ cup orange juice

2 tablespoons vodka, optional

Slice of lime, for garnish

Slice of orange, for garnish

Fill a 12 ounce glass with crushed ice and pour in cranberry juice, orange juice and vodka. Stir. Garnish with lime and orange slices.

*SERVES 1*

# Strawberry Avocado Walnut Salad

**DRESSING**

1 cup vegetable oil

¼ cup sugar

½ cup raspberry vinegar

2 cloves garlic, minced

½ teaspoon salt

½ teaspoon paprika

¼ teaspoon ground black pepper

**SALAD**

½ cup walnuts, coarsely chopped and toasted

1 pint strawberries, hulled and sliced

1 large (or 2 medium) avocado

1 cup shredded Monterey Jack cheese

1 head romaine lettuce

1 head Boston or red leaf lettuce

Combine oil, sugar, raspberry vinegar, garlic, salt, paprika, and pepper in a large jar. Cover tightly and shake vigorously. Set aside. Preheat oven to 350°. Toast walnuts in oven for about 10 minutes or until golden brown. Tear romaine lettuce and Boston lettuce into bite-sized pieces. Place romaine lettuce, Boston lettuce, strawberries, avocado, Monterey Jack cheese, and toasted walnuts in a large bowl. Just prior to serving, pour desired amount of dressing over salad and toss gently.

*SERVES 12*

Left over dressing keeps well in the refrigerator for about 1 week.

# Crab and Artichoke Stuffed Mushrooms

2 (6 ounce) cans crabmeat

1 (14 ounce) can artichoke hearts, drained and finely chopped

1 cup mayonnaise (or ½ cup mayonnaise and ½ cup plain yogurt)

½ cup grated Parmesan cheese

¼ teaspoon lemon pepper seasoning

⅛ teaspoon salt

30 large fresh mushroom caps

Preheat oven to 400°. In a bowl, combine crabmeat, artichoke hearts, mayonnaise, Parmesan cheese, lemon pepper seasoning and salt. Clean mushroom caps and remove stems. Fill the caps with the crabmeat mixture. Place the caps in a lightly greased shallow baking dish. Bake for 10 minutes or until hot and bubbly.

*SERVES 30 APPETIZERS*

# Triangle Treasures

¼ cup olive oil

½ cup chopped onion

2 eggs

1 (10 ounce) package frozen chopped spinach, thawed and well drained

16 ounces feta cheese, crumbled

½ cup chopped fresh parsley

2 tablespoons fresh oregano, chopped or 1 teaspoon dried oregano leaves

Salt and pepper to taste

1 (16 ounce) package frozen phyllo dough, thawed to room temperature

1 cup butter, melted

Preheat oven to 375°. Heat oil over medium high heat in a small skillet and add onion; cook and stir until translucent and golden. In a large separate bowl beat eggs on medium high speed with electric mixer until light and lemon colored. Combine onions, spinach, feta cheese, parsley, and oregano with eggs; stir until well blended. Season with salt and pepper. Remove phyllo from package, unroll and place on large sheet of waxed paper. Fold phyllo crosswise into thirds. Use scissors (or sharp paring knife) to cut along folds and into thirds. Cover phyllo with a damp clean kitchen towel. (Phyllo dries out quickly if not covered.) Lay a strip of phyllo on flat surface; brush immediately with melted butter. Fold strip in half lengthwise; brush again with butter. Place 1 rounded teaspoon of spinach filling on end of strip; fold over one corner to make a triangle. Continue folding end to end as you would a flag, keeping edges straight. Brush top with butter. Repeat process until all spinach filling is used. Place triangles in a single layer, seam side down, on ungreased baking sheet. Bake for 20 minutes or until lightly brown. Serve warm.

*SERVES 60 APPETIZERS*

# Green Asparagus with Black Olive Tapenade

2 bunches green asparagus
3 tablespoons olive oil
4 ounces black olive tapenade
Salt and freshly ground black pepper,
    to taste

4 ounces fresh goat cheese, crumbled
¼ cup whole almonds, toasted and
    coarsely chopped

Prepare asparagus by holding spears individually by the tip and base and bend each until it snaps. Discard ends that are hard and woody. Heat olive oil in a large sauté pan. Cook asparagus over medium heat for about 10 minutes, stirring often. When asparagus is tender, add black olive tapenade and a light touch of salt and pepper. (Keep in mind that tapenade is already salty.) Toss until asparagus is well coated. Sprinkle goat cheese and almonds on top of asparagus and serve warm.

Black olive tapenade may be purchased at a grocery store.

# Baked Ham with Mango Chutney Glaze

6 garlic cloves, peeled
¾ cup mango chutney
½ cup Dijon mustard
1 cup firmly packed light brown sugar

¼ cup freshly squeezed orange juice
Zest of 1 orange
1 (14-16 pound) fully cooked spiral
    cut smoked ham

Preheat oven to 350°. Mince garlic in the bowl of a food processor fitted with a steel blade. Add the chutney, mustard, brown sugar, orange juice and orange zest. Process until smooth. Place ham in heavy roasting pan. Pour the glaze over the ham and bake for 1 hour until the ham is fully heated and the glaze is well browned. Serve hot or at room temperature.

*SERVES 20*

# Rosemary and Cheese Breadsticks

¼ cup grated Parmesan cheese
⅓ cup grated Gruyère cheese
1 teaspoon fresh rosemary leaves, chopped

1 (11 ounce) can refrigerated breadstick dough
Sea salt, finely ground, optional

Preheat oven to 350°. Line 2 baking sheets with parchment paper. In food processor, combine the Parmesan cheese, Gruyère cheese and rosemary. Set aside. Separate the dough strips. Using a pizza cutter or a sharp knife, cut each strip in half lengthwise to form thin strips. Coat each dough strip with the cheese mixture, pressing gently. Twist each cheese-covered dough strip and place on prepared baking sheets. Sprinkle with salt if desired. Bake about 10-15 minutes or until the breadsticks are golden brown. Serve warm.

Asiago cheese can be substituted for Gruyère cheese.

# Coconut Macaroons

14 ounces sweetened shredded coconut
1 (14 ounce) can sweetened condensed milk

1 teaspoon vanilla extract
2 egg whites, at room temperature
¼ teaspoon kosher salt

Preheat oven to 350°. Combine the coconut, milk and vanilla in a large bowl. In a separate bowl, whip the egg whites and salt on high speed with an electric mixer fitted with whisk beaters until they form medium firm peaks. Carefully fold the egg whites into the coconut mixture. Line sheet pans with parchment paper and drop the batter onto pans using a medium ice cream scoop. Bake for 25-30 minutes until golden brown. Cool and serve. Store covered at room temperature.

*SERVES 20 COOKIES*

# Lime Tart with Blackberries and Blueberries

### LIME CURD

3 eggs

3 egg yolks

1 cup sugar

¾ cup fresh lime juice

6 tablespoons unsalted butter,
cut into 6 pieces

### CRUST

½ cup unsalted butter, at room
temperature

¼ cup sugar

1 egg yolk

1¼ cups all-purpose flour

1 large pinch of salt

### TOPPING

2 (6 ounce) containers fresh
blackberries

1 (6 ounce) container fresh blueberries

1 tablespoon blackberry jam

To make Lime Curd, set fine metal strainer over medium bowl and set aside. Whisk eggs, egg yolks, and sugar in another medium metal bowl to blend. Whisk in lime juice. Set bowl over large saucepan of gently simmering water (do not allow bottom of bowl to touch water). Whisk constantly until curd thickens and instant read thermometer inserted into curd registers 178° to 180° (about 5 minutes). Immediately pour curd through prepared strainer set over bowl. Add butter to warm strained curd; let stand 1 minute, then whisk until blended and smooth. Press plastic wrap directly onto surface of curd, covering completely. Refrigerate until cold, about 4 hours. Pressing plastic wrap directly onto the surface of the lime curd makes sure that skin does not form as the curd chills.

To make the crust, using an electric mixer, beat butter and sugar in medium bowl until well blended, 1-2 minutes. Add egg yolk; beat to blend. Add flour and salt and mix on low speed until mixture resembles large peas. Using hands, knead in bowl just until dough comes together. Transfer dough to 9 inch tart pan with removable bottom. Break dough into pieces, then press dough evenly up sides and onto bottom of pan. Cover and chill 1 hour. Keep chilled until baked. Preheat oven to 350°. Uncover crust and bake until golden brown, about 35 minutes. Cool completely in pan on rack.

To assemble, remove outer-ring from tart pan and place crust on serving plate. Spread lime curd evenly in baked crust. Arrange blackberries in 2 concentric circles just inside edge of tart. Mound blueberries in center of tart. Place blackberry jam in small microwave

## Lime Tart, continued

safe bowl. Heat in microwave until jam is melted, about 15 seconds. Whisk to loosen and blend, adding water by teaspoonfuls if too thick. Brush jam over berries. Brushing the berries with a little blackberry jam gives the fruit topping a shiny pastry shop finish. Tart can be made up to 8 hours ahead. Chill uncovered.

*SERVES 8-10*

Lime curd can be made up to 2 days ahead. Keep chilled. Purchased lime curd may be substituted. Crust can be made up to 1 day ahead.

# Berry Berry Cool Pie

1 (14 ounce) can sweetened condensed milk

½ cup lemon juice

2 cups assorted fresh berries (raspberries, blueberries and blackberries)

1 (8 ounce) container frozen whipped topping, thawed

1 (6 ounce) graham cracker pie crust

In a large bowl stir together milk and lemon juice. Fold in the berries and then fold in whipped topping. Spoon mixture into crust. Freeze 5 hours. Let stand 30-40 minutes before serving. Garnish as desired. Store leftovers covered in freezer.

*SERVES 6-8*

# Tuscan Potato Bake

2 pounds red potatoes
¼ cup butter
3 to 4 cloves garlic, minced
1 ½ teaspoons fresh thyme minced or
½ teaspoon dried thyme, crushed
1 cup buttermilk
½ teaspoon salt
¼ teaspoon black pepper

1 cup shredded fontina cheese
1 cup Parmesan cheese, divided
⅓ cup crumbled blue cheese
½ cup panko style bread crumbs
¼ teaspoon dried Italian seasonings,
crushed
1 tablespoon olive oil
Parsley, snipped, optional

Preheat oven to 400°. Lightly grease a 2 quart square baking dish. Scrub potatoes; cut into 1 inch pieces. In large saucepan cook potatoes in salted boiling water for 12-15 minutes or until tender; drain. In 12 inch skillet, melt butter over medium heat and add garlic and thyme; stir and cook for 1 minute. Add potatoes to skillet and coarsely mash. Stir in buttermilk, salt and pepper. Fold in fontina cheese, ½ of Parmesan cheese and the blue cheese. Spread potato mixture evenly in baking dish. In a small bowl, combine remaining Parmesan cheese, panko crumbs, Italian seasoning and olive oil; toss with fork. Sprinkle over potato mixture. Bake for 20 minutes or until bubbly and golden brown. Garnish with parsley.

*SERVES 8-10*

To keep potatoes from budding, place an apple in the bag with the potatoes.

Our Scholarship Program was developed and initiated in club year 2002-2003. This program helps the non-traditional students improve their lives and the lives of their families and, consequently, our community.

# Champagne Punch

½ cup sugar
2 (10 ounce) packages frozen sliced
   peaches

2 bottles champagne
1 cup Grand Marnier® liqueur
1 bottle dry white wine

Combine sugar and Grand Marnier® in punch bowl; stir until sugar dissolves. Place peach slices in punch bowl. Pour in champagne and wine until peaches separate. Serve in punch cups with a peach slice in each cup.

*SERVES 20*

# Cantaloupe Balls à la Orange

¼ cup frozen orange juice concentrate,
   slightly thawed and undiluted
2 tablespoons light corn syrup

1 tablespoon cherry-flavored liqueur
4 cups ripe cantaloupe balls
6 fresh mint sprigs

In a medium bowl, combine the orange juice, corn syrup and liqueur and mix well. Add cantaloupe balls and toss lightly to combine. Refrigerate 2 hours. Spoon the mixture into dessert glasses and garnish with mint.

*SERVES 4-6*

# Very Fancy Brunch Bacon

1 pound thick sliced bacon
2 teaspoons cinnamon

¼ cup light brown sugar

Preheat oven to 200°. Cut bacon into thirds vertically; separate pieces. Combine cinnamon and brown sugar. Press pieces of bacon into mixture; coating both sides and shaking off excess. Twist each piece if desired. Place on foil lined pan. Bake 60 minutes. Drain well. To store: place bacon between wax paper layers in containers lined with foil that are airtight. May be frozen.

*SERVES 10-12*

# Antipasto Squares

¼ pound Virginia ham
¼ pound salami
¼ pound large pepperoni, thinly sliced
8 slices Swiss cheese
8 slices Provolone cheese

1 medium jar peeled roasted red peppers, drained
2 packages refrigerated crescent rolls (may use reduced fat)
¼ cup grated Parmesan cheese
2 eggs

Spray 9x13 inch pan with vegetable cooking spray. Unroll and spread 1 package crescent rolls on bottom of pan, gently sealing perforations. Layer as follows: ham, Swiss cheese, pepperoni, Provolone cheese and salami. Place the roasted red peppers on top of the salami. Beat eggs and add Parmesan cheese to eggs. Pour half of egg mixture over roasted red peppers. Top with remaining package of crescent rolls, then brush with remaining egg mixture. Cover with foil and bake at 350° for 30 minutes; remove foil and bake an additional 10 minutes or until the top is golden brown. Let rest for a few minutes before cutting into squares.

*SERVES 12-15*

# South of the Border Breakfast

1 (8.5 ounce) package corn muffin mix, including ingredients listed on package
3 cups cubed white bread, in ½ inch cubes
1 cup onion, chopped
8 ounces ground turkey sausage
1½ teaspoons Italian seasoning

2½ cups fat free milk
1 teaspoon ground cumin
¼ teaspoon ground black pepper
1 (10 ounce) can diced tomatoes and green chilies, undrained
1 (8 ounce) carton egg substitute
1 cup shredded Monterey Jack cheese, divided

Prepare corn muffin mix according to package directions and cool. Crumble in large bowl and stir in white bread cubes. Brown sausage and onion. Add Italian seasoning to sausage mixture; crumble and drain. In bowl, combine milk, cumin, pepper, tomatoes and egg substitute; stir with a whisk until well blended. Combine milk and sausage mixtures and stir into bread mixture. Spoon half of mixture into 11x7 inch greased glass baking pan. Top with half of the Monterey Jack cheese. Spoon remaining mixture over the cheese. Cover and refrigerate for at least 8 hours or overnight. Preheat oven to 350°. Bake uncovered for 20 minutes or until set. Top with remaining Monterey Jack cheese and bake an additional 20 minutes. Let stand 10 minutes before serving.

*SERVES 8*

# Spinach and Bacon Quiche

**CRUST**

½ cup butter

1 (3 ounce) package cream cheese, at room temperature

1 cup flour

Salt, to taste

**FILLING**

12 slices bacon, cooked and crumbled over bottom of crust, optional

2 cups milk

½ cup biscuit baking mix

4 eggs, slightly beaten

¼ teaspoon salt

½ teaspoon black pepper

1 cup grated Swiss cheese

⅓ cup chopped onion

½ box frozen chopped spinach, thawed and well drained, optional

Preheat the oven to 350°. To make the crust, blend butter, cream cheese, flour and salt in mixing bowl with pastry blender or fork. Work into ball, then push into quiche pan until pan bottom and sides are covered. For the filling, combine milk, baking mix, eggs, salt, pepper, Swiss cheese, onion and spinach; pour into crust and bake for 50-65 minutes, or until set.

*SERVES 6-8*

# Fruit Casserole

4 (15.5 ounce) cans fruit, any combination, well drained

1 stick butter, crumbled

1 cup brown sugar

1 tablespoon cornstarch

1 teaspoon cinnamon or to taste

1 teaspoon nutmeg or to taste

Preheat the oven to 325°. In a 9x12 inch baking dish, combine the drained fruit. In a medium bowl, combine the butter, brown sugar, cornstarch, cinnamon and nutmeg until it is a crumbly streusel topping. Sprinkle streusel topping over fruit. Bake for 1 hour.

*SERVES 10*

# BLT Salad

1 pound sliced bacon, cut into 1 inch
  pieces
¼ cup butter, cubed
4 slices white bread, crust removed
  and cut into 1 inch cubes
½ cup mayonnaise
3 to 5 tablespoons fresh basil, minced

2 tablespoons red wine vinegar
½ teaspoon black pepper
½ teaspoon garlic, minced
6 cups romaine lettuce, torn into
  bite-sized pieces
1½ cups grape tomatoes

In a large skillet cook bacon over medium heat until crisp. Using a slotted spoon, remove to paper towels; drain, reserving 2 tablespoons drippings. Set bacon and drippings aside. To make croutons, in another large skillet, melt butter. Add bread cubes; cook over medium heat for 4-5 minutes or until golden brown, stirring frequently. Remove to paper towels; cool. For dressing, in a small bowl, whisk the mayonnaise, basil, vinegar, pepper, garlic and reserved drippings. In a large bowl combine the romaine lettuce, tomatoes and bacon. Drizzle with dressing and toss to coat. Top with croutons.

*SERVES 8*

# Tomato Basil Squares

1 package refrigerated pizza dough
2 cups shredded mozzarella cheese
¼ cup grated Parmesan cheese
2 tablespoons fresh basil, minced

⅔ cup mayonnaise
1 clove garlic, crushed
4 Roma tomatoes, thinly sliced

Preheat oven to 375°. Press pizza dough into a greased baking sheet; sprinkle with mozzarella cheese. Arrange tomato slices in a grid pattern on top of cheese. In a bowl combine Parmesan cheese, basil, mayonnaise and garlic. Spread mixture carefully on top of tomatoes. Bake for 15-18 minutes or until golden brown. Cool slightly before cutting into squares.

*SERVES 25-30*

# Lemon Curd Pie

1 graham cracker pie shell

2 (8 ounce) packages cream cheese, at room temperature

4 eggs, at room temperature

½ cup sugar

8 ounces lemon curd, purchased or homemade

Preheat oven to 350°. In a food processor (or with a mixer), combine cream cheese, eggs and sugar for 30 seconds until smooth. Spoon the lemon curd onto the bottom of the graham cracker pie shell. Next spread the cream cheese mixture over the curd. Bake for 45-50 minutes. Cool and serve at room temperature.

*SERVES 6-8*

Cranberry or orange curd may be substituted for the lemon curd.

# Coconut Cake

1 (18.5 ounce) box white cake mix, plus ingredients listed on directions

½ (14 ounce) can sweetened condensed milk

1 (8 ounce) can cream of coconut milk

1 (8 ounce) container frozen whipped topping, thawed

1 (10 ounce) package sweetened flaked coconut

Mix cake as directed on box. Pour into 9x13 inch pan and bake as directed on box (if using a glass pan, lower temperature by 25°). Let cake cool for 30 minutes. Make holes 1 inch apart in cake with end of wooden spoon. Pour condensed milk over top of cake and then pour cream of coconut milk over the top of cake. Let cool completely and then spread whipped topping over cake. Sprinkle with coconut. Refrigerate 6 hours or more before serving.

*SERVES 10-12*

# Berry Pizza Pie

1 (18.5 ounce) box white cake mix
1¼ cups quick cooking rolled oats, divided
½ cup butter, room temperature, divided
1 egg
½ cup chopped nuts
¼ cup firmly packed brown sugar
½ teaspoon cinnamon
1 (21 ounce) can prepared fruit pie filling, any variety

Preheat oven to 350°. Grease pizza pan. In large bowl, combine cake mix, 1 cup oats and 6 tablespoons butter at low speed until crumbly. Reserve ½ cup crumbs for topping and set aside. To remaining crumb mixture, blend in egg. Press egg crumb mixture into prepared pizza pan. Bake for 12 minutes. In same large bowl, add remaining ¼ cup rolled oats, 2 tablespoons butter, nuts, sugar and cinnamon to reserved crumb mixture. Beat until well mixed. Spread pie filling on baked crust, sprinkle with reserved crumb mixture. Return to oven and bake 15-20 minutes or until crumbs are light golden brown. Cool completely. Garnish with your choice of fruit, icing or cream cheese decorations.

*SERVES 10-15*

# Delicious Cucumber Dip

2 cucumbers, peeled, seeded and diced
1 (8 ounce) package cream cheese, room temperature
1 teaspoon lemon juice
1 tablespoon sirachi sauce (in the Oriental section of the grocery store)
2 to 3 tablespoons fresh dill, chopped
Salt and pepper, to taste

Mix all ingredients and refrigerate. Serve with tortilla or vegetable chips.

*2 CUPS*

# Piña Colada Punch (Non-Alcoholic)

2 cans cream of coconut milk
3 large cans pineapple juice

2 (2 liter) bottles ginger ale
carbonated beverage

Chill all liquids. Blend together cream of coconut milk and pineapple juice in a punch bowl. Add ginger ale and stir.

*SERVES 60-80*

A frozen fruit ice ring may be used as garnish.

# Chili Cheesecake

1 cup crushed tortilla chips
3 tablespoons butter, melted
2 (8 ounce) packages cream cheese, room temperature
2 eggs
1 (4 ounce) can diced green chilies
1 fresh jalapeño pepper, cored, seeded, and diced

4 ounces shredded Colby cheese
4 ounces shredded Monterey Jack cheese
¼ cup sour cream
Tomatoes, chopped
Green onions, chopped
Black olives, diced

Preheat oven to 325°. In medium bowl, combine tortilla chips and butter. Press into bottom of 8 or 9 inch springform pan. Bake 15 minutes, remove from oven, leaving oven on. In large bowl, blend cream cheese and eggs. Add green chilies, jalapeño, Colby cheese and Monterey Jack cheese. Pour over crust and bake 30 minutes. Do not overcook. Remove from oven and cool in pan 5 minutes. Run knife around inside edge and remove sides from pan. Spread sour cream over top and decorate with tomatoes, green onions, and olives. Serve with tortilla chips.

*SERVES 12-15*

# Watermelon Fire and Ice Salsa

3 cups watermelon, diced and seeded
2 tablespoons fresh lime juice
½ cup green bell pepper, chopped
2 teaspoons fresh cilantro, chopped

1 tablespoon green onions, chopped
1 tablespoon jalapeño pepper, chopped
½ teaspoon garlic salt

Drain the watermelon in a colander. In a large bowl combine the drained watermelon, lime juice, green bell pepper, cilantro, green onions, jalapeño and garlic salt. Mix well and serve with tortilla chips.

*3 CUPS*

# Bacon Wrapped Jalapeños

20 whole fresh jalapeños, 2-3 inches in size
2 (8 ounce) packages cream cheese, room temperature

1 package dry buttermilk ranch salad dressing mix
1 pound thin sliced bacon, cut into thirds

Preheat oven to 375°. Cut jalapeños in half lengthwise and clean out with a spoon. Combine cream cheese and dry dressing mix; fill jalapeño halves with cheese mixture. Wrap jalapeño with bacon pieces and secure with toothpick. (At this point, you can freeze them uncooked for use later.) Bake on a broiler pan in oven for 20-25 minutes or until the bacon is crispy and brown.

*SERVES 20*

# Marinated Asparagus

2 pounds asparagus, tenderly cooked and drained
2 tablespoons lemon juice
1 tablespoon Dijon mustard
¼ teaspoon salt
⅛ teaspoon black pepper

1 clove garlic, minced
⅓ cup olive oil
2 tablespoons Parmesan cheese
1¼ tablespoons red wine vinegar
1 small jar pimento strips, drained

In a bowl, combine the lemon juice, mustard, salt, pepper and garlic. Slowly combine the olive oil, Parmesan cheese and red wine vinegar into the mustard mixture. Add the pimento strips. Pour mixture over asparagus and marinate in refrigerator.

*SERVES 6-8*

# Chicken Enchiladas

### ENCHILADA SAUCE

2 tablespoons vegetable or canola oil

2 tablespoons all-purpose flour

2 tablespoons chili powder

1 teaspoon ground cumin

1 (14 ounce) can chicken broth

1 (8 ounce) can tomato sauce

1 teaspoon salt

¼ teaspoon garlic powder

### FILLING

2 cups cooked chicken, shredded

½ cup green onions, thinly sliced

¾ cup shredded Cheddar cheese, divided

¾ cup shredded Monterey Jack cheese, divided

¼ cup sour cream

1 (4 ounce) can diced green chilies

Vegetable or canola oil, as needed

¼ cup fresh cilantro, chopped

Salt and black pepper, to taste

12 (6 inch) corn tortillas

Nonstick cooking spray

Sour cream for garnish

Green onions, chopped, for garnish

Fresh cilantro, chopped, for garnish

Preheat oven to 350°. To make the enchilada sauce, heat oil in large saucepan, stir in flour and chili powder and cook for 1 minute. Add cumin, broth, sauce, salt and garlic powder and mix. Bring to a boil and simmer for 10 minutes. To make enchiladas: in a medium bowl, combine chicken, green onions, ½ cup Cheddar cheese, ½ cup Monterey Jack cheese, sour cream, chilies and cilantro. Stir in ½ cup enchilada sauce. Season with salt and pepper. Set aside. Heat ½ inch oil in large pan, fry tortillas, 1 at a time, until softened (10 seconds per side). Drain on paper towels. Spray 9x13 inch baking dish with nonstick cooking spray. Spread small amount of enchilada sauce in bottom of dish. Spread 2 heaping tablespoons of chicken mixture in each tortilla and roll up. Place seam side down, side by side, in prepared dish. Pour remaining enchilada sauce over top. Sprinkle with ¼ cup Cheddar cheese and ¼ cup Monterey Jack cheese. Bake until bubbly about 15-20 minutes. Garnish with extra sour cream, sliced green onions and chopped cilantro.

*SERVES 4-6*

3 cups of canned enchilada sauce may be substituted for the above enchilada sauce.

# Southwestern Cornbread Salad

1 (6 ounce) package Mexican cornbread mix, plus ingredients listed on package

1 (1 ounce) envelope dry buttermilk ranch salad dressing mix plus ingredients listed on envelope

1 head romaine lettuce, shredded

2 large tomatoes, chopped

1 (15 ounce) can black beans, rinsed and drained

1 (15 ounce) can whole kernel corn with red and green peppers, drained

1 (8 ounce) package shredded Mexican four cheese blend

6 bacon slices, cooked and crumbled

6 green onions, chopped

Prepare cornbread according to package directions, cool and crumble. Set aside. Prepare salad dressing according to package directions; set aside. Layer a large serving bowl with half of each: cornbread, lettuce, tomatoes, beans, corn, cheese, bacon and onions; spoon half of dressing evenly over top. Repeat layers with remaining ingredients and dressing. Cover and chill at least 2 hours.

*SERVES 10-12*

# Pistachio Cake

**CAKE**

1 box white or yellow cake mix

¾ cup vegetable oil

3 eggs

1 cup lemon lime soda

1 (3.4 ounce) pistachio instant pudding package

½ cup chopped pistachios, optional

**TOPPING**

2 packets whipped topping mix

1 (3.4 ounce) package pistachio instant pudding

1½ cups milk

½ cup chopped pistachios, optional

Preheat oven to 350°. Combine cake mix, vegetable oil, eggs, soda and pudding mix in a large mixer bowl and beat at medium speed for 3 minutes; add nuts. Pour in a greased and floured 9x13 inch cake pan. Bake for 40-50 minutes. Cool cake before spreading topping. In a mixing bowl combine the whipped topping mixes, pudding mix, and milk. Beat until thick; spread on cooled cake and sprinkle with nuts. Cake must be stored in refrigerator.

*SERVES 12-15*

# Toffee Pecan Cookies

| | |
|---|---|
| 1 cup pecan halves, broken in half | ¾ cup sugar |
| 2 cups all-purpose flour | ¼ cup firmly packed brown sugar |
| 1 cup baking soda | 1 egg |
| ¼ teaspoon salt | 1 teaspoon vanilla extract |
| 6 tablespoons butter, at room temperature | 6 (1.4 ounce) chocolate covered toffee candy bars, coarsely broken |
| 6 tablespoons vegetable shortening | |

Preheat oven to 350°. Place pecans in a single layer in a shallow pan. Bake for 7 minutes or until toasted; cool. Stir together flour, baking soda and salt in a medium bowl. In a separate bowl, beat butter and shortening on medium speed with an electric mixer until creamy. Add sugar and brown sugar to butter mixture and beat until smooth. Combine egg and vanilla with butter mixture. Gradually add flour mixture, beating just until each addition is incorporated. Stir in pecans and toffee bits. Drop dough by ¼ cupfuls, 2-3 inches apart, onto parchment paper lined baking sheets. Bake for 17 minutes or until edges are slightly browned. Cool on baking sheets 2 minutes. Remove to wire racks and cool completely.

*16 COOKIES*

# Monterey Shrimp Dip

| | |
|---|---|
| 1 (8 ounce) package shredded Monterey Jack cheese with peppers | 1 (2.25 ounce) can sliced ripe black olives, drained |
| ¾ cup mayonnaise | ¼ cup green onions, chopped |
| 2 (4 ounce) cans shrimp, drained | |

Combine cheese, mayonnaise, shrimp, olives and green onions and place in a 1 quart casserole. Microwave at high 3 minutes or until cheese melts; stirring after each minute. Serve immediately with tortilla chips.

*3¼ CUPS*

# Fruit Trifle

1 (5.1 ounce) package instant vanilla pudding mix

2 cups skim milk

½ (8 ounce) package light cream cheese, at room temperature

1 (8 ounce) carton peach low fat yogurt

6 cups purchased angel food cake, cut into 1 inch cubes

2 cups fresh peaches, peeled and sliced (about 2)

2 cups ripe bananas, sliced (about 2)

1 cup kiwi fruit, peeled and sliced (about 3)

Combine pudding mix and milk; beat at low speed with an electric mixer for 2 minutes or until well blended and thickened. Add cream cheese and yogurt; beat well. Cover and chill at least 30 minutes. Line the bottom of a 2½ quart straight sided glass bowl or trifle bowl with 2 cups cake cubes. Spoon 1⅓ cups pudding mixture over cake cubes; arrange ⅔ cup peaches, ⅔ cup bananas and ⅓ cup kiwi over the pudding mixture. Repeat procedure with remaining ingredients, ending with kiwi. Save enough of the pudding mixture to "frost" the very top of the trifle. Cover and chill at least 3 hours or overnight.

*SERVES 10-12*

Other fruits may be used; one combination is strawberries, blueberries and grapes.

Johnson County Young Matrons

It's easy to become a member. Go to jcym.net and learn more. You won't regret it.

# Beer with a Punch

1 (12 ounce) can frozen pink lemonade concentrate, thawed

3 (12 ounce) bottles chilled beer (not dark in color)

¾ cup vodka, chilled

Combine the lemonade, beer and vodka. Serve.

*SERVES 6-8*

# Shoe Peg Corn

2 (14.5 ounce) cans shoe peg corn (or any white corn), drained

1 (8 ounce) package cream cheese, at room temperature

6 tablespoons butter, melted

1 (4 ounce) can chopped green chilies

Combine cream cheese and melted butter; add corn and green chilies to cream cheese mixture. Pour into a greased 1½ quart casserole pan. Bake at 350° for 30 minutes.

*SERVES 6-8*

# Fiery Beef Burgers

2 pounds lean ground beef
¾ cup shredded Cheddar cheese
¼ cup chopped fresh cilantro
1 teaspoon cumin
2 cloves garlic, minced

1 teaspoon kosher salt
2 jalapeño peppers, seeded and minced
8 hamburger buns

In a large bowl, lightly mix the meat with the cheese, cilantro, cumin, garlic, salt and jalapeño peppers using your fingertips. Shape into 8 patties. Preheat grill on medium high then brush or spray grids with vegetable oil. Place patties on the grill and sear 2 minutes per side. Reduce heat to low and continue cooking another 2 minutes per side until juicy but cooked through. Lightly toast the buns during the last 2 minutes of cooking time.

*SERVES 8*

# Chunky Gazpacho Salad

½ English cucumber, sliced into rounds and quartered

1 container grape tomatoes, halved

1 orange pepper, seeded and cut into quarter sized pieces

½ sweet onion, sliced into very thin half moons

4 to 6 ribs celery hearts including leafy tops, sliced into ½ inch chunks

3 to 4 tablespoons fresh cilantro, chopped

1 tablespoon red wine vinegar

Juice of 1 lime

2 teaspoons hot pepper sauce

¼ cup extra virgin olive oil

Kosher salt and freshly ground black pepper to taste

Combine cucumber, tomatoes, pepper, onion and celery in a bowl. Sprinkle with cilantro. In a small bowl, combine vinegar, lime juice and hot pepper sauce; whisk in olive oil in a steady stream. Pour oil mixture over vegetable mixture and toss well. Season with salt and black pepper. Refrigerate for several hours or overnight. Set out salad on counter for 20 minutes before serving.

Great as a leftover...it becomes an even tastier marinated salad.

# Oven Fries with Herbs and Pecorino

2 large baking potatoes, cut into 4x½ inch sticks

¼ cup extra virgin olive oil

1 garlic clove, minced

1 teaspoon sage, minced

1 teaspoon rosemary, minced

¼ cup freshly grated Pecorino Romano cheese

Salt and freshly ground black pepper, to taste

Preheat oven to 425°. In a large bowl, toss the potato sticks with the olive oil until evenly coated. Spread the potato sticks on a rimmed baking sheet in a single layer and bake in the upper third of the oven, turning once or twice with a spatula until they are golden and crispy, about 30 minutes. Sprinkle the minced garlic, sage and rosemary over the fries and toss well. Roast for about 5 minutes longer, until the herbs are fragrant and the garlic is lightly browned. Transfer the fries to a large bowl and toss with the grated cheese. Season with salt and pepper and serve.

*SERVES 4*

# Shrimp Quesadillas

3 quarts water
1 tablespoon shrimp boil seasoning
2 teaspoons Ancho chili powder
1 pound medium fresh shrimp
1 (10 ounce) can diced tomatoes with green chilies, drained
1 cup shredded sharp Cheddar cheese

1 cup shredded Monterey Jack cheese with peppers
4 (10 inch) flour tortillas
½ cup butter, divided
Shredded lettuce for garnish, optional
Sour cream for garnish, optional
Lemon wedges for garnish, optional

In a large Dutch oven, bring 3 quarts water, shrimp seasoning and chili powder to a boil over high heat. Add shrimp and cook for 3 minutes or until pink and firm. Drain and rinse with cold water. Peel shrimp and put in a food processor and pulse 2-3 times or until coarsely chopped. Spoon shrimp into a large bowl; add tomatoes, Cheddar cheese and Monterey cheese, stirring to combine. Spoon shrimp mixture evenly over half of each tortilla; fold each in half. In a large skillet, melt 1 tablespoon butter over medium heat. Add 1 quesadilla, cook for 4-5 minutes per side or until tortilla is crisp. Repeat procedure with remaining butter and quesadillas. Cut each quesadilla into 4 wedges to serve. Garnish with shredded lettuce, sour cream and lemon wedges, if desired.

*SERVES 4*

A pizza cutter is a great tool for cutting quesadillas!

# Frozen Lemon Pie

1 (14 ounce) can low fat sweetened condensed milk
1 (8 ounce) frozen whipped topping, thawed
½ cup plus 2 tablespoons lemon juice

½ teaspoon vanilla extract
1 large size premade shortbread or graham cracker pie crust
1 lemon, sliced or made into curls for garnish

Combine milk, whipped topping, lemon juice and vanilla in a bowl and mix well. Pour mixture into crust. Freeze overnight. Garnish with lemon curls or slices.

*SERVES 6-8*

# Roasted Cherry Tomatoes

1 pint cherry tomatoes
Extra virgin olive oil
Kosher salt and freshly ground black
  pepper, to taste

10 fresh basil leaves, cut into thin
  strips, chiffonade style
Sea salt, to taste

Preheat oven to 400°. Toss the tomatoes lightly with olive oil on a baking sheet. Spread them out into 1 layer and sprinkle generously with kosher salt and black pepper. Roast for 15-20 minutes or until the tomatoes are soft. Transfer the tomatoes to a serving platter and sprinkle with basil and sea salt. Serve warm or at room temperature.

These tomatoes can be served as part of an antipasto platter.

# Thumbprint Cookies

¼ cup butter, softened
¼ cup shortening
¼ cup firmly packed brown sugar
1 egg, separated
½ teaspoon vanilla extract

1 cup all-purpose flour
¼ teaspoon salt
¾ cup finely chopped nuts
Jelly or jam of choice

Preheat oven to 350°. Mix thoroughly butter, shortening, sugars, egg yolk and vanilla. Work in flour and salt until dough holds together. Shape dough by teaspoonfuls into 1 inch balls. Dip each ball into slightly beaten egg whites then roll in nuts. Place on ungreased baking sheet; press thumb deeply into center of each ball. Bake about 10 minutes or until lightly browned. Remove from baking sheet and cool. When cool, add a dollop of jelly or jam into each indentation.

*SERVES 36*

# Salty Dog

Coarse kosher salt

Ice cubes

½ cup vodka or gin, divided

¾ cup fresh grapefruit juice, divided

Pour salt onto small plate. Moisten rims of 2 highball glasses. Gently dip rims into salt to coat lightly. Fill glasses with ice cubes. Pour ¼ cup vodka or gin over ice cubes in each glass. Divide grapefruit juice in half and pour each half into a glass. Serve.

*SERVES 2*

# Saffron Rice Pilaf

2½ cups low salt chicken broth or water

Saffron, pinch (about 30 threads)

1 tablespoon extra virgin olive oil

1 medium onion, small diced (about 1¼ cups)

1 red bell pepper, cored, seeded and small diced (about 1 cup)

1½ cups long-grain white rice

1 teaspoon kosher salt, more as needed

Cayenne pepper, pinch

¼ cup fresh Italian flat leaf parsley, roughly chopped and divided

1 clove garlic, minced (about 1½ teaspoons)

¼ cup slivered almonds, toasted

1 tablespoon fresh oregano, roughly chopped

On the stovetop or in the microwave, heat the broth until hot. Add the saffron, cover, and let sit for 15-20 minutes. In a heavy based 3 quart saucepan with a tight lid, heat the oil over medium heat. Reduce the heat to medium low and add the onions and bell peppers. Cook, stirring occasionally, until soft but not browned, about 5 minutes. Add the rice, salt and cayenne pepper and stir well to coat each grain with oil. Toast for a full 5 minutes, stirring regularly to keep the grains separated and to prevent them from sticking to the bottom of the pan (the rice may turn opaque before 5 minutes are up but keep going). Reduce the heat to low if there are any signs of scorching. Stir in the garlic and 2 tablespoons parsley. Add in the saffron broth, stir once, and bring to a boil over medium heat. Cover, reduce the heat to low, and cook for 18 minutes. Remove from the heat and let the pilaf sit, still covered, for 5 minutes. Once the pilaf has rested, remove the lid and fluff the rice with a fork. Using the fork, gently fold in the almonds, the remaining 2 tablespoons parsley and the oregano. Taste for seasoning and adjust as needed.

*SERVES 6-8*

# Blue Crab and Avocado Cocktail

1 pound lump blue crabmeat
Juice of 3 limes
2 avocados, seeded, peeled and diced
1 medium tomato, diced and divided
2 green onions, diced

1 tablespoon fresh cilantro, coarsely
 chopped
¾ cup mayonnaise
1 cup romaine lettuce, shredded
Cilantro, for garnish
Lime wedges, for garnish

Place 6 martini glasses in the refrigerator to chill. Drain crabmeat and gently check for pieces of shell or cartilage and discard. In a small bowl, combine lime juice with the avocados. In a small bowl, gently combine crabmeat, tomato (reserving ½ cup for garnish), green onions, cilantro and mayonnaise until just mixed together to avoid breaking up crabmeat. Gently fold avocado mixture into crabmeat mixture until combined. Place 2-3 tablespoons lettuce in bottom of each martini glass. Add equal parts of crab mixture to glasses. Garnish with reserved diced tomato, a sprig of cilantro and a lime wedge.

*SERVES 6*

# Hot Onion Soufflé

3 (8 ounce) packages cream cheese, at
 room temperature
1 (8 ounce) container grated Parmesan
 cheese

1 (12 ounce) package frozen chopped
 onions, thawed and squeezed dry
½ cup mayonnaise
Green onions, for garnish, optional
Paprika, for garnish, optional

Place ingredients in a bowl and beat just until well combined. Spoon into a shallow baking dish and bake at 425° for 15 minutes. Serve with corn chips or tortilla strips.

*3 CUPS*

To make this dish more colorful, bake in a colorful baking dish or garnish the top with chopped green onions or paprika.

# Spinach Salad with Grapes and Shrimp

## SALAD

8 cups fresh spinach, cleaned and dried

2 cups seedless green or red grapes

1 pound cooked small shrimp

1 cup celery, bias cut

½ English cucumber, sliced thin

¼ cup green onions, sliced

2 teaspoons sesame seeds, toasted

## SESAME VINAIGRETTE DRESSING

½ cup rice or white vinegar

4 tablespoons olive oil

2 tablespoons toasted sesame oil

2 tablespoons sugar

2 teaspoons garlic, minced

2 teaspoons fresh ginger, peeled and grated

1 teaspoon salt

1 teaspoon black pepper

In a large bowl, combine spinach, grapes, shrimp, celery, cucumbers, onions and sesame seeds. In a blender, combine vinegar, olive oil, sesame oil, sugar, garlic, ginger, salt and pepper until emulsified. Toss with salad mixture just before serving.

*SERVES 8*

# Pesto Cheesecake

½ cup bread crumbs

3 tablespoons butter, melted

1 (8 ounce) package cream cheese, at room temperature

2 eggs

1 (8 ounce) container pesto (skim off top oil if any)

1 cup sour cream

Sun-dried tomatoes, for garnish

Preheat oven to 325°. Combine crumbs and butter then spread in bottom of a 9 inch springform or tart pan. Combine cream cheese, eggs, pesto and sour cream and pour mixture over top of crumbs. Bake for 30 minutes. Garnish middle of baked pesto with sun-dried tomatoes and serve with crackers.

*SERVES 10-12*

# Roasted Pencil Asparagus

2 pounds pencil asparagus, woody
   ends trimmed, rinsed and patted
   dry
3 tablespoons extra virgin olive oil

1¼ teaspoons kosher salt
½ teaspoon freshly ground black
   pepper
3 tablespoons fresh lemon juice

Preheat oven to 400°. In a large bowl, toss the asparagus with the olive oil and season with the salt and pepper. Transfer to a large baking sheet with low sides and drizzle the lemon juice over the asparagus. Place pan in the oven and roast until the asparagus are tender and beginning to caramelize around the edges, about 20 minutes. Remove from the oven, adjust the seasoning if necessary; serve either hot or at room temperature.

*SERVES 6-8*

# Roasted Salmon with Shallot and Grapefruit Sauce

4 (5 to 6 ounces each) skinless salmon
   fillets
¼ teaspoon salt, plus more to taste
2 ruby red grapefruits
2 teaspoons olive oil
1 tablespoon green onion, minced

1 teaspoon fresh ginger, peeled and
   grated
2½ teaspoons honey
Cayenne pepper, pinch
2 teaspoons fresh lemon juice
2 tablespoons fresh basil, thinly sliced,
   chiffonade style

Preheat oven to 350°. Season the salmon with the salt; place in a baking dish and roast until just cooked through, about 18 minutes. While the salmon is cooking, prepare the sauce. Peel and section 1 grapefruit. Then, with a paring knife, remove each segment of fruit from its membrane and cut the segments in half. Set the segments aside. Juice the other grapefruit and set the juice aside. In a medium skillet, heat the oil over medium heat. Add the onions and cook, stirring, until softened, about 2 minutes. Add the ginger, grapefruit juice, honey and cayenne pepper and bring to simmer. Cook until the sauce is reduced by about half, about 10 minutes. Add the lemon juice and season with salt. Right before serving, toss the grapefruit pieces and basil into the sauce. Place the salmon on a serving dish, spoon the sauce over it, and serve.

*SERVES 4*

# Raspberry Orange Trifle

1 (16 ounce) purchased pound cake
1 (12 ounce) jar raspberry jam
2 half pints fresh raspberries, rinsed and dried
½ cup Grand Marnier® liqueur or orange juice
1 (12 ounce) frozen whipped topping, thawed

¼ cup powdered sugar, sifted
1 tablespoon orange zest
1 (3.4 ounce) package vanilla pudding (not instant)
1¾ to 2 cups milk (use amount given on pudding directions)

In medium saucepan, combine pudding mix, milk and orange zest. Bring to a boil over medium heat. Remove from heat and cover surface with plastic wrap and cool for 1 hour. Meanwhile, in a chilled bowl, combine whipped topping and powdered sugar. Beat at medium speed with mixer until soft peaks form. Fold half the whipped topping mixture into the cooled pudding mixture. Cut the pound cake into 1 inch slices and spread each slice with raspberry jam, using all the jam. Cut into 1 inch squares. Place half of the cake cubes (jam side up) in a 2½-3 quart trifle bowl; sprinkle ¼ cup Grand Marnier® (or juice) over cake cubes. Top with half each of the pudding mixture and raspberries. Repeat the layers of cake, liqueur (or juice), pudding mixture and raspberries. Spread the remaining whipped topping mixture on top of trifle. Cover with plastic wrap and chill overnight or at least 8 hours.

*SERVES 6*

To help your cake retain its freshness, store half an apple in the container with the cake.

Women join for a variety of reasons but all have at least one common goal: giving back to our society.

# Mini Chocolate Chip Angel Cakes

11 egg whites
1 cup plus 2 tablespoons cake flour
1½ cups sugar, divided
1¼ teaspoons cream of tartar
½ teaspoon salt

1 teaspoon vanilla extract
¾ cup semisweet mini chocolate chips
1 cup powdered sugar
2 tablespoons 1% milk

Preheat oven to 375°. Place egg whites in a large mixing bowl and allow to stand at room temperature 30-60 minutes. Line regular size muffin tins with paper bake cups, set aside. Sift together flour and ½ cup sugar three times, set aside. In a separate large bowl, beat egg whites until foamy. Add cream of tartar and salt. Beat until soft peaks form. Add vanilla. Add remaining sugar, 2 tablespoons at a time, to egg white mixture, beating well after each addition. Beat until glossy stiff peaks form. Fold flour mixture in to egg white mixture ½ cup at a time. Fold in chocolate chips. Place ⅓ cup batter into each paper cup. Bake 15-17 minutes or until light brown and cakes spring back when lightly touched. Remove to wire rack immediately to cool. Whisk together powdered sugar and milk until smooth. Brush onto cakes. Let stand at room temperature until set.

*SERVES 3 DOZEN*

If you don't have enough batter to fill all the cupcake tins, pour 1 tablespoon of water into the unfilled spots to help preserve the life of your pan.

Informational programs are provided at most meetings. These help foster awareness of the needs and civic responsibilities of our community.

# Zucchini Squares

3 cups zucchini, sliced paper thin
½ cup onion, finely chopped
½ cup grated Parmesan cheese
2 tablespoons fresh parsley, minced
½ teaspoon salt
½ teaspoon seasoning salt, optional
½ teaspoon oregano (or dill)

Black pepper, to taste
¼ cup oil (if too dry, add another ¼ cup)
4 eggs, slightly beaten
1 cup biscuit baking mix
1 clove garlic, crushed

Preheat oven to 350°. Combine zucchini and onions and place in a 9x13 inch baking pan. In a separate bowl, combine Parmesan cheese, parsley, salt, seasoning salt, oregano, pepper, oil, eggs, biscuit mix and garlic. Pour mixture over zucchini and onions. Bake for 25-30 minutes or until lightly browned (may take up to 45 minutes). Cut into squares. Cool or serve warm.

*SERVES 48*

# Caprese Salad

¼ cup roasted red peppers, finely diced (rinse and drain well if from can or jar)
¼ cup mixed black and green olives, roughly chopped
¼ cup grilled red onion, diced

1 tablespoon capers
1 tablespoon chopped fresh parsley
1 tablespoon chopped fresh basil
2 tablespoons extra virgin olive oil
1 tablespoon red wine vinegar
Salad greens, enough for 8 salads

Combine peppers, olives, onions, capers, parsley, basil, olive oil and vinegar. Place over salad greens.

*SERVES 8*

Another way to use the caprese is to layer slices of tomato and fresh mozzarella over arugula, top with the caprese and finish by drizzling balsamic vinegar on top.

# Mamma's Caponata

1 large eggplant, peeled and chopped
¼ cup plus 2 tablespoons olive oil, divided
2 medium onions, chopped
2 celery ribs, chopped
2 (14.5 ounce) cans diced tomatoes, undrained
⅓ cup chopped ripe black olives

¼ cup red wine vinegar
2 tablespoons sugar
2 tablespoons capers, drained
½ teaspoon salt
½ teaspoon black pepper
French bread baguettes, sliced and toasted

In a Dutch oven, sauté eggplant in ¼ cup oil until tender. Remove from the pan and set aside. In the same pan, sauté onions and celery in remaining oil until tender. Stir in tomatoes and eggplant. Bring to a boil. Reduce heat, simmer uncovered for 15 minutes. Add the olives, vinegar, sugar, capers, salt and pepper. Return to a boil. Reduce heat, simmer uncovered for 20 minutes or until thickened. Serve warm or at room temperature with baguettes.

*6 CUPS*

# Beef, Pork and Mushroom Lasagna

2 tablespoons olive oil
2 cloves garlic, chopped
½ pound lean ground beef
½ pound ground pork
Kosher salt and freshly ground black pepper, to taste
1 (10.5 ounce) can cream of mushroom soup

½ cup whipping cream
1 package ready cooked lasagna noodles
1 pound shredded Parmesan cheese
1 pound shredded mozzarella cheese
Butter, to grease pan

Preheat oven to 350°. In a medium saucepan placed over medium heat, add olive oil, garlic, beef and pork. Season the meat with salt and pepper. Cook meat thoroughly and drain fat. To meat mixture, add soup and cream; stir well and heat. When mixture is hot, remove from heat. To assemble, butter inside of 9x13 inch pan and cover the bottom with 1 layer of noodles. Spoon ¼ of meat and mushroom mixture over pasta. Repeat process until 1 inch from top of dish. Top with Parmesan cheese and mozzarella cheese. Cover with foil and bake for 35 minutes, removing foil for last 5 minutes to brown cheese.

*SERVES 12-14*

# Italian Breadsticks

**DOUGH**

1 package active dry yeast

1½ cups plus 2 tablespoons warm water, divided

4¼ cups all-purpose flour, plus more for dusting

2 tablespoons unsalted butter, at room temperature

2 tablespoons sugar

1 tablespoon salt

**TOPPING**

3 tablespoons unsalted butter, melted and divided

½ teaspoon kosher salt, divided

⅛ to ¼ teaspoon garlic powder

Dried oregano, pinch

Make the dough by placing ¼ cup warm water in the bowl of a mixer, sprinkle in the yeast and set aside until foamy, about 5 minutes. Add the flour, butter, sugar, salt and 1¼ cups plus 2 tablespoons warm water; mix with the paddle attachment until a slightly sticky dough forms, 5 minutes. Knead the dough by hand on a floured surface until very smooth and soft, 3 minutes. Roll into a 2 foot long log, cut into 16 (1½ inch long) pieces. Knead each piece slightly and shape into a 7 inch long breadstick; arrange 2 inches apart on a parchment lined baking sheet. Cover with a cloth, let rise in a warm spot until almost doubled, about 45 minutes. Preheat oven to 400°. To make the topping brush the breadsticks with 1½ tablespoons melted butter and sprinkle with ¼ teaspoon of kosher salt. Bake until lightly golden, about 15 minutes. Meanwhile, combine the remaining ¼ teaspoon kosher salt with the garlic powder and oregano. Brush the warm breadsticks with the remaining 1½ tablespoons melted butter and sprinkle with the flavored salt.

*16 BREADSTICKS*

## TO MAKE BAGUETTE TOASTS:

1 baguette and ¾ cup olive oil

• Cut baguette diagonally into ½ inch slices. Brush both sides with oil, placing close together on baking sheet, and bake at 400° for 4 minutes. Turn slices and bake 3-4 minutes longer or until toasted. Can be stored in an airtight container up to 2 days. Makes 2 dozen.

# Penne with Sausage, Artichokes and Sun-Dried Tomatoes

¾ cup oil pack sun-dried tomatoes, sliced and drained (reserve 2 tablespoons of oil)

1 pound Italian hot sausages, casings removed

2 (8 ounce) packages frozen artichoke hearts

2 cloves garlic, chopped

1¾ cups chicken broth

½ cup dry white wine

1 (16 ounce) package penne pasta

½ cup shredded Parmesan cheese, plus additional for garnish

⅓ cup fresh basil, chopped

¼ cup fresh Italian parsley, chopped

8 ounces water packed fresh mozzarella cheese, drained and cubed, optional

Salt and freshly ground black pepper, to taste

Heat the oil from the tomatoes in a heavy large frying pan over medium high heat. Add the sausages and cook until brown, breaking up the meat into bite-sized pieces with a fork, about 8 minutes. Transfer the sausage to a bowl. Add the artichokes and garlic to the same skillet and sauté over medium heat until the garlic is tender, about 2 minutes. Add the broth, wine and sun-dried tomatoes. Boil over medium high heat until the sauce reduces slightly, stirring occasionally, about 8 minutes. Meanwhile bring a large pot of salted water to a boil. Cook the penne pasta in boiling water until tender but still firm to the bite, stirring often, about 6 minutes. Drain the pasta (do not rinse). Add the pasta, sausage, ½ cup Parmesan cheese, basil and parsley to the artichoke mixture. Toss until the sauce is almost absorbed by the pasta. Stir in the mozzarella cheese, optional. Season, to taste, with salt and pepper. Serve with Parmesan cheese on the side.

*SERVES 6-8*

One pound of pasta will serve four as a first course; six as an accompaniment to a meat and three if it's the entire meal.

# Rich and Cheesy Vegetable Lasagna

## TOMATO SAUCE

2 tablespoons olive oil

1 medium onion, finely chopped

4 cloves fresh garlic, crushed

1 teaspoon dried oregano

1 teaspoon dried basil

1 teaspoon dried parsley

1 (24 ounce) can crushed tomatoes

¼ teaspoon salt

## VEGETABLE LAYER

¼ cup plus 2 tablespoons olive oil, divided

3 cloves fresh garlic, minced and divided

½ teaspoon dried thyme

1 medium zucchini, cut into bite-sized pieces

1 medium yellow squash, cut into bite-sized pieces

½ cup button mushrooms, sliced ¼ inch thick

2 portobello mushrooms, sliced ¼ inch thick

## NOODLES

6 lasagna noodles

## CHEESES

1 cup ricotta cheese

1 pound mozzarella cheese, sliced

½ cup grated Parmesan cheese

Preheat oven to 350°. Make the sauce by sautéing onion in 2 tablespoons olive oil over medium heat until translucent, about 5 minutes. Add 4 cloves crushed garlic and sauté 1 more minute. Add oregano, basil, parsley, tomatoes and salt. Simmer until thickened, about 15 minutes. In a small bowl, combine ¼ cup olive oil, 1 garlic clove and thyme. Add zucchini and squash and marinate for about 5 minutes. Place mixture on a sheet pan and roast in preheated oven for 10 minutes. Meanwhile, heat 2 tablespoons oil in a large skillet over medium heat. Add 2 cloves garlic and sauté about 1 minute. Add button and portobello mushrooms and sauté until tender. Gently combine mushroom and zucchini mixtures. Prepare lasagna noodles according to package directions. Line the bottom of a buttered 9x13 inch pan with 3 lasagna noodles. Spread half of the ricotta cheese over the noodles. Spread half of the vegetable mixture over ricotta cheese. Lay half of the mozzarella cheese over vegetables. Spoon half of the tomato sauce over mozzarella cheese. Repeat these layers, then sprinkle Parmesan cheese on the top. Bake for 40 minutes. Let stand about 10 minutes before serving.

*SERVES 12*

# Seafood Lasagna

**WHITE SAUCE**

¼ cup flour
¼ cup butter

2 cups milk
⅔ cup white wine

**NOODLES**

12 lasagna noodles, cooked as directed on the package and drained

**CHEESE MIXTURE**

1 cup onions, chopped
2 tablespoons butter
1 (8 ounce) package cream cheese, at room temperature
1½ cups creamy cottage cheese (either small or large curd)

1 egg, slightly beaten, at room temperature
2 teaspoons dried basil
½ teaspoon salt
Black pepper, pinch

**SEAFOOD MIXTURE**

1 pound shrimp, cleaned, deveined, cooked and cut lengthwise
1 (7.5 ounce) can crabmeat, drained

⅔ pound scallops (cut large ones in half)
¼ cup grated Parmesan cheese
Parsley, for garnish

Preheat oven to 350°. Make the white sauce by melting ¼ cup butter in saucepan; whisk in flour and milk until smooth. Cook until thickened and then add white wine. Set aside. Sauté onions in 2 tablespoons melted butter. In a bowl, combine onions, cream cheese, cottage cheese, egg, basil, salt and pepper. Blend until smooth. Set aside. For the seafood mixture combine shrimp, crabmeat and scallops. Set aside. In a greased 9x13 inch baking pan, assemble the lasagna by spreading ⅓ of the white sauce on the bottom of the pan, laying 4 lasagna noodles on the white sauce, spreading ⅓ of the cheese mixture over the noodles and topping noodles with ⅓ of seafood mixture. Repeat layers two more times. Top with Parmesan cheese. Bake for 45-60 minutes until bubbly and slightly browned. Garnish with chopped parsley if desired. Let set for 15 minutes before serving.

*SERVES 12*

# Lemon Pound Cake

### CAKE

| | |
|---|---|
| 2 cups sugar | 2 cups all-purpose flour |
| ½ cup shortening | ¼ teaspoon salt |
| ½ cup butter, room temperature | ½ cup milk |
| 4 teaspoons lemon zest | 1 teaspoon vanilla extract |
| 5 eggs | |

### LIMONCELLO CREAM

| | |
|---|---|
| 2 cups whipping cream | ¼ cup Limoncello liqueur |
| ½ cup powdered sugar | |

### TOPPINGS

| | |
|---|---|
| Fresh blueberries | Fresh blackberries |
| Fresh strawberries | Lemon zest, for garnish |

Preheat oven to 300°. Spray a 10 inch round cake pan with nonstick cooking spray; line with parchment paper. In a large bowl, combine sugar, shortening, butter and lemon zest. Beat at medium speed with an electric mixer until creamy. Add eggs, 1 at a time, beating well after each addition. In a small bowl, sift together flour and salt. Gradually add flour mixture to butter mixture, alternately with milk, beating to mix well. Beat in vanilla. Spoon batter into prepared pan. Bake for 50-60 minutes or until a wooden pick inserted in center comes out clean. Cool in pan for 10 minutes. Remove to wire rack and cool completely. Prepare Limoncello cream by beating cream at high speed with an electric mixer until soft peaks form. Gradually add powdered sugar, beating until stiff peaks form. Beat in Limoncello. Cover and chill until ready to spread over top of cake. Top with fresh berries. Garnish with lemon zest, if desired.

*SERVES 10-12*

# White Chocolate Raspberry Bars

½ cup butter
2 cups white chocolate chips, divided
2 eggs
½ cup sugar
1 cup flour

½ teaspoon salt
1 teaspoon almond extract
½ cup raspberry jam
⅓ cup sliced almonds

Preheat oven to 350°. Grease and flour a 9x13 inch baking pan. Melt butter in saucepan on low heat. Add 1 cup white chocolate chips; DO NOT STIR. Remove from heat and set aside. Beat eggs in a mixer bowl until foamy. Add sugar gradually, beating until blended. Stir in white chocolate mixture. Add flour, salt and almond extract. Mix at low speed just until moistened. Pour half the mixture into prepared pan. Bake for 15 minutes or until light brown. Heat jam in a saucepan over low heat. Spread jam over warm baked layer. Spoon remaining mixture over jam. Sprinkle with 1 cup white chocolate chips and almonds. Return to oven and bake 25-30 minutes or until toothpick inserted in center comes out clean.

*SERVES 12-15*

# Tiramisu Brownie Squares

1 (19-21 ounce) box brownie mix
   plus ingredients to make cake-like
   brownies
1 cup milk
¼ cup instant coffee granules
1 (12 ounce) container frozen whipped
   topping, thawed and divided

2 (3.4 ounce) packages cheesecake
   instant pudding
2 cups chocolate sandwich cookies,
   coarsely chopped in food processor
   (approximately 20 cookies)
2 tablespoons semisweet chocolate,
   grated
¼ teaspoon cinnamon

Preheat oven to 350°. Prepare brownie mix according to package directions for cake-like brownies; pour batter into lightly greased 9x13 inch pan, spreading batter evenly. Bake 25-30 minutes or until cake tester inserted in center comes out clean. Remove from oven and cool completely. In large bowl, combine milk and instant coffee granules; stir until dissolved. Add ½ of the whipped topping and all the pudding mix; whisk until smooth. Fold cookies into pudding mixture. Spread pudding mixture evenly over baked brownies. Pipe remaining whipped topping in diagonal rows, ¼ inch apart over filling. Sprinkle grated chocolate and cinnamon over piped whipped topping. Refrigerate at least 30 minutes. Cut into 20 squares.

*20 BROWNIES*

# Bowtie Pasta with Asparagus

| | |
|---|---|
| 1 pound box bowtie pasta | 2 teaspoons lemon zest |
| 2 pounds asparagus tips (3 bundles) | 2 tablespoons lemon juice |
| 6 ounces thin prosciutto (cut into strips) | ⅔ cup Italian leaf parsley, chopped |
| | 3 tablespoons butter |
| 1 cup green onions, sliced | ½ cup shredded Parmesan cheese |

Cook pasta according to box directions, drain. Cook asparagus in boiling salted water for 3-4 minutes; drain asparagus and set aside. In small pan, add butter and cook prosciutto in pan until crispy; add onions and cook 1 minute longer. Combine pasta, asparagus, prosciutto, onions, lemon zest, lemon juice, parsley and Parmesan cheese.

*SERVES 6-8*

# Chicken Spaghetti Casserole

| | |
|---|---|
| 1 (16 ounce) package spaghetti | 1 (12 ounce) jar chicken gravy |
| 4½ cups cooked chicken (1 prepared rotisserie chicken or 4 chicken breasts) | 2 (10 ounce) cans tomatoes with chilies, undrained |
| | 2 cups shredded Monterey Jack and Cheddar cheese blend |
| 2 tablespoons olive oil | |
| 1 cup onions, chopped | ½ teaspoon salt |
| 1 cup parsley, chopped | ½ teaspoon pepper |
| 1 cup celery, chopped | 1 sleeve buttery crackers, crushed |
| 1 tablespoon garlic, minced | |

Preheat oven to 350°. Lightly grease a 3 quart casserole dish; set aside. In boiling water cook spaghetti for approximately 8 minutes or until done; drain and set aside. Chop and shred the chicken. In a medium saucepan heat olive oil over medium heat. Add onions, parsley, celery and garlic, cook 3-4 minutes or until onions are translucent. In large bowl combine spaghetti, chicken, onion mixture, chicken gravy, tomatoes, cheese, salt and pepper. Pour into prepared casserole dish. Top with crushed crackers. Cover loosely with foil. Bake for 20 minutes. Remove foil and bake 10 minutes to brown the top.

*SERVES 12-15*

# Mac's Meatballs

1 pound ground beef
1 pound ground pork
1 cup fresh white bread crumbs
(approximately 4 slices with crusts
removed)
¼ cup seasoned dry bread crumbs
2 tablespoons fresh Italian parsley,
chopped
½ cup grated Parmesan cheese

2 teaspoons kosher salt
½ teaspoon freshly ground black
pepper
¼ teaspoon ground nutmeg
¾ cup warm water
1 egg, beaten
Vegetable oil
Olive oil

Place the ground meats, fresh bread crumbs, dry bread crumbs, parsley, Parmesan cheese, salt, pepper, nutmeg, egg and ¾ cup warm water in a bowl. Combine very lightly with a fork. Using your hands, lightly form the mixture into 2 inch meatballs; this will make approximately 14-16 meatballs. Pour equal amounts of vegetable oil and olive oil into a large skillet to a depth of ¼ inch. Heat the oil. Very carefully in batches, place the meatballs in the oil and brown them on all sides over medium low heat, turning carefully with a spatula or fork. Each batch takes about 10 minutes.

*SERVES 4*

May be frozen and reheated with favorite spaghetti sauce by covering and simmering on low heat for 25 to 30 minutes.

Ways & Means earnings have come from homes tour, boutiques, theatre nights, style shows (such as modeling movie star gowns for a local store in 1962-63), garage sales, food tastings, consumer surveys, fun social events, plant sales; the list goes on.

# Baked Jalapeño Matchsticks

8 jalapeño peppers, seeded and very
thinly sliced

2 medium onions, thinly sliced

½ cup low fat buttermilk

1 (5.75 ounce) package hot and spicy
shaking and baking mix

Butter flavored cooking spray

Preheat oven to 400°. Place aluminum foil on baking pan with the dull side of the aluminum facing up. Dip vegetables in the buttermilk and then toss them in a plastic bag with the hot and spicy mix. Place vegetables on baking pan and sprinkle the leftover mix on top. Then spray vegetables with butter flavored cooking spray. Bake for 25-30 minutes or until tender.

*SERVES 4*

# Crab Rangoon Dip

1 (8 ounce) package cream cheese,
softened

6 ounces imitation crabmeat

2 tablespoons milk

¼ teaspoon garlic powder

¼ cup green onions, both white and
green parts

1 teaspoon dried parsley

Salt and black pepper to taste

¼ cup sweet and sour sauce

1 (12 ounce) package wonton
wrappers

Cooking spray

Parmesan cheese (or 5 spice powder)

Preheat oven to 350°. Cut wontons into strips, spray lightly with cooking spray, sprinkle with Parmesan or 5 spice powder and toast until lightly browned. Set aside to cool. Combine all remaining ingredients. Refrigerate until serving time. At serving time, heat the cream cheese mixture in a microwave and serve with wonton strips.

*SERVES 8*

May substitute corn chips for wonton strips if in a pinch for time.

# Tangy Orange Ball

5 ounces orange flavored drink crystals

12 ounces cream cheese, softened

⅓ cup milk

¾ cup chopped pecans

Sliced red and green apples for dipping (about 4 apples)

Combine cream cheese, milk and drink crystals until smooth. Create a ball with this mixture and roll in chopped pecans. Refrigerate until 30 minutes before serving. Place on serving dish with apples surrounding the ball.

*SERVES 8*

Dip apples in orange juice to prevent browning.

# Creamy Bacon Dip

1 (8 ounce) carton fat free plain yogurt

6 tablespoons light mayonnaise

¼ cup green onions minced, both white and green parts

¼ cup crumbled, cooked bacon

¼ teaspoon paprika

8 drops hot sauce

2 garlic cloves, crushed

Tortilla chips

Place yogurt in a bowl lined with several layers of heavy duty paper towels. Spread yogurt out in a ½ inch layer on the towels. Set aside for 5 minutes so that paper towels can absorb the excess liquid. Scrape yogurt into a bowl using a rubber spatula. Add all remaining ingredients except the chips. Chill until serving time. Serve with tortilla or corn chips.

*SERVES 8*

# Hot Swiss Cheese and Onion Dip

3 sweet onions, coarsely chopped
1 clove garlic, minced
2 tablespoons butter
2 cups Swiss cheese, shredded

1 cup mayonnaise
½ teaspoon hot sauce
½ cup Parmesan cheese, shredded

Preheat oven to 350°. Sauté onions and garlic in butter until soft. Remove from heat and add the remaining ingredients. Mix and place in an 8x8 inch glass baking dish. Bake for 20 minutes. Serve with assorted crackers.

*SERVES 20-24*

# Artichoke Hummus

2 cups chickpeas, cooked and drained
1 (14 ounce) can artichoke hearts, drained
3 to 6 garlic cloves, add according to taste
Extra virgin olive oil

White pepper to taste
Paprika to taste
Ground cumin to taste
Kosher salt to taste
Pita wedges for serving

Place all ingredients except the olive oil and pita wedges into a food processor. While the processor is running, slowly drizzle in the oil until all ingredients are blended but not smooth. Serve with pita wedges.

*SERVES 10*

# Spinach and Chèvre Dip

1 (10 ounce) package frozen, chopped spinach, thawed and squeezed dry
1 cup (8 ounces) plain yogurt
½ cup goat cheese, crumbled

¼ cup Dijon mustard
2 tablespoons fresh basil, chopped
1 garlic clove, chopped
¼ teaspoon black pepper

Place all ingredients into a food processor or blender and process until well blended but slightly chunky. Cover and refrigerate until 1 hour before serving. Place on serving dish with vegetables or assortment of crackers.

# Cajun Shrimp and Artichoke Dip

1 cup mayonnaise

1 cup sour cream

2 tablespoons Cajun seasoning

8 ounces of shrimp, cooked, cleaned, deveined and coarsely chopped

2 (6 ounce) jars marinated artichoke hearts, drained and chopped

⅓ cup sun-dried tomatoes, drained and coarsely chopped

3 green onions, green and white parts finely chopped

Salt and black pepper to taste

Mix mayonnaise, sour cream and Cajun seasoning together in a medium bowl. Add shrimp, tomatoes, artichoke hearts and green onions, mixing well. Season with salt and pepper. Cover and refrigerate 1 hour or overnight. Transfer to a serving bowl and serve with chips, vegetables or baguette slices.

*SERVES 3½ CUPS*

# Avocado-Goat Cheese Spread

2 ripe avocados, peeled, pitted and cut into chunks

4 ounces cream cheese, softened

4 ounces creamy goat (chèvre) cheese, softened

2½ tablespoons lime juice

1 tablespoon shallots, minced

1 tablespoon garlic, minced

¼ teaspoon ground cumin

¼ teaspoon salt

2 teaspoons jalapeño pepper, seeded and diced (more to increase heat)

1½ tablespoons cilantro, chopped

Process avocado, goat cheese and cream cheese in a food processor by pulsing for 30-60 seconds. Add lime juice, shallots, garlic, cumin, salt, jalapeños and cilantro and process to mix well. Taste to see if you want to add more jalapeños. Mound in non-reactive bowl (not copper or aluminum) and refrigerate. Bring to room temperature before serving. Crackers or pita chips are great for serving this spread.

*SERVES 8-10*

May be made a day ahead of serving.

# True Tapenade

6 ounces black olives
1½ ounces anchovy fillets
1½ ounces tuna in oil, drained

3 ounces capers
1-2 tablespoons olive oil

Use a mortar and pestle or a small food processor to crush all ingredients except the olive oil. Add 1 tablespoon olive oil and check for desired consistency. You may choose to add the second tablespoon. Keep in a tightly covered container.

*SERVES APPROXIMATELY 1 CUP*

# Quick and Easy Tapenade

10 ounces Kalamata olives
  (or black olives)
1 teaspoon oregano
½ teaspoon basil

½ to 1 teaspoon balsamic vinegar
¾ teaspoon sugar
2 teaspoons extra virgin olive oil

Combine all ingredients except olive oil in a food processor. Scraping sides of the processor bowl frequently, process until the mixture becomes a paste. With processor running, drizzle the olive oil into the processor.

Can be poured over cream cheese, fish or pasta.

169

# Baked Brie Parcels

1 (16 ounce) package Phyllo dough sheets, thawed

⅔ cup unsalted butter, melted

1 pound Brie cheese

1½ cups whole cranberry sauce

Heat oven to 400°. Place 1 sheet of phyllo on clean work surface. Brush with melted butter. Top with another sheet and brush with butter. Repeat 2 more times. Cut into 16 even squares. Make 16 balls of Brie and place 1 ball on each square of phyllo. Top with ½ teaspoon of cranberry sauce. Bring up corners of the phyllo to the center and twist them to secure the parcel. Place on lightly oiled baking sheet and bake for 18-20 minutes or until lightly golden brown.

*SERVES 8*

# Chicken Enchilada Dip

3 cups chicken breast (grilled, canned or rotisserie), finely chopped

2 (8 ounce) packages cream cheese, softened

2 cups Cheddar cheese, grated

1 teaspoon garlic, minced

1½ tablespoons chili powder (or to taste)

1 teaspoon cumin

1 teaspoon oregano

1 teaspoon paprika

½ bunch cilantro, chopped

4 green onions, both white and green chopped

1 (14.5 ounce) can tomatoes with green chilies, undrained

Place chicken, cilantro, green onions and tomatoes in bowl. Set aside. Mix cream cheese, Cheddar, garlic, chili powder, cumin, oregano and paprika together. Fold chicken mixture into this mixture. Refrigerate until serving. It is best served after chilling overnight. Serve with tortilla or rice chips.

*SERVES 6 CUPS*

Our membership comes for the entire Kansas City area as well as those who have once lived here and now live away.

# Artichoke Dip

1 (14 ounce) can artichoke hearts, drained
1 cup Parmesan cheese, grated
1 cup mayonnaise
1 cup mozzarella cheese, grated

2 (3 ounce) cans green chilies, chopped
1 green onion, chopped white and green parts
Dash of garlic salt
Cooking spray

Preheat oven to 350°. Spray glass pie plate with cooking spray. Combine all ingredients and place in pie plate. Bake for 30 minutes or until lightly browned. Serve with crackers, chips or breadsticks.

*SERVES 8-10*

# Smoked Salmon Bites

30 slices cocktail pumpernickel bread, diagonally sliced to form a triangle
1 (10 ounce) container crème fraîche

⅓ pound smoked salmon, thinly sliced and in bite-sized pieces
Dill sprigs for garnish

Spread crème fraîche over each piece of bread. Top with smoked salmon and garnish with small sprig of dill.

*SERVES 60 PIECES*

# Louisiana Crab Dip with Crudités

1 (8 ounce) package cream cheese, softened
½ cup sour cream
3 tablespoons horseradish
2 tablespoons chopped parsley

1 tablespoon coarse ground mustard
2 teaspoons pepper sauce
1 pound lump crabmeat, cleaned
Fresh vegetables of your choice

Combine cream cheese, sour cream, horseradish, parsley, mustard and pepper sauce. Once they are well mixed, gently add in the crabmeat. Refrigerate until serving. Use any combination of raw vegetables or crackers for serving.

*SERVES 12*

# King Ranch Casserole

1 (12 ounce) package corn chips

1 cup hot chicken broth

1 medium or large frying chicken, boned and cut-up

1 large onion, chopped

1 green pepper, chopped

8 ounces grated Cheddar cheese, divided

1 (10.5 ounce) can cream of mushroom soup

1 (10.5 ounce) can cream of chicken soup

1 (10 ounce) can tomatoes with green chilies

½ teaspoon chili powder

½ teaspoon salt

½ teaspoon pepper

Preheat oven to 350°. Wilt corn chips in hot chicken broth then spread in bottom of 9x13 inch casserole. Evenly distribute chicken on top, then onion, green pepper and half of the cheese. In saucepan, heat together the soups, tomatoes and seasonings. Pour sauce mixture over ingredients in casserole, and top with remaining cheese. Bake for 30 minutes. If casserole seems dry add a little of the chicken broth.

*SERVES 8-12*

May use boneless, skinless chicken breasts in place of frying chicken.

# Zesty Ham Roll-Ups

1 (8 ounce) package cream cheese, softened

2 tablespoons Dijon mustard

3 green onions, chopped

6 (8 inch) flour tortillas

12 to 18 large spinach leaves, no stems

1 (12 ounce) jar whole, roasted red peppers, drained and sliced

¾ pound thin sliced deli ham

Lettuce for garnish

Combine cream cheese and mustard. Add green onion and mix well. Spread ¼ cup cream cheese mixture on each tortilla to within ¼ inch of edge. Cover with 2-3 spinach leaves. Press down. Top with 1-2 pepper slices and 2 ham slices. Roll up in jelly roll fashion. Place in lidded container with seam side down. Refrigerate at least 1 hour. Cut in 1 inch diagonal slices. Serve on a lettuce lined platter.

# Cheesy Herb Coins

2 (4 ounce) packages crumbled blue cheese, softened
½ cup butter, softened
1⅓ cups all-purpose flour

⅓ cup toasted, ground walnuts
1 egg white, beaten
Tiny fresh herb sprigs
(rosemary, thyme, sage)

Beat cheese and butter at medium speed with an electric mixer until creamy. Add flour and nuts, beat until blended. Shape the dough into 2 (8 inch) logs. Wrap logs in wax paper, and chill 2 hours or until firm. Preheat oven to 350°. Cut into ¼ inch thick slices, and place on lightly greased baking sheets. Brush lightly with beaten egg white. Press herb sprigs firmly into each slice. Bake for 12-15 minutes or until golden brown. Cool 1 minute on baking sheets, remove to wire racks to cool completely

*SERVES 4 DOZEN*

Chill logs of dough overnight and slice and bake the next day.

# Blueberry Oatmeal Crisp

**FRUIT**

3 pints blueberries
½ cup sugar

Juice and finely grated zest of 1 lemon
3 tablespoons flour

**TOPPING**

1 cup all-purpose flour
1 cup firmly packed light brown sugar
⅔ cup rolled oats
½ teaspoon cinnamon

¼ teaspoon salt
½ cup plus 2 tablespoons cold, unsalted butter, cut into small pieces

Preheat oven to 400°. Mix the berries, sugar, flour, lemon juice and zest in a large bowl. Butter a 9x13 inch glass pan. For the topping, combine the flour, brown sugar, oats, cinnamon and salt in the food processor. Add the butter and pulse until the mixture is clumpy. Transfer the berries to the baking dish. Spread the crumbs evenly over the fruit. Bake for 30 minutes until bubbly hot. Serve at any temperature, but let cool at least 10 minutes.

*SERVE 10*

# Green Bean Salad with Feta

¾ cup olive oil
¼ cup white wine vinegar
1 clove garlic, minced
½ teaspoon salt
¼ teaspoon pepper

2 pounds green beans
1 small purple onion, thinly sliced
1 (4 ounce) package feta cheese, crumbled
1 cup coarsely chopped walnuts, toasted

Combine oil, vinegar, garlic, salt and pepper. Whisk until blended. Trim stem end of green beans, snap or for prettier presentation, leave whole. Arrange beans in steamer over boiling water for 10-12 minutes, or until tender crisp. Immediately plunge into cold water to stop cooking process. Drain and pat dry. Combine beans, onion and cheese in a large bowl, toss well. Cover and chill, if desired. Pour oil mixture over bean mixture, cover and chill 1 hour. Add walnuts and toss just before serving.

*SERVES 8*

# Peanut Butter Fudge Bars

1 cup creamy peanut butter
1 (18.5 ounce) box yellow cake mix
½ cup melted butter
2 eggs
1 (14 ounce) can sweetened condensed milk
2 tablespoons melted butter

2 teaspoons vanilla extract
½ teaspoon salt
1 (12 ounce) package semisweet chocolate chips
1 cup coconut
1 cup finely chopped walnuts

Preheat oven to 350°. Combine cake mix, peanut butter, ½ cup melted butter and eggs. Stir until blended. Press ⅔ of mixture into a 9x13 inch ungreased pan. In a separate bowl, combine condensed milk, 2 tablespoons melted butter, vanilla and salt. Stir in chocolate chips, coconut and walnuts. Spread over cake mix layer. Crumble reserved ⅓ of dough over the top. Bake 25-35 minutes or until golden brown. Cool overnight and cut into squares.

*SERVES 18*

# Quick Broccoli Salad

1 large bunch broccoli, washed and cut into bite-size pieces
¾ cup oil

¾ cup sugar, may use a little less
⅓ cup cider vinegar
1 package zesty Italian salad dressing

Mix all together and pour over broccoli. Marinate overnight.

# Summer Sensations

# Whole Lot of Love

Blueberry Lemonade, page 181
Spinberry and Cheese Salad, page 182
Spicy Egg Casserole, page 182
Sausage Stars, page 181
Blueberry French Toast, page 183
Mixed Fruit Compote, page 183
Fruit Salsa with Tortilla Crisps, page 184
Blackberry Peach Coffee Cake, page 185
Orange Cream Cake, page 186
Lemon Pound Cake Muffins, page 186

# Taste of the Southwest

White Strawberry Sangría, page 187
Not Your Mama's Nachos, page 188
Avocado Salsa, page 187
Gazpacho, page 188
Shrimp and Avocado Salad, page 189
Layered Southwestern Salad, page 189
Flank Steak with Salsa Verde, page 190
Fast and Easy Green Chili Rice, page 191
Margarita Key Lime Pie with Gingersnap Crust, page 191
Carmelitas, page 190
Grilled Peaches with Berry Sauce, page 192

## Substitutions
Cold Avocado Soup, page 192
Southwest Chicken Lasagna, page 193
Zippy Corn on the Cob, page 193

# Summer Soiree

Raspberry Beer Cocktail, page 194
BLT Bites, page 194
Gazpacho Blanca, page 195
Watermelon and Strawberry Salad, page 194
Hot Chicken Salad, page 195
Zucchini Casserole, page 196
Onion Cheese Corn Muffins, page 196
Kansas Rhubarb, page 197
Orange Coconut Cookies, page 196

## Substitutions

Mango Chicken Salad, page 197
Berries Romanoff, page 197

# Fourth of July

Watermelon Margaritas, page 198
Black Bean Salsa, page 199
Broccoli Slaw, page 200
State Fair Potato Salad, page 198
Crunchy Chili Onion Rings, page 199
Grilled Burgers with Lemon Butter, page 201
Spicy Hot Dogs, page 200
Georgia Peach Ice Cream, page 202
Maple Nut Coffee Ice Cream Dessert, page 203
White Chocolate Cookie and Cream Fudge, page 203

## Substitutions

Grilled Sweet Potatoes, page 202
Kahlúa Ice Cream Bars, page 201

# It's Greek To Me

Mocktail, page 204
Layered Greek Dip, page 205
Hot Feta Cheese Dip, page 204
Simple Antipasto Platter, page 204
Watermelon Feta Salad, page 205
Greek Orzo and Grilled Shrimp Salad with Dill Vinaigrette, page 206
Greek Chicken Pasta, page 206
Spinach Phyllo, page 207

## Substitutions
Greek Salad, page 208
Mediterranean Layered Dip, page 209
Chocolate Mocha Cream Cake, page 209
Greek Caesar Salad, page 208

# Beef on the Barbie

Bourbon Slush, page 210
Smokey Cheese Round with Avocado Mango Salsa, page 211
Southwestern Caesar Salad, page 212
Marinated Vegetables, page 210
Grilled Beef Tenderloin with Ancho Jalapeño Butter, page 213
Molasses Cookies, page 213
Blueberry Cream Cheese Dessert, page 214

## Substitution
Mexican Spice-Rubbed Rib-Eyes with Lime Butter, page 214

# Sunset on the Deck

Pomegranate Margaritas, page 215
Hot Corn Dip, page 215
Crab Soup, page 216
Sour Cream Biscuits, page 217
Swannie's Coleslaw, page 216
Cauliflower Salad, page 217
Grilled Prosciutto Wrapped Shrimp, page 217
Peaches and Ice Cream Sandwich Bars, page 218
Kansas Mud Brûlée, page 219

## Substitution
Chilled Cucumber Soup, page 218

# Girls' Weekend at the Lake

Egg Salad Sandwiches, page 220
Fresh Veggies with Buttermilk Herb Dip, page 221
Better Than Sex Cake, page 221
Summer Martini, page 222
Phyllo Pizza with Feta, Basil and Tomatoes, page 222
Mango-Spinach Salad with Warm Bacon Vinaigrette, page 220
Farm Fresh Pasta with Bacon, page 223
Bacon and Herb Cupcakes, page 223
Vanilla Cake with Buttercream, Berries and Jam, page 224
Stuffed Filet Mignon with Merlot Mushroom Sauce, page 225
Parmesan Polenta Cakes, page 226
Peanut Butter and Banana Bread, page 226
Maple French Toast and Bacon Cupcakes, page 227
Peanut Butter Banana Cream Pie, page 228

## Substitutions
Sweet Pea Casserole, page 229
Prosciutto-Melon Bites with Lime Drizzle, page 225
Hash Brown Cakes, page 229

# Taste of Tuscany

Baked Ravioli Bites, page 230
Skinny Fettuccini Alfredo, page 232
Sweet Potato Risotto, page 230
Puff Pastry Pizza with Chorizo, page 233
Pork Loin with Fontina, Prosciutto and Sun-Dried Tomato, page 231
Mesclun Green Salad with Camembert Cheese, page 232
Hazelnut, Ricotta & Lemon Pesto, page 233
Fresh Tomato-Olive Sauce, page 234
Short Ribs with Tagliatelle, page 235
Focaccia Versiliese, page 238
Berry Tiramisu, page 236

# Seaside Sampler

Tonga Mai Tai, page 239
Shrimp Pâté, page 239
Tomato Relish Salad, page 240
Spring Peas with Dates and Walnuts, page 240
Herbed Rice with Raisins, page 241
Lemon-Peppered Broiled Fish, page 241
Cedar Plank Salmon with Maple-Ginger Glaze, page 242
Grilled Citrus Salmon, page 243
Butterhorns, page 244
Glacé Fruit, page 243

## Substitutions
Oven-Fried Fish, page 242
Easy Roasted Asparagus, page 243
Marinated Vegetables, page 244

# Blueberry Lemonade

1 large can frozen lemonade
2 cups blueberry vodka

Blueberries for garnish

Make lemonade by instructions. Add vodka. Mix and enjoy. Garnish with fresh blueberries.

*SERVES 8-10*

# Sausage Stars

1 (16 ounce) package wonton shells
1 pound mild breakfast sausage
1 cup prepared ranch dressing
1 (6 ounce) can black olives, sliced

1½ cups Cheddar cheese, shredded
1½ cups mozzarella cheese, shredded
½ cup red bell pepper, chopped

Preheat oven to 350°. Spray muffin pans with cooking spray. Press a wonton shell in each muffin cup. Spray shells lightly with cooking spray. Bake 5 minutes or until lightly browned. When done, remove shells from pans. Set aside and cook remaining shells. Some may break or not be stuffable. Fry sausage until browned and drained. Combine sausage, ranch dressing, olives, cheeses and pepper. Arrange baked wonton shells on an ungreased cookie sheet. Stuff each shell about ¾ full with sausage mixture. Bake 5-7 minutes or until bubbly.

*SERVES 25-30*

Egg roll wrappers cut in fourths may be substituted for wonton shells. The shells may be made ahead and frozen until needed.

# Spicy Egg Casserole

1 pound mild ground pork sausage

1 small onion, chopped

½ green bell pepper, chopped

2 (10 ounce) cans diced tomatoes with green chilies, undrained

8 (10 inch) flour tortillas, torn into bite-size pieces

3 cups (12 ounces) shredded Monterey Jack cheese with peppers or Monterey Jack cheese

6 eggs

2 cups milk

1 teaspoon salt

½ teaspoon pepper

¼ cup chopped fresh cilantro

Preheat oven to 350°. Cook sausage in a large skillet over medium-high heat, stirring until crumbled and is no longer pink. Drain and return to skillet. Add chopped onion and bell pepper to sausage; sauté over medium-heat 5 minutes or until vegetables are tender. Stir in tomatoes with green chilies; reduce heat. Cover and simmer 10 minutes. Layer half each of tortilla pieces, sausage mixture and cheese in a lightly greased 9x13 inch baking dish. Repeat layers. Whisk together eggs, milk, salt and pepper; pour over layers in dish. Bake uncovered for 25-30 minutes or until lightly browned and set in center. Sprinkle with cilantro before serving.

*SERVES 8-10*

# Spinberry and Cheese Salad

6 cups fresh baby spinach

1 cup fresh blackberries

1 cup cherry tomatoes, halved

1 green onion, sliced

2 tablespoons chopped walnuts, toasted

⅓ cup oil

1 tablespoon balsamic vinegar

2½ teaspoons honey

1 garlic clove, minced

1 teaspoon Dijon mustard

¼ teaspoon salt

¼ teaspoon pepper

⅔ cup crumbled feta cheese

In a large salad bowl, combine the spinach, blackberries, tomatoes, onion and walnuts. In a small bowl, whisk the oil, vinegar, honey, garlic, mustard, salt and pepper. Drizzle over salad and toss to coat. Sprinkle with cheese.

*SERVES 8*

# Blueberry French Toast

| | |
|---|---|
| 12 slices day old bread | 12 eggs |
| 2 (8 ounce) packages cream cheese | 2 cups milk |
| 1 cup fresh or frozen blueberries | ⅓ cup maple syrup |

**GREAT BLUEBERRY SAUCE**

| | |
|---|---|
| 1 cup sugar | 2 tablespoons cornstarch |
| 1 cup blueberries | 1 cup water |
| 1 tablespoon sweet butter | |

Slice bread into cubes. Place half the cubes into a greased 9x13 inch pan. Cut cream cheese into small cubes and layer over the bread cubes in your pan. Top with the blueberries and cover with the remaining bread cubes. Set aside. In mixing bowl, beat eggs until nice and light. Add milk and syrup; mix well. Pour this mixture over the bread mixture. Cover with foil and refrigerate overnight. Remove from the refrigerator 15-20 minutes before baking. Preheat oven to 350°. Bake covered for 30 minutes. Uncover and bake for another 25-30 minutes or until golden brown. To make sauce: in a saucepan, over medium heat, combine the sugar and cornstarch. Add the water and bring to a boil. Whisk as you continue to let it boil for about 3 minutes. Stir in the blueberries and lower the heat to a simmer. Allow to simmer gently for 10 minutes or until berries burst. Fold in the butter and allow to melt. Serve on the side.

*SERVES 12*

# Mixed Fruit Compote

| | |
|---|---|
| 3 red grapefruits | 3 tablespoons honey |
| 4 blood oranges | ¼ cup fresh mint leaves |
| 3 navel oranges | ½ cup pomegranate seeds |
| 1 cup sugar | Garnish: fresh mint sprigs |

Peel the fruit and separate into sections; catching juice in a bowl. Pour juice into a glass measuring cup, adding water if necessary, to measure ¾ cup; reserve fruit in bowl. Combine juice, sugar, honey and mint in a medium saucepan; bring to a boil over medium heat. Boil 5 minutes, stirring occasionally. Remove from heat and let cool, uncovered, 45 minutes. Remove and discard mint. Pour syrup over fruit; gently stir in pomegranate seeds. Cover and chill until ready to serve. Garnish, if desired.

*SERVES 8*

# Fruit Salsa with Tortilla Crisps

1 cup finely chopped strawberries

1 medium orange, peeled and finely chopped (⅓ cup)

2 large or 3 small kiwi, peeled and finely chopped (⅔ cup)

½ cup finely chopped fresh pineapple or 1 (8 ounce) can crushed pineapple (juice pack), drained

¼ cup thinly sliced green onions

¼ cup finely chopped yellow or green bell pepper

1 tablespoon lime or lemon juice

1 fresh jalapeño chili pepper, seeded and chopped, optional

**TORTILLA CRISPS**

½ cup sugar

1 teaspoon cinnamon

¼ cup melted butter

12 (7 or 8 inch) flour tortillas

In a bowl combine strawberries, orange, kiwi, pineapple, green onions, pepper, lime juice, and, if desired, jalapeño pepper. Cover and chill for 6-24 hours. Serve with cinnamon tortilla crisps. To make crisps, preheat oven to 350°. Combine ½ cup sugar and 1 teaspoon cinnamon. Brush ¼ cup melted butter or margarine over 12 (7 or 8 inch) flour tortillas. Sprinkle tortillas with cinnamon-sugar mixture. Cut each tortilla into 8 wedges. Bake for 7-10 minutes until dry and crisp. Store in airtight container for 4 days or freeze for up to 3 weeks.

*SERVES 12*

If you plan to chill salsa for more than 6 hours, stir in strawberries just before serving.

JCYM has supported a vast array of philanthropies in our 50 year history with time and money. Over one hundred non-profit agencies have benefited from our generosity.

# Blackberry Peach Coffee Cake

½ cup butter, softened

1 cup sugar

2 eggs

2 cups all-purpose flour

2 teaspoons baking powder

½ teaspoon salt

⅔ cup milk

2 teaspoons vanilla extract

2 cups peeled and sliced fresh, firm, ripe peaches (about 2 large peaches)

1 cup fresh blackberries

Powdered sugar

Fresh blackberries and sliced peaches for garnish

**STREUSEL TOPPING**

½ cup butter, softened

½ cup sugar

½ cup firmly packed light brown sugar

⅔ cup all-purpose flour

1 teaspoon cinnamon

½ teaspoon nutmeg

Preheat oven to 350°. Prepare streusel topping by beating butter at medium speed until creamy. Gradually add sugars, beating well. Add flour, cinnamon and nutmeg until blended, and set aside. Beat butter at medium speed with an electric mixer until creamy; gradually add sugar, beating well. Add eggs, one at a time, beating until blended after each addition. Combine flour, baking powder and salt; add to butter mixture alternately with milk, beginning and ending with flour mixture. Beat at low speed until blended after each addition. Stir in vanilla. Pour batter into a greased and floured 9 inch springform pan; top with sliced peaches and blackberries. Sprinkle streusel topping over fruit. Bake for 1 hour 10 minutes to 1 hour 20 minutes or until center of cake is set. A wooden pick inserted in center will not come out clean. Cool completely on a wire rack (about 1½ hours). Dust with powdered sugar. Garnish, if desired.

*SERVES 8*

For Peach Coffee Cake only, omit blackberries, and increase peaches to 3 cups sliced (about 3 large peaches). Proceed with recipe as directed.

# Orange Cream Cake

1 (16.5 ounce) roll refrigerated sugar cookies

2 tablespoons grated orange zest

2 (8 ounce) packages cream cheese, softened

¼ cup sugar

½ cup sweet orange marmalade

1 teaspoon orange-flavored liqueur or ¼ teaspoon orange extract

2 eggs

3 tablespoons whipping cream

2 drops orange food coloring

1½ teaspoons butter

½ cup white vanilla baking chips

Preheat oven to 350°. Press cookie dough evenly on bottom and 1 inch up sides of ungreased 9x13 inch glass baking dish. (If dough is sticky, use floured fingers.) Sprinkle evenly with orange zest. In medium bowl, beat cream cheese, sugar, marmalade and liqueur with electric mixer on high speed about 1 minute or until well blended. Add eggs, beat about 2 minutes or until well blended and mixture is creamy. Spread evenly in crust. Bake 29-36 minutes or until crust is golden brown and center is set. Cool 1 hour. In small microwavable bowl, microwave whipping cream and food coloring uncovered on high about 30 seconds or just until boiling. Add butter and baking chips; stir until chips are melted. Spread mixture evenly over bars. Refrigerate about 1½ hours or until chilled and firm. Cut into 24 squares. Cover and refrigerate any remaining dessert.

*SERVES 24*

# Lemon Pound Cake Muffins

½ cup butter, softened

1 cup sugar

2 eggs

½ cup sour cream

1 teaspoon vanilla extract

½ teaspoon lemon extract

1¾ cups all-purpose flour

½ teaspoon salt

¼ teaspoon baking soda

**GLAZE**

2 cups powdered sugar

3 tablespoons lemon juice

Preheat oven to 400°. In a large bowl, cream the butter and sugar until light and fluffy. Add eggs, one at a time, beating well after each addition. Beat in the sour cream and extracts. Combine the flour, salt and baking soda; add to creamed mixture just until moistened. Fill greased or paper-lined muffin cups ¾ full. Bake for 18-20 minutes or until a toothpick inserted near the center comes out clean. Cool for 5 minutes before removing from pan to a wire rack. Combine glaze ingredients; drizzle over muffins. Serve warm.

*SERVES 12*

# White Strawberry Sangría

2 (750 milliliter) bottles dry white wine
1 cup strawberry schnapps
½ cup sugar

4 cups sliced fresh strawberries
Ice cubes
Whole strawberries, optional

In a gallon container or 2 (2 quart) pitchers, stir together wine, strawberry schnapps and sugar until sugar is dissolved. Add sliced strawberries. Cover and chill for 1-4 hours. Serve in glasses over ice. If desired, garnish with whole strawberries.

*SERVES 6-8*

For non-alcoholic version, use 7 cups white grape juice in place of the wine and use ½ cup lemon juice and ½ cup strawberry flavored syrup (such as a syrup for coffee) in place of the strawberry schnapps. Omit the sugar. Prepare as directed above.

# Avocado Salsa

1 (10-16 ounce) package frozen corn, thawed
1 small sweet red onion, chopped
1 red bell pepper, chopped
2 (2.25 ounce) cans sliced olives
1 tablespoon dried oregano

½ teaspoon salt
½ teaspoon pepper
¼ cup olive oil
⅓ cup lemon juice
4 avocados, chopped

In a large bowl, combine thawed corn, onion, red pepper and sliced olives. In a small bowl whisk oregano, salt, pepper, olive oil and lemon juice. Pour over mixture in large bowl and refrigerate overnight. Before serving, stir avocados in and serve with chips

*SERVES 8-10*

Peppers with 3 bumps on the bottom are sweeter and better for eating. Peppers with 4 bumps on the bottom are firmer and better for cooking.

# Not Your Mama's Nachos

2 (15 ounce) cans black beans
1 lime, juice only
¼ cup finely chopped white onion
1 tablespoon extra virgin olive oil
1 teaspoon chopped garlic
¼ cup chopped cilantro
¼ teaspoon cumin
¼ teaspoon salt
¼ teaspoon black pepper

20 ounces soft goat cheese, crumbled
1 cup whipping cream
2 avocados, chopped
1 cup chopped fresh spinach
1 small jar salsa or pico de gallo, optional
1 small jalapeño, chopped, optional
Chips and lime wedges for serving

In a medium saucepan, combine black beans, juice from lime, onion, olive oil, garlic, cilantro, cumin, salt and pepper. Cover and warm over medium-low heat for 5 minutes. Remove from heat. In a medium bowl, stir goat cheese into cream. Cover and microwave on high for 90 seconds. Whisk until creamy. Set aside. To assemble, place a handful of tortilla chips on plates. Drizzle with goat cheese sauce and top with black bean mixture, avocado, pico de gallo or salsa, spinach and chopped jalapeños, optional. Serve with lime wedges.

*SERVES 8-10*

# Gazpacho

½ green onion
1 green bell pepper, chopped
½ cup chopped celery
1 cucumber, peeled and chopped
3 large tomatoes, peeled and chopped
5 tablespoons red wine vinegar

4 tablespoons olive oil
2 teaspoons salt or to taste
½ teaspoon black pepper
4 cups tomato juice
2 avocados, chopped
Sour cream as garnish

Put onion, green pepper, celery, cucumber and tomatoes in food processor and pulse until chunky. Pour this in a large pan and add vinegar, olive oil, salt, pepper, tomato juice and avocados. Serve cold with sour cream.

*SERVES 4-6*

# Shrimp and Avocado Salad

1 pound large shrimp, uncooked, peeled and deveined
1 garlic clove, minced
½ teaspoon chili powder
¼ teaspoon salt
¼ teaspoon ground cumin
2 teaspoons olive oil

5 cups hearts of romaine salad mix
1 cup corn, fresh or frozen, thawed
1 cup frozen peas, thawed
½ cup red bell pepper, chopped
1 medium avocado, peeled, thinly sliced

**CILANTRO VINAIGRETTE**

7 tablespoons olive oil
¼ cup minced fresh cilantro
¼ cup lime juice
1½ teaspoons sugar

1 small garlic clove, minced
½ teaspoon salt
¼ teaspoon black pepper

In a large skillet, cook the shrimp, garlic, chili powder, salt and cumin in oil over medium heat for 3-4 minutes or until shrimp turn pink. Set aside. In a large bowl, combine the romaine, corn, peas and red pepper. Divide among 4 serving plates. Top each with shrimp and avocado. In a small bowl, whisk the vinaigrette ingredients and drizzle over salads.

*SERVES 4*

# Layered Southwestern Salad

⅓ cup fresh cilantro, chopped
½ cup lime juice
½ cup olive oil
½ cup sour cream
1 teaspoon sugar
½ teaspoon salt
½ teaspoon pepper
1 (16 ounce) package romaine lettuce, shredded
5 plum tomatoes, chopped

1 (15 ounce) can black beans, rinsed and drained
1 small red onion, chopped
1 (8 ounce) package shredded Mexican 4 cheese blend
1 (15 ounce) whole kernel corn with red and green peppers, drained
1 (6 ounce) can sliced ripe olives, drained
2 cups crushed tortilla chips
Fresh cilantro leaves, for garnish

Process cilantro, lime juice, olive oil, sour cream, sugar, salt and pepper in a blender or food processor until smooth, stopping to scrape down sides. Layer lettuce and remaining ingredients in a 3 quart glass bowl. Pour vinaigrette over salad just before serving and gently toss. Garnish, if desired, and serve immediately.

*SERVES 8-10*

# Flank Steak with Salsa Verde

2 cups fresh parsley, loosely packed
3 green onions, coarsely chopped
2 tablespoons capers, drained
Zest and juice of ½ lemon
2 anchovy fillets
2 cloves garlic, smashed
½ teaspoon Dijon mustard

⅓ cup olive oil, extra virgin plus more for the grill
Kosher salt
1 flank steak (about 1½ pounds)
Freshly ground black pepper
2 or 3 tomatoes

To make the salsa verde, pulse the parsley, green onions, capers, lemon zest and juice, anchovies, garlic, mustard and olive oil in a food processor until slightly chunky. Pour into bowl and season with salt. Preheat a grill to high or place a grill pan over high heat. Pierce the steak all over with a fork and season with salt and pepper. Oil the grill or pan. Grill the steak 4-5 minutes per side for medium rare, turning once. Transfer to a cutting board and let rest for 5 minutes.

Slice the tomatoes and season with salt and pepper. Thinly slice the steak against the grain. Serve with the tomatoes and salsa verde.

*SERVES 4*


# Carmelitas

1 cup all-purpose flour
1 cup quick-cooking oats
¾ cup firmly packed brown sugar
½ teaspoon baking soda
¼ teaspoon salt
¾ cup butter, softened

1 (12 ounce) jar caramel ice cream topping
3 tablespoons all-purpose flour
6 ounces chocolate chips
½ cup chopped pecans

Preheat oven to 350°. Mix flour, oats, sugar, soda, salt and butter in a large mixing bowl, then use a pastry cutter to combine. Press about ⅔ of mixture in an 8x8 inch greased foil baking pan. Bake for 10 minutes. Mix 3 tablespoons of flour into caramel and spread over crust, then sprinkle with chocolate chips and pecans. Sprinkle remaining oat mixture and pat down lightly. Bake an additional 25-30 minutes. Cool completely. Cut into squares.

*SERVES 8-12*

# Fast and Easy Green Chili Rice

2 cups sour cream
2 cups uncooked instant rice
2 (4 ounce) cans diced green chilies
   including the liquid

16 ounces grated Monterey Jack cheese

Preheat oven to 350°. Grease a large casserole dish. Combine all ingredients and place in the casserole dish. Bake for 30 minutes.

*SERVES 6-8*

# Margarita Key Lime Pie with Gingersnap Crust

4 eggs
½ cup fresh lime juice
¼ cup orange liqueur
¼ cup tequila

2 (14 ounce) cans sweetened
   condensed milk
2 teaspoons lime zest
2 cups whipping cream

**GINGERSNAP CRUST**
¾ cup flaked coconut, toasted
18 gingersnap cookies, crumbled
3 tablespoons unsalted butter, melted

Garnishes: lime rind curls, sweetened
   whipped cream

Preheat oven to 350°. For the crust, stir together coconut, cookie crumbs and melted butter. Press into bottom and up sides of a 9 inch pie plate. Bake for 8 minutes. Cool on a wire rack. Combine eggs, lime juice, orange liqueur, sweetened condensed milk and tequila in a heavy saucepan over medium heat, stirring often, 20 minutes or until temperature reaches 165°. Remove from heat. Stir in lime zest. Cool completely. Beat whipping cream at high speed with an electric mixer until soft peaks form. Fold into egg mixture. Spoon into gingersnap crust. Freeze 2 hours or until firm. Let stand 20 minutes before cutting. Garnish, if desired.

*SERVES 6-8*

# Grilled Peaches with Berry Sauce

½ (10 ounce) package frozen raspberries in syrup, slightly thawed

1½ teaspoons lemon juice

2 medium fresh peaches, peeled and halved

5 teaspoons brown sugar

¼ teaspoon cinnamon

½ teaspoon vanilla extract

1 teaspoon butter

In a blender or food processor, process raspberries and lemon juice until puréed. Strain and discard seeds. Cover and chill. Place the peach halves, cut side up, on a large piece of heavy duty foil (about 18x12 inch). Combine brown sugar and cinnamon. Sprinkle into peach centers. Sprinkle with vanilla. Dot with butter. Fold foil over peaches and seal. Grill over medium-hot coals for 15 minutes or until heated through. To serve, spoon the raspberry sauce over peaches.

*SERVES 4*

# Cold Avocado Soup

3 large avocados, peeled, pitted and cut into ½ inch pieces

1½ cups chicken stock

¼ cup green onions, minced

2 tablespoons fresh lemon juice

2 tablespoons fresh cilantro, minced, plus 6 sprigs

1½ teaspoons salt, divided

½ teaspoon cayenne pepper

1 cup whipping cream

1 tablespoon olive oil

1 cup corn kernels, fresh or frozen

½ teaspoon cumin

In batches in a food processor, purée the avocados, chicken stock, green onions, lemon juice, cilantro, 1 teaspoon of the salt and the cayenne. Pour into a soup tureen or large pitcher and stir in the cream just before serving. In a small skillet, heat the oil over medium-high heat. Add the corn kernels, cumin and remaining ½ teaspoon salt and cook until fragrant and golden brown, about 5 minutes, stirring occasionally. Remove from the heat and garnish each serving of soup with 2 tablespoons of toasted corn and 1 sprig of cilantro.

*SERVES 4-6*

# Southwest Chicken Lasagna

2 cups deli-roasted chicken, shredded
1 tablespoon lime juice
1½ teaspoons chili powder
1 teaspoon salt
½ teaspoon black pepper
1 small onion, chopped
2 cloves garlic, minced
1 tablespoon oil

1 (16 ounce) jar salsa
1 (15 ounce) can chili with beans
1 (4.5 ounce) can chopped green chilies
10 (6 inch) flour tortillas
1 (12 ounce) package shredded Mexican cheese blend

Preheat oven to 350°. Combine chicken, lime juice, chili powder, salt and pepper. Set aside. Sauté onion and garlic in oil on medium high heat for 3-4 minutes until tender. Add salsa, chili and green chilies. Reduce heat and simmer for 3-4 minutes. Spray a 9x13 inch baking dish. Put a small amount of salsa on the bottom. Layer with 3 tortillas, salsa, chicken and cheese. Repeat with 2 more layers ending with the cheese on top. Bake for 25-30 minutes. Let stand 5-10 minutes before serving.

*SERVES 12-15*


# Zippy Corn on the Cob

6 medium ears sweet corn, shucked
½ cup butter, melted
2 tablespoons Dijon mustard
1 tablespoon fresh parsley, minced

½ teaspoon salt
¼ teaspoon pepper
2 teaspoons prepared horseradish

Place ears of corn on a large sheet of double-layer heavy-duty foil. In a small bowl, combine the remaining ingredients and brush over corn. Fold foil around corn and seal tightly. Grill covered over medium heat for 25-30 minutes or until corn is tender, turning once.

*SERVES 6*

Johnson County Young Matrons

Many of our members donate over 100 hours of personal service annually.

193

# Raspberry Beer Cocktail

¾ cup frozen or fresh raspberries

3½ (12 ounce) bottles beer, chilled

1 (12 ounce) container frozen
  raspberry lemonade concentrate,
  thawed

½ cup vodka

Lemon and lime slices, for garnish

Stir together all ingredients. Serve over ice. Garnish, if desired.

*SERVES 6*

# BLT Bites

16 to 20 cherry tomatoes

1 pound bacon, cooked and crumbled

½ cup mayonnaise

⅓ cup green onion, chopped

3 tablespoons grated Parmesan
  cheese

2 tablespoons snipped parsley

Choose tomatoes that will stand upright. Cut a thin slice off the top of each tomato and scoop out pulp and discard. Invert tomatoes on a paper towel to drain. In a small bowl combine remaining ingredients. Mix well. Spoon this mixture into each of the tomatoes and chill several hours before serving.

*SERVES 8-10*

# Watermelon and Strawberry Salad

6 (½ inch) squares watermelon

3 strawberries, quartered

1 tablespoon crumbled feta cheese

1 tablespoon extra virgin olive oil

1 teaspoon fresh lemon juice

⅓ cup baby salad greens or spring mix

Salt and pepper to taste

Mix watermelon, strawberries, cheese, olive oil and lemon juice. Add salt and pepper to taste. Place salad greens on a plate, top with fruit and dressing.

*SERVES 1*

# Gazpacho Blanca

3 medium cucumbers, peeled, seeded and coarsely chopped
3 cups chicken broth
3 cups sour cream or 2 cups sour cream and 1 cup plain yogurt
3 tablespoons white vinegar

2 teaspoons salt or to taste
2 cloves garlic, crushed (more if desired)
Condiments such as tomatoes, slivered almonds, chopped green onions or parsley

Whirl cucumber chunks in a food processor a short time with a little chicken broth leaving cucumber in small chunks. Do in two batches. Pour into large mixing bowl. Add remaining broth, sour cream, vinegar, salt and garlic. Stir just enough to mix. Chill thoroughly (2-3 hours). Before serving, stir well. Pour into chilled bowl and pass condiments.

*SERVES 8*

Add an additional cup of sour cream to make it thicker.

# Hot Chicken Salad

2 cups cooked chicken, diced
½ cup almonds, toasted
1 cup butter, melted
2 teaspoons grated onion
2 cups celery, sliced
½ teaspoon salt

2 tablespoons lemon juice
½ cup Cheddar cheese, grated
¼ teaspoon black pepper
¼ teaspoon paprika
1 cup potato chips, crushed

Preheat oven to 350°. Mix all the ingredients except the potato chips. Spread in a greased 8x8 inch baking dish. Top with crushed potato chips. Bake for 15-20 minutes. Double for 9x13 inch pan. To prevent over- browning, cover with foil and remove foil the last few minutes of heating.

*SERVES 6-8*

# Zucchini Casserole

1 large onion, chopped
6 cups zucchini, cubed and unpeeled
½ cup green pepper, chopped
2 tablespoons oil
2 cups tomatoes, chopped
(drained if canned)
½ cup saltine cracker crumbs

1 tablespoon garlic powder
1 cup shredded mozzarella cheese
1 cup shredded sharp Cheddar cheese
½ cup Parmesan cheese
½ teaspoon oregano
¼ teaspoon Italian seasoning
1 teaspoon salt

Preheat oven to 350°. Sauté zucchini, green pepper and onion in oil. Add rest of ingredients. Put in a greased 2½-3 quart casserole. Bake for 45 minutes.

*SERVES 6-8*

# Onion Cheese Corn Muffins

1 cup yellow cornmeal
1 cup all-purpose flour
2 tablespoons sugar
1 tablespoon baking powder
1 teaspoon salt

1 cup milk
2 eggs, beaten
½ cup chopped green onion
½ cup cottage cheese
½ cup shredded Cheddar cheese

Preheat oven to 400°. Mix all dry ingredients. Mix all moist ingredients and combine the mixtures. Stir until just moistened. Spoon into lined muffin tins and bake for 15 minutes. Serve warm with butter.

*SERVES 12*

# Orange Coconut Cookies

1 cup shortening
1 cup white sugar
1 cup firmly packed brown sugar
2 eggs
1 cup coconut
2 cups all-purpose flour

1 teaspoon baking soda
1 cup quick-cooking oats
1 cup chopped orange slice candy
½ teaspoon almond extract
Orange candy for decoration

Preheat oven to 375°. Cream shortening with brown and white sugars. Add eggs and almond extract and combine until smooth. Add dry ingredients, coconut and chopped candies. Drop by spoonfuls on sprayed baking pan. Bake for 12 minutes. Decorate with half orange slice cut lengthwise placed on warm cookie.

*SERVES 3 DOZEN*

# Kansas Rhubarb

2 pounds frozen rhubarb, thawed
   or 8 cups sliced fresh
3 cups sugar, divided
6 tablespoons butter, softened
2 cups all-purpose flour

2 teaspoons baking powder
1 teaspoon salt, divided
1 cup whole or 2% milk
2 tablespoons cornstarch
¾ cup boiling water

Preheat oven to 350°. In a 9x13 inch greased metal baking pan, distribute the rhubarb. Cream together butter with 1 cup of sugar. Mix together flour, baking powder and ½ teaspoon salt. Add flour mixture to sugar mixture, alternating with the milk. Spread the mixture over rhubarb. Mix 2 cups sugar with cornstarch and ½ teaspoon salt and sprinkle over batter. Pour boiling water over the top, making sure to wet the whole pan. Bake 1 hour. Serve warm with ice cream.

*SERVES 12*

# Berries Romanoff

1 (16 ounce) carton sour cream
2 tablespoons Kahlúa
3 cups assorted fresh berries such
   as raspberries, blueberries,
   strawberries or blackberries

¼ cup firmly packed brown sugar
1 tablespoon Grand Marnier®
Fresh mint sprigs

In a small bowl, combine brown sugar, Kahlúa, sour cream and Grand Marnier®. Cover and chill for 4-24 hours. To serve, layer sour cream sauce and fruit in parfait glasses. Garnish with mint.

*SERVES 4*

# Mango Chicken Salad

4 cups cooked chicken breast, diced
1 cup celery, chopped
1 (9 ounce) jar mango chutney
1 (20 ounce) can pineapple tidbits in
   juice, drained

½ cup almond slivers, toasted
1½ cups red and green seedless
   grapes, halved
¾ cup mayonnaise
1½ teaspoons curry powder

Mix all of the above ingredients. Serve on a lettuce leaf, as a sandwich or on small sandwich rounds.

*SERVES 6-8*

# Watermelon Margaritas

2 teaspoons sugar
1 lime wedge
3½ cups cubed, seeded watermelon
½ cup tequila
2 tablespoons sugar

3 tablespoons fresh lime juice
1 tablespoon triple sec
Lime wedges or watermelon balls, optional
Crushed ice

Place 2 teaspoons sugar in a saucer. Rub the rims of 6 glasses with 1 lime wedge; spin rim of each glass in sugar to coat. Set prepared glasses aside. Combine watermelon, tequila, sugar, lime juice and triple sec in a blender; process until smooth. Fill each prepared glass with ½ cup crushed ice. Add ½ cup margarita to each glass. Garnish with lime wedges or melon balls, if desired.

*SERVES 6*

After you have squeezed a lemon, lime or orange for its juice, wrap and freeze the rind. When a recipe calls for the zest of a fruit you won't have to grate a fresh one.

# State Fair Potato Salad

3½ pounds red-skinned potatoes, peeled, cut into ¾-inch pieces
¼ cup juice from jar of sweet pickles
¾ cup mayonnaise
⅓ cup buttermilk
4 teaspoons Dijon mustard

1 teaspoon sugar
½ teaspoon ground black pepper
3 hard-boiled eggs, peeled, chopped
½ cup chopped red onion
½ cup chopped celery
½ cup chopped sweet pickles

Place potatoes in large pot of cold salted water and bring to a boil, cook until just tender, about 10 minutes. Drain; transfer to large bowl. Drizzle pickle juice over potatoes and toss gently. Cool to room temperature. Whisk mayonnaise, buttermilk, mustard, sugar and pepper in medium bowl to blend. Pour over potatoes. Add eggs, onion, celery and pickles and toss gently to blend. Season to taste with salt. Can be made 8 hours ahead. Chill. Bring to room temperature before serving.

*SERVES 6-8*

# Black Bean Salsa

1 (15.5 ounce) can black beans, drained and rinsed

1 (11 ounce) can shoe peg corn, drained

5-6 Roma tomatoes, seeded and finely diced

1 avocado, finely diced

½ red onion, finely diced

1 garlic clove, crushed

1 teaspoon cumin

2 tablespoons chopped cilantro or 1 tablespoon dried cilantro

1 tablespoon olive oil

Juice of ½ to 1 lime

1 teaspoon red wine vinegar

¼ teaspoon cayenne pepper

¼ teaspoon salt

Mix together all ingredients and chill for 1 hour. Serve with tortilla chips.

# Crunchy Chili Onion Rings

6 cups vegetable oil (for deep-frying)

1 pound Vidalia onions, peeled, cut into ⅓ inch thick slices, then separated into rings

3 cups buttermilk

2 cups all-purpose flour

1 cup yellow cornmeal

3 tablespoons chili powder

2 tablespoons ground cumin

1 tablespoon salt

1 teaspoon cayenne pepper

Chopped fresh cilantro, optional

Pour vegetable oil into heavy, large, deep skillet. Heat oil to 375°. Combine onion rings and buttermilk in large bowl. Mix flour, cornmeal, chili powder, cumin, salt and cayenne in another large bowl. Remove ⅓ of onion rings from buttermilk; add to flour mixture and toss well to coat. Add coated onion rings to oil; fry until golden brown, adjusting heat as needed to maintain oil temperature, about 3 minutes. Using tongs, transfer onion rings to paper towels to drain. Repeat with remaining onion rings in 2 more batches. Transfer onion rings to platter. Sprinkle with cilantro, if desired, and serve.

*SERVES 4-6*

# Broccoli Slaw

½ cup apple cider
¾ cup sugar
½ teaspoon salt
½ teaspoon mustard seed
3 tablespoons vegetable oil

1 (16 ounce) package broccoli slaw
2 Gala or Granny Smith apples, chopped
1 cup dried cranberries

Combine the apple cider, sugar, salt and mustard seed in a small saucepan. Bring to a boil for 1 minute until sugar dissolves. Remove from heat and cool, whisk in oil. Combine slaw mix, apples and cranberries in a large bowl. Pour dressing over slaw and toss well. Cover and chill.

*8 CUPS*

# Spicy Hot Dogs

2 tablespoons olive oil
3 poblano chiles, cut into ½ inch wide strips
1 large onion (about 12 ounces), sliced
6 hot dogs or flavored sausages
1 cup purchased salsa verde (tomatillo salsa)

⅓ cup chopped fresh cilantro
6 hot dog buns
2 ounces hot pepper Monterey Jack cheese, thinly sliced
Crumbled Cotija cheese or feta cheese
1 cup water

Heat oil in large nonstick skillet over medium-high heat. Add poblanos and onion: sprinkle with salt. Sauté until chiles soften, 10 to 12 minutes. Transfer mixture to bowl. Add hot dogs to same pan. Add 1 cup water and cover. Boil until heated through, about 5 minutes. Meanwhile, preheat broiler. Combine salsa verde and cilantro in small bowl. Place a hot dog in each bun; place on baking sheet. Cover each with slices of cheese. Broil until cheese melts, about 2 minutes. Top with chili-onion mixture; then Cotija cheese and salsa.

*SERVES 6*

# Grilled Burgers with Lemon Butter

6 tablespoons butter, room temperature

1 tablespoon finely chopped fresh tarragon

1 tablespoon finely chopped fresh basil

1 tablespoon finely chopped fresh Italian parsley

1 teaspoon finely grated lemon peel

1 teaspoon fresh lemon juice

1½ pounds ground beef

Vegetable oil for brushing

4 sesame seed hamburger buns

1 large tomato, thinly sliced crosswise

1 bunch arugula

Salt and black pepper to taste

Mix butter, all herbs, lemon peel and lemon juice in small bowl. Season with salt and pepper. Measure ⅓ cup herb butter; transfer to sheet of plastic wrap (reserve remaining butter mixture in bowl for spreading on buns). Using plastic wrap as aid, form butter mixture into 3 inch long log; wrap plastic around to seal. Freeze until firm, about 30 minutes. Cut crosswise into 4 rounds. Flatten rounds into 2 inch diameter disks. Divide meat into 4 equal pieces. Using damp hands, form each piece into ball. Using thumb, make deep wide indentation in center of each ball. Press a lemon-butter round flatly into indentation, then press meat securely over butter to enclose. Flatten each burger into 3½ inch diameter patty, leaving butter rounds horizontal in center of each burger. DO AHEAD. Herb butter and burgers can be made 6 hours ahead. Place burgers on baking sheet, cover with plastic wrap and chill. Cover and chill herb butter in bowl; bring to room temperature before continuing. Brush barbecue rack with oil. Prepare barbecue (high heat). Sprinkle both sides of burgers with salt and pepper. Spread remaining butter mixture over cut sides of buns. Grill burgers until cooked through, 4-6 minutes per side. Grill buns until slightly charred, about 1 minute per side. Place burgers on bun bottoms. Top with tomato slices and arugula leaves. Cover with bun tops and serve.

*4 BURGERS*

# Kahlúa Ice Cream Bars

1 box 12 ice cream sandwiches

1 (8 ounce) container frozen whipped topping, thawed

Kahlúa

3-6 full size chocolate toffee bars, crushed

Chocolate syrup

Line a 9x13 inch pan with ice cream sandwiches, cutting to fit as needed. Poke holes in them, pour Kahlúa over them. Cover with whipped topping. Sprinkle with crushed toffee bars. Freeze. When ready to serve, pour chocolate sauce mixed with Kahlúa over the top.

*SERVES 10-12*

# Georgia Peach Ice Cream

4 cups peeled, diced fresh peaches
(about 8 small ripe peaches)

1 cup sugar

1 (12 ounce) can evaporated milk

1 (3.75 ounce) package instant vanilla
pudding

1 (14 ounce) can sweetened condensed
milk

4 cups half and half

Combine peaches and sugar. Let stand 1 hour. Process peach mixture in a food processor until smooth, stopping to scrape sides down. Stir together evaporated milk and pudding mix in large bowl, stir in peach purée, condensed milk and half and half. Pour mixture into freezer container of 4 quart electric ice cream freezer and freeze according to manufacturer's instructions. Spoon into airtight container and freeze until firm.

*SERVES 8*

Soft, ripe peaches lend the smoothest texture and the best flavor.

# Grilled Sweet Potatoes

3 sweet potatoes, unpeeled

Kosher salt

2 teaspoons finely grated lime zest

¼ teaspoon cayenne pepper

¼ cup canola oil

Freshly ground black pepper

¼ cup finely chopped fresh cilantro

Parboil the potatoes by placing in a pot of cold water and boil until fork tender. Let cool. Slice each potato lengthwise into eighths. Preheat a grill to medium or place a cast iron grill pan over medium heat. Mix 1 tablespoon salt, lime zest and cayenne in a small bowl. Brush the potato wedges with the oil and season with salt and pepper. Grill until golden brown on all sides (including the skin) and just cooked through, about 1½ minutes per side. Transfer to a platter. Immediately season with the salt mixture and sprinkle with cilantro.

*SERVES 4*

# Maple Nut Coffee Ice Cream Dessert

2 pints coffee ice cream
1 cup salted mixed nuts, coarsely chopped

½ cup medium to dark amber maple syrup, warmed
Rolled wafer cookies for garnish

Top 2 scoops of coffee ice cream with chopped salted mixed nuts. Drizzle nuts and ice cream with warm maple syrup. Garnish with rolled wafer cookies and serve.

*SERVES 4*

Serve this dessert in cocktail or martini glasses for a fancy finish.

# White Chocolate Cookie and Cream Fudge

1 cup sugar
¾ cup butter
1 (5 ounce) can evaporated milk
2 (12 ounce) packages white chocolate morsels

1 (7 ounce) jar marshmallow crème
3 cups coarsely crushed cream-filled chocolate sandwich cookies (about 25 cookies) divided
¼ teaspoon salt

Line a greased 9 inch square pan with aluminum foil and set aside. Combine sugar, butter and milk in a medium saucepan. Cook over medium high heat, stirring constantly until mixture comes to a boil. Cook 3 minutes, stirring constantly. Remove from heat; add white chocolate morsels, marshmallow creme, 2 cups crushed cookies and salt. Stir until morsels melt. Pour fudge into prepared pan. Sprinkle remaining 1 cup cookies over fudge, gently pressing cookies into fudge. Cover and chill until firm (about 1-2 hours). Lift uncut fudge in aluminum foil from pan. Remove foil and cut fudge into squares.

*4 POUNDS*

# Mocktail

3 cups pineapple juice
1 (14 ounce) can sweetened condensed
milk

½ (12 ounce) can frozen orange juice,
thawed and undiluted
½ teaspoon coconut extract
1 (32 ounce) bottle chilled ginger ale

Combine all ingredients except ginger ale. Stir. Refrigerate up to 1 week. To serve, use ½ cup juice mixture with ⅓ cup or more of ginger ale. You may add rum if desired.

*SERVES 10-12*

# Hot Feta Cheese Dip

1 pound feta cheese
4 tablespoons extra virgin olive oil
6 tablespoons milk

4 tablespoons wine vinegar
½ teaspoon chili powder
1 clove garlic, crushed

Preheat oven to 350°. Place all ingredients in food processor or blender and blend until nice and creamy. Place in a baking dish. Bake until bubbly, about 20 minutes. Serve with pita slices or thinly sliced French bread. This may also be served at room temperature.

*SERVES 8*

# Simple Antipasto Platter

1 (5 ounce) log goat cheese
2 tablespoons chopped fresh parsley
1 (16 ounce) jar pickled okra, drained
1 (8 ounce) jar Kalamata olives,
drained and rinsed

1 (7 ounce) jar roasted red bell
peppers, drained and cut into pieces
4 ounces sliced salami
Assorted crackers and breadsticks

Roll goat cheese log in parsley; place on a serving platter. Arrange okra, olives, peppers and salami on platter around goat cheese. Serve with crackers or breadsticks.

*SERVES 8*

# Layered Greek Dip

1 (8 ounce) package cream cheese, softened
1½ cups hummus

1 tablespoon lemon juice
1 teaspoon Italian seasoning
3 cloves garlic, minced

**TOPPINGS**

1 cup chopped cucumber, drained
1 cup chopped tomato, drained
½ cup Kalamata olives, pitted and chopped

½ cup crumbled feta cheese
⅓ cup chopped green onions

Combine cream cheese, hummus, lemon juice, Italian seasoning and garlic. Spread in a 9 inch pie pan or shallow serving dish, cover and refrigerate 2-24 hours. Combine the topping ingredients, cover and refrigerate for up to 24 hours. Just before serving spread vegetable cheese mixture over cream cheese mixture. Serve with tortilla chips, pita, crackers or vegetables.

*SERVES 12*

# Watermelon Feta Salad

1 small red onion
2 limes, juiced
1 cup crumbled feta cheese
½ medium watermelon, cut into 1 inch cubes and seeded

1 bunch parsley
1 small bunch mint, chopped
¼ cup Kalamata olives
Olive oil
Freshly ground black pepper to taste

Quarter or slice a red onion, put into a bowl with freshly-squeezed lime juice. Combine feta and melon in a large bowl. Add large sprigs of parsley and a handful of chopped mint. Pour onions along with the juice into the salad bowl. Add olive oil to taste and about ¼ cup of pitted Kalamata olives. Season salad with a dash of freshly ground pepper and toss gently. To save time, use precut watermelon.

*SERVES 8*

# Greek Orzo and Grilled Shrimp Salad with Dill Vinaigrette

¾ pound orzo cooked al dente

1 large cucumber; seeded, quartered lengthwise and sliced

3 green onions, thinly sliced

1 pint grape tomatoes, halved

¼ cup chopped fresh dill plus extra for garnish

¼ cup white wine vinegar

3 tablespoons Dijon mustard

½ cup olive oil plus additional for brushing shrimp

Salt and freshly ground black pepper

½ pound feta cheese, crumbled

16 medium shrimp, peeled and deveined

Combine orzo, cucumber, green onions and tomatoes in a large bowl. Place dill, vinegar and mustard in a small bowl; whisk until blended. Season with salt and pepper to taste. Pour the vinaigrette over the orzo mixture and stir well to combine. Gently fold in the feta cheese. Heat grill to high. Brush shrimp with oil and season with salt and pepper. Grill for approximately 2 minutes per side or until just cooked through. Divide orzo salad among 4 plates and top with shrimp. Garnish with additional dill.

*SERVES 4*

# Greek Chicken Pasta

2 cups uncooked penne pasta

¼ cup butter, cubed

1 large onion, chopped

¼ cup all-purpose flour

1 (14.5 ounce) can reduced-sodium chicken broth

3 cups cubed rotisserie chicken

1 (7.5 ounce) jar marinated quarter artichoke hearts, drained

1 cup (4 ounces) crumbled feta cheese

½ cup chopped oil-packed sun-dried tomatoes

⅓ cup sliced pitted Greek olives

2 tablespoons minced fresh parsley

Cook pasta according to directions and drain. In a large ovenproof skillet, melt butter. Add onion, sauté until tender. Stir in flour until blended; gradually add broth. Bring to a boil; cook and stir for 2 minutes or until thickened. Stir in the chicken, artichoke hearts, cheese, tomatoes and olives. Stir pasta into the pan. Broil 3-4 inches from the heat for 5-7 minutes or until bubbly and golden brown. Sprinkle with parsley.

*SERVES 5*

# Spinach Phyllo

½ pound sliced mushrooms
2 medium onions, finely chopped
1 tablespoon butter
3 ounces cream cheese
1 (10 ounce) package chopped spinach, thawed with liquid removed
1 teaspoon salt

Juice of ½ lemon
2 tablespoons flour
1 egg, lightly beaten
½ cup sour cream
½ pound phyllo sheets (thawed overnight in refrigerator)
Butter flavored cooking spray
1 pound thinly sliced Swiss cheese

Preheat oven to 350°. Sauté onions and mushrooms with butter in a large pan. Stir in the cream cheese and heat until melted. Add the spinach to the mixture and stir. Stir in the lemon juice, salt and flour. In a small bowl, mix the sour cream and the egg. Add this mixture to the spinach mixture. Set aside. Place phyllo sheets on flat surface and place a 7x12 inch baking dish on top of the phyllo. Cut around the shape of the dish and discard the excess phyllo. Spray the baking dish and each of the 4 layers of phyllo with butter flavored cooking spray. Place these 4 layers in the dish and top with ½ of the spinach mixture, cover with ½ cheese slices. Repeat this process with 4 more layers of phyllo. Top with the last 4 sheets of phyllo sprayed with cooking spray. Score the top of the phyllo into serving pieces. Bake for approximately 35 minutes or until golden brown.

*SERVES 15*

The proper method is to spread melted butter over each of the phyllo sheets but the faster method is to use the cooking spray.

Johnson County Young Matrons

All proceeds from Ways & Means activities (i.e. Homes Tour, etc.) is returned to our philanthropies annually. Membership dues provide funds for operating expenses.

# Greek Salad

1 package romaine hearts, sliced into ¼ to ½ inch strips
1 English cucumber, sliced into half moons
1 box grape tomatoes, halved
1 Bermuda onion, sliced into paper thin half moons
1 can chickpeas, drained and rinsed
1 (14.5 ounce) can black olives, sliced and drained
1 jar Greek pepperocini, sliced
1 (8 ounce) container Greek feta cheese crumbles
Greek dressing, to taste

Toss the salad ingredients, add salad dressing to taste. This salad can be served the second day.

*SERVES 10-12*

To reduce the strong taste of onions in a salad, dice them and put in the refrigerator overnight before using.

# Greek Caesar Salad

¾ cup olive oil
¼ cup lemon juice
¼ cup egg substitute
2 cloves garlic, pressed
1 teaspoon dried oregano
¼ teaspoon salt
⅛ teaspoon pepper
1 head romaine lettuce, torn
¾ cup Kalamata olives
1 small red onion, thinly sliced
½ cup crumbled feta cheese
Croutons

Whisk together olive oil, lemon juice, egg, garlic, oregano, salt and pepper in a small bowl. Cover and chill up to 2 days. Combine lettuce, olives, onion and cheese in a large bowl; gradually add enough olive oil mixture to coat leaves, tossing gently. Sprinkle with croutons and serve with remaining olive oil mixture.

*SERVES 6*

# Mediterranean Layered Dip

1 (8 ounce) package cream cheese, softened
½ cup mayonnaise
½ cup basil pesto

½ cup chopped marinated artichoke hearts
1 cup chopped roasted red peppers
½ cup Italian blend grated cheese
½ cup crumbled feta cheese

Cream together cream cheese and mayonnaise. Spread on bottom of 9 inch pie pan or other serving dish. Add the other ingredients in layers as listed. Great served with pita chips or multi-grain crackers.

*SERVES 6*

# Chocolate Mocha Cream Cake

**CAKE**

2 cups all-purpose flour
1 cup sugar
1 cup firmly packed dark brown sugar
¾ cup unsweetened cocoa
1½ teaspoons baking soda
1½ teaspoons baking powder
½ teaspoon salt

1 cup reduced-fat mayonnaise
3 tablespoons canola oil
1 cup hot strong brewed coffee
2 teaspoons vanilla extract
⅓ cup semisweet chocolate morsels
Cooking spray

**MOCHA CREAM**

¼ cup boiling water
1 tablespoon instant coffee granules
1 (7 ounce) jar marshmallow creme

1 (8 ounce) container frozen light whipped topping, thawed
⅓ cup light chocolate syrup

Preheat oven to 350°. To prepare cake combine flour, sugar, brown sugar, cocoa, baking soda, baking powder and salt. Add mayonnaise and oil, beat with a mixer at low speed until well blended. Slowly add brewed coffee and vanilla; beat with a mixer at low speed 1 minute or until well blended. Stir in chocolate, pour batter into a 9x13 inch baking pan coated with cooking spray. Bake for 30 minutes or until a wooden pick inserted in center comes out clean. Cool completely in pan on a wire rack. To prepare mocha cream, combine water and coffee granules to dissolve. Add marshmallow creme, beat with a mixer at low speed until smooth. Fold in whipped topping. Spread mocha cream over top of cake; drizzle with chocolate syrup. Chill until ready to serve.

*SERVES 16*

# Bourbon Slush

1 (6 ounce) can frozen orange juice, undiluted
1 (6 ounce) can frozen lemonade, undiluted
2½ cups water

1 cup sugar
1 cup bourbon
2 teabags, orange pekoe
1 cup water

Boil 2 teabags in 1 cup water for 5 minutes or until very strong. Mix all ingredients and freeze. This may be mixed with a lemon-lime beverage or ginger ale if desired.

*SERVES 10*

# Marinated Vegetables

1 (12 ounce) package fresh broccoli florets
4 medium carrots, cut into thin (2 inch) sticks
1 yellow, orange, or red bell pepper, cut into thin strips
1 pound fresh button or baby portobello mushrooms
1 (5.75 ounce) jar pimiento-stuffed Spanish olives, drained
1 cup pitted Kalamata olives, drained

¾ cup white wine vinegar
2 tablespoons sugar
1 teaspoon salt
½ teaspoon freshly ground black pepper
½ teaspoon dried oregano
½ cup olive oil
1 (12 ounce) jar roasted red bell peppers, drained and cut into ½ inch thick strips

Combine broccoli, carrots, pepper, mushrooms, Spanish olives and Kalamata olives in a large bowl. Combine vinegar, sugar, salt, pepper and oregano in a small saucepan; bring to a boil. Reduce heat and cook 1 minute or until sugar dissolves. Remove from heat; whisk in oil. Pour over vegetables in bowl; toss gently to coat. Add roasted red bell pepper, toss gently. Transfer vegetables to a 2-gallon zip-top plastic freezer bag. Seal and chill 8 hours, turning bag occasionally. Drain vegetables, reserving marinade. Arrange vegetables on a serving platter; drizzle with a small amount of reserved marinade if desired.

*SERVES 15-18 APPETIZERS*

# Smokey Cheese Round with Avocado Mango Salsa

2 (8 ounce) packages cream cheese, softened
2 (8 ounce) blocks pepper jack cheese, shredded
16 ounces smoked Cheddar cheese, shredded

6 green onions, minced
2 (4.5 ounce) cans chopped green chilies, drained
1 (1.25 ounce) envelope taco seasoning mix

### AVOCADO MANGO SALSA

¼ cup hot jalapeño jelly
¼ cup fresh lime juice
2 large mangoes, peeled and diced

2 large avocados, diced
1 large red bell pepper, diced
¼ cup chopped fresh cilantro

Combine cream cheese, pepper jack cheese, Cheddar cheese, onion, chilies and seasoning mix in a large bowl. Divide into two equal portions and shape each into a ball. Cover and chill 8 hours or freeze up to 1 month and thaw in the refrigerator for 8 hours. For salsa, whisk together jelly and lime juice in a large bowl. Add remaining ingredients, stir until blended. Cover and chill 8 hours. Place cheese balls or rounds on a serving plate and top evenly with Avocado Mango Salsa; serve with chips or cracker of choice.

*SERVES 18*

Substitute 1 (26 ounce) jar refrigerated mango pieces, drained, for fresh mango.

Small group activities provide opportunities to relax and enjoy an hour or two of lively discussion as well as a fun activity plus allow members to develop closer friendships with others.

# Southwestern Caesar Salad

## CHILI CROUTONS

⅓ cup unsalted butter, melted

1 teaspoon chili powder

¼ teaspoon cumin

¼ teaspoon salt

½ loaf French bread, cut into ½-inch cubes

## SOUTHWESTERN CAESAR DRESSING

3 teaspoons minced garlic

2 shallots, peeled

4 anchovy fillets

2 fresh jalapeño peppers, cored and seeded

2 cups loosely packed, chopped cilantro

½ cup red wine vinegar

½ cup freshly grated Romano cheese

1 egg yolk

½ teaspoon freshly ground black pepper

1 teaspoon lemon juice

Salt to taste

1 cup olive oil

## SALAD

1 teaspoon olive oil

2 cups (about 3 ears) fresh corn kernels or frozen corn kernels, thawed

3 romaine lettuce hearts or 2 large heads romaine lettuce, torn into bite sized pieces, chilled

2 red bell peppers, roasted, peeled, seeded and cut into thin strips

½ cup drained, chopped oil-packed sun-dried tomatoes

¼ cup freshly grated Romano cheese

Preheat oven to 350°. In large bowl, combine melted butter, chili powder, cumin and salt; stir to blend. Add bread cubes and toss to coat. Spread in single layer on baking pan. Bake 8-10 minute until crisp and golden brown, stirring occasionally. Remove from oven and set aside to cool. In food processor or blender combine garlic, shallots, anchovies, jalapeños, cilantro, vinegar, Romano cheese, egg yolk, pepper, lemon juice and salt to taste. Blend until smooth. With processor running slowly, add 1 cup olive oil and blend until smooth. Cover and chill. In skillet, heat 1 teaspoon olive oil over medium heat. Add corn and cook 4 minutes. Remove with slotted spoon and set aside. In large bowl, combine lettuce and half the dressing. Toss to coat. Add cooled croutons and toss. Arrange roasted bell pepper strips in spoke pattern around edge of bowl and sprinkle with reserved corn, sun-dried tomatoes and Romano cheese. Pass remaining dressing.

*SERVES 4-6 AS A MAIN DISH OR 8-10 AS A SIDE DISH*

Grilled chicken breast strips may be added for a main course salad. To roast peppers, place on baking sheet, broil until skin is lightly charred, turning occasionally (about 10 minutes). Place in brown paper sack and allow to cool. Gently remove skin.

# Grilled Beef Tenderloin with Ancho Jalapeño Butter

1 cup unsalted butter, softened
2 medium shallots, minced
2 jalapeño peppers, minced
3 teaspoons ancho chile powder
Kosher salt
2 tablespoons dark brown sugar

1 tablespoon sweet smoked paprika
1 teaspoon freshly ground black pepper
2½ pounds beef tenderloin, tied
8 thick slices of crusty bread

Prepare grill for indirect grilling with coals on 1 side and heat to 450°. In a large bowl, mix the butter, shallots, jalapeños and chile powder, season with salt. Transfer to a sheet of plastic wrap and roll into a ½ inch thick log, refrigerate for 15 minutes. In a bowl mix the brown sugar, paprika, pepper and 1 tablespoon of salt. Rub the beef with the spice mixture. Oil the grate and grill the beef directly over the coals, turning, until charred, 12 minutes. Move beef away from the coals. Cover and grill for 25 minutes, or until an instant-read thermometer inserted in the thickest part of the beef registers 130°. Transfer to a carving board; let rest for 10 minutes. Grill the bread directly over the coals until toasted. Spread the bread with half of the ancho-jalapeño butter. Slice the remaining butter and transfer to a plate. Slice the beef and serve with the toasts and ancho-jalapeño butter.

*SERVES 8*


# Molasses Cookies

¾ cup butter or shortening
½ cup sugar
½ cup unsulphured molasses
½ cup smooth peanut butter
1 egg

2 cups all-purpose flour, sifted
¼ teaspoon salt
¼ teaspoon baking soda
2 teaspoons baking powder

Preheat oven to 375°. Cream together butter and sugar, add molasses and beat well. Add egg and blend well. Sift together flour, salt, baking soda and baking powder; beat into wet mixture. Drop by tablespoonfuls onto an ungreased baking sheet. Bake for 10-12 minutes. Cool and store in sealed container.

*SERVES 36*

# Blueberry Cream Cheese Dessert

**CRUST**

1½ cups crushed butter crackers

⅓ cup sugar

⅓ cup butter

**FILLING**

1 (8 ounce) package cream cheese, softened

1 (14.5 ounce) can sweetened condensed milk

⅓ cup lemon juice

1 teaspoon vanilla extract

1 can blueberry pie filling

1 (16 ounce) container frozen whipped topping, thawed

Preheat oven to 350°. For the crust combine the crackers and sugar. Melt butter and stir into cracker mixture. Grease bottom of a 9x9 inch pan. Press mixture into bottom of pan and bake for 8 minutes. Cool completely before adding filling. For the filling, beat cream cheese until smooth. Gradually add condensed milk and beat until smooth. Add lemon juice and vanilla and beat until combined. Pour over cooled crust. Gently spoon pie filling over cream cheese mixture. Layer whipped topping over pie filling 1 spoonful at a time, gently spreading as you go to avoid smearing pie filling into topping. Refrigerate until serving.

*SERVES 8*

# Mexican Spice-Rubbed Rib-Eyes with Lime Butter

4 tablespoons unsalted butter, softened

1 small garlic clove, minced

¼ teaspoon finely grated lime zest

1 tablespoon fresh lime juice

Kosher salt

1½ teaspoons sweet paprika

1½ teaspoons ground cumin

1½ teaspoons chipotle powder

4 (12 ounce) 1 inch thick boneless rib-eye steaks

Vegetable oil for the grill

Prepare grill. In a small bowl combine the butter, garlic, lime zest, lime juice and a pinch of salt. In another bowl combine the paprika, cumin and chipotle powder with 1½ teaspoons of kosher salt. Rub the mixture all over the steaks. Oil the grate and grill the steaks over moderately high heat, turning once, until slightly charred and medium-rare, about 12 minutes. Transfer the steaks to plates and top with the lime butter. Let the steaks stand for 3-4 minutes before serving.

*SERVES 4*

# Pomegranate Margaritas

Lime juice

Margarita salt

½ cup powdered sugar

½ cup pomegranate juice

½ cup tequila

½ cup orange liqueur

4 tablespoons fresh lime juice

6 cups ice

Dip rims of glasses into lime juice and then into salt. Set aside. Combine sugar and remaining ingredients in a blender. Process until smooth. Pour into prepared glasses.

*SERVES 4-6*

# Hot Corn Dip

2 tablespoons unsalted butter. divided

3 (11 ounce) cans niblets corn, drained

½ teaspoon salt

⅛ teaspoon freshly ground black
   pepper

1 cup finely chopped yellow onions

½ cup finely chopped red bell pepper

¼ cup chopped green onions, white
   and green parts

1 (4.5 ounce) can chopped green
   chilies, drained

½ to 1 cup mayonnaise

1 cup Monterey Jack cheese, shredded

1 cup sharp Cheddar cheese, shredded

2 teaspoons minced garlic

Tortilla chips

Preheat oven to 350°. Melt 1 tablespoon butter in a large heavy skillet over medium high heat. Add the corn, salt and pepper. Cook, stirring occasionally, until the corn turns deep golden brown, about 5 minutes. Transfer to a bowl. Melt the remaining butter in the skillet. Add the yellow onions and bell peppers and cook, stirring often, until the yellow onions are wilted, about 2 minutes. Add the green onions, green chilies and garlic; cook for 2 minutes or until the vegetables are softened; stir often. Transfer to the bowl with the corn. Add the mayonnaise, ½ the Monterey Jack cheese and ½ of Cheddar cheese. Mix well. Pour into an 8-inch square baking dish and sprinkle the remaining cheese on top. Bake 10-12 minutes or until bubbly and golden brown. Serve hot with tortilla chips.

*SERVES 12-15*

# Crab Soup

1 pound fresh lump crabmeat
4 slices applewood-smoked bacon
1 cup diced onion
1 cup diced celery
½ cup diced green bell pepper
½ cup diced red bell pepper
2 cups diced red potato
4 cups vegetable broth
2 cups spicy-hot vegetable juice
2 bay leaves
1 teaspoon seafood seasoning
½ teaspoon paprika
2 cups seeded, diced tomatoes
2 cups fresh corn kernels
½ cup chopped fresh flat-leaf parsley
½ teaspoon freshly ground black pepper
Sour Cream Biscuits

Drain crabmeat and remove any bits of shell. Set aside. Cook bacon in a large Dutch oven until crisp; remove bacon and drain on paper towels, reserving drippings in pan. Crumble bacon and set aside. Sauté onion, celery, green and red peppers in hot drippings 11 minutes or until tender. Stir in potato, vegetable broth, vegetable juice, bay leaves, seafood seasoning and paprika; bring to a boil. Reduce heat and simmer, uncovered, 25 minutes or until potatoes are tender. Stir in tomatoes and corn; cook 15 minutes. Stir in crabmeat and cook for 5 minutes. Add parsley. Remove bay leaves. Sprinkle with black pepper and serve immediately with warm Sour Cream Biscuits.

*SERVES 13*

# Swannie's Coleslaw

**SLAW**
1 medium bag shredded cabbage
2 medium onions, sliced very thin
¾ cup sugar
2 teaspoons celery seeds

**DRESSING**
1½ teaspoons salt
1 tablespoon sugar
1 teaspoon prepared mustard
1 cup cider vinegar
1 cup vegetable oil

Layer cabbage, onions, sugar and celery seeds in a 9x13 inch pan, ending with cabbage. Put salt, sugar, mustard and vinegar in a saucepan. Bring to a rolling boil and add oil. Return mixture to rolling boil. Pour hot dressing over slaw. DO NOT STIR. Cover and refrigerate overnight.

*SERVES 10*

# Sour Cream Biscuits

2 cups self-rising flour                        1 cup butter, melted
1 (8-ounce) container sour cream

Preheat oven to 350°. Stir together all ingredients just until blended. Spoon batter into lightly greased miniature muffin pans, filling to the top. Bake for 10-12 minutes or until lightly brown and serve warm.

*SERVES 18*


# Cauliflower Salad

1 head cauliflower, chopped                     1 pound bacon
1 red onion, chopped                            1 cup mayonnaise
2 cups grated Cheddar cheese                    1 head lettuce, chopped
½ cup sugar

Fry bacon until crispy; crumble. Add all ingredients but lettuce and chill. Add lettuce when ready to serve.

*SERVES 6-8*


# Grilled Prosciutto Wrapped Shrimp

24 large shrimp, cleaned and deveined           12 slices prosciutto, thinly sliced and
                                                cut in half lengthwise (24 pieces)

**MARINADE**
¼ cup white wine                                1 teaspoon fresh oregano, minced
¼ cup olive oil                                 1 teaspoon fresh thyme, minced
1½ teaspoons Dijon mustard                      2 teaspoons minced garlic
1 tablespoon chopped fresh parsley

Wrap each shrimp with a prosciutto slice. If necessary, secure with toothpick. Mix together all marinade ingredients. Place the wrapped shrimp in the marinade for 2-4 hours or more in refrigerator, using either a glass dish or sealed zip-top plastic bag. Grill shrimp for 2-3 minutes on each side depending upon size of shrimp and temperature of grill.

*SERVES 12*

# Peaches and Ice Cream Sandwich Bars

10-14 rectangular ice cream
sandwiches
2 pints mango sorbet or peach sorbet,
softened

1 (8 ounce) carton sour cream
1 cup whipping cream
¾ cup powdered sugar
2 cups blueberries or raspberries

Place ice cream sandwiches in bottom of 9x13 inch pan or 3-quart rectangular baking dish, cutting to fit as necessary. Spread sorbet on top of ice cream sandwiches. Freeze about 15 minutes or until sorbet is firm. In medium bowl, combine sour cream, whipping cream and powdered sugar. Beat with electric mixer on medium speed until mixture thickens and holds soft peaks. Spread on top of sorbet. Cover and freeze for at least 4 hours or until firm. Let stand at room temperature for 10 minutes. Top with blueberries.

*SERVES 12*

# Chilled Cucumber Soup

2 tablespoons butter
1 cup chopped onions
4 cups cucumber, peeled, seeded
and chopped

6 cups low-fat chicken broth
Salt and pepper to taste
¼ cup fresh dill or parsley for garnish

Melt butter in a large saucepan and sauté onions and cucumbers until soft. Add the broth and cover; simmer for about 10 minutes. Place mixture into a blender and purée until smooth, may need to do several batches. Add salt and pepper to taste. Chill for at least 4 hours. Garnish with chopped dill or parsley.

*SERVES 6-8*

If you prefer a thicker soup, add 2 tablespoons of flour to the cooked onions and cucumbers. Add broth slowly to that mixture to prevent lumping.

# Kansas Mud Brûlée

2 cups whipping cream
1 (4 ounce) bar sweet baking
 chocolate
⅓ cup sugar
6 egg yolks
¼ cup Kahlúa®

⅓ cup marshmallow creme
1½ tablespoons semisweet chocolate
 mini-morsels
¾ teaspoon milk
3 tablespoons brown sugar

Preheat oven to 275°. Combine cream, chocolate and sugar in a small heavy saucepan; cook over low heat, stirring constantly, until chocolate melts. Process egg yolks in blender at high speed; with blender running, add chocolate mixture in a slow, steady stream. Add liqueur and pulse until blended. Pour into 6 (6 ounce) lightly greased ramekins or custard cups and place in a 9x13 inch baking pan. Add hot water to pan to depth of 1 inch. Bake for 55 minutes or just to set. Remove ramekins from pan and transfer to a wire rack to cool; cover and chill thoroughly. Combine marshmallow cream, mini-morsels and milk, stirring well. Spoon a small amount onto each custard. Sprinkle brown sugar over marshmallow layer and place custards in 9x13 inch baking pan. Broil 3½ inches from heat (with electric oven door partially open) 2-3 minutes or until brown sugar melts.

*SERVES 6*

To broil custards 3½ inches from heat, invert jelly roll pan and place it beneath the 9x13 inch pan holding the custards on the top oven rack.

JCYM
Johnson County Young Matrons

Members support our philanthropic agencies with an average of over 20,000 volunteer hours annually.

# Egg Salad Sandwiches

6 eggs
2 celery stalks, diced
1 shallot, finely chopped
2 tablespoons sliced chives

⅓ cup garlic aïoli or mayonnaise
1 teaspoon salt
1 teaspoon ground black pepper
12 slices pumpernickel bread

**GARNISH**

4 tablespoons crème fraîche or sour
  cream

1 cup whipping cream
1 small red onion, cut into slivers

Place eggs in a deep bottom pot, cover with water and bring to a boil. Simmer for 12 minutes, drain, and put eggs in ice water, chill completely. Peel and roughly chop eggs. Place in a medium mixing bowl. Add celery, shallot, chives, aïoli and salt and pepper; whisk until creamy. Spread mixture onto bread, making a sandwich, slice off crust and cut into desired size. To garnish sandwiches, whip crème fraîche and cream into firm peaks, top with onion.

*36 TEA SANDWICHES*

# Mango-Spinach Salad with Warm Bacon Vinaigrette

4 thick bacon slices, diced
½ medium red onion, thinly sliced
¼ cup red wine vinegar
1 tablespoon lime juice
1 tablespoon honey

1 (9 ounce) package fresh spinach
1 mango, peeled and diced
½ cup crumbled queso fresco
  (fresh Mexican cheese)
Salt and pepper to taste

Cook bacon over medium high heat 6-8 minutes and drain on paper towels, reserving 1 tablespoon drippings in skillet. Sauté onion in hot drippings 2-3 minutes or until tender. Add vinegar, lime juice and honey; cook 2 minutes, stirring to loosen particles from bottom of skillet. Place spinach in a serving bowl. Add warm vinaigrette and toss to coat. Top with mango, queso fresco and bacon; season with salt and pepper. Serve immediately.

*SERVES 4*

# Fresh Veggies with Buttermilk Herb Dip

1 cup plain whole-milk yogurt

1 cup sour cream

1 cup freshly grated Parmigiano-Reggiano cheese

⅓ cup buttermilk

1 cup fresh chives, thinly sliced

2 tablespoons fresh dill, chopped

2 tablespoons fresh thyme, chopped

1 small clove garlic, minced and mashed into paste with a pinch of salt

1 tablespoon cider vinegar

¼ teaspoon hot chili sauce; more to taste

1½ teaspoons kosher salt

1½ teaspoons coarsely ground black pepper

**VEGGIES**

1 pound pickling cucumbers, cut into spears 3-4 inches long and ½ inch thick

1 pound small, slender carrots, peeled and cut into 3-4 inch lengths and halved if thick

1 pint grape or cherry tomatoes

In a large bowl, whisk yogurt, sour cream, cheese, buttermilk, chives, dill, thyme, garlic and vinegar. Season with chili sauce, salt and pepper to taste. Sit for 15 minutes. Arrange the veggies on a large platter, with dip in center.

*SERVES A CROWD*

# Better Than Sex Cake

1 (18.5 ounce) box German chocolate cake mix, plus ingredients listed on package

1 (14 ounce) sweetened condensed milk

1 (12 ounce) caramel ice cream topping

1 (16 ounce) container frozen whipped topping, thawed

3 chocolate toffee bars, crushed

Preheat oven to 350°. Prepare cake mix according to package instructions, pour into 9x13 inch pan, bake for 25-30 minutes. Mix together caramel topping and condensed milk. While warm poke holes with wooden spoon handle. Pour caramel mixture over warm cake. When cool, spread with whipped topping and top with crushed toffee bars.

*SERVES 15*

# Summer Martini

¾ ounce freshly squeezed lemon juice　　1½ ounces vodka
½ ounce simple syrup　　Lemon wedges
¼ ounce triple sec liqueur

Rim glass with lemon and coat with sugar. Fill shaker with lemon juice, simple syrup, triple sec and vodka. Shake 8 times. Garnish with lemon wedge, serve in a martini glass.

*1 SERVING*

Simple syrup is made by boiling equal parts sugar and water until sugar is dissolved.

# Phyllo Pizza with Feta, Basil and Tomatoes

½ cup shredded part-skim mozzarella cheese
½ cup finely crumbled reduced fat feta cheese
¼ cup grated fresh Parmigiano-Reggiano cheese
1 tablespoon chopped fresh oregano
¼ teaspoon salt

⅛ teaspoon freshly ground black pepper
10 (18x14 inch) sheets frozen phyllo dough, thawed
Cooking spray
2 cups thinly sliced plum tomatoes
⅓ cup thinly sliced green onions
¼ cup fresh basil leaves

Preheat oven to 375°. Combine mozzarella, feta, Parmigiano-Reggiano cheeses, oregano, salt and pepper. Cut phyllo sheets in half crosswise. Working with 1 phyllo sheet (cover remaining dough to keep from drying out), place phyllo sheet on a baking sheet coated with cooking spray. Coat phyllo sheet with cooking spray. Repeat with 2 more sheets of phyllo. Sprinkle with 2 tablespoons cheese mixture. Repeat layers 5 times, ending with 2 phyllo sheets. Coat top phyllo sheet with cooking spray; sprinkle with 2 tablespoons cheese mixture. Arrange tomato slices on top of cheese mixture, leaving a 1 inch border. Sprinkle with onions and remaining 6 tablespoons cheese mixture. Bake for 20 minutes or until golden. Sprinkle with basil leaves.

*6 SERVINGS*

# Farm Fresh Pasta with Bacon

1 (16 ounce) package orecchiette pasta
1 cup frozen sweet peas
1½ cups fresh snow peas
8 radishes, cut into wedges
2 large carrots, grated
2 green onions, thinly sliced
⅓ cup parsley, coarsely chopped

¼ cup lemon juice
¼ cup olive oil
Salt and pepper to taste
6 thick bacon slices, cooked and crumbled
½ cup crumbled goat cheese, optional

Cook pasta according to package directions, adding sweet peas and snow peas during last minute of cook time. Drain. Toss pasta mixture with radishes, carrots, onions ,parsley, lemon juice and olive oil. Sprinkle bacon and, if desired, goat cheese on top.

*SERVES 6-8*

Bow-tie pasta may be substituted for orechiette pasta.

# Bacon and Herb Cupcakes

1½ cups sour cream
½ cup cooked bacon, finely crumbled
½ cup butter, melted
¼ cup fresh herbs (parsley, thyme, oregano), finely chopped

2 cups self-rising flour
6 ounces cream cheese, softened
Garnishes: assorted fresh herbs, cooked and crumbled bacon
Dash of white pepper

Preheat oven to 375°. Stir together sour cream, bacon, butter, herbs, onions, pepper, and flour until blended. Mixture will be thick. Spoon batter into lightly greased miniature muffin pans. Bake for 26-28 minutes or until golden brown. Remove cupcakes from pans to wire rack, cool completely, about 30 minutes. Top cupcakes with cream cheese. Garnish, if desired.

*SERVES 32*

# Vanilla Cake with Buttercream, Berries and Jam

2½ cups all-purpose flour
⅓ cup cornstarch
3½ teaspoons baking powder
1 teaspoon salt
¾ cup vegetable oil
½ cup milk
1 tablespoon vanilla extract
4 egg whites

¼ teaspoon cream of tartar
1½ cups sugar
1 cup strawberry jam
3 cups sliced fresh strawberries, raspberries, blackberries and or blueberries, stemmed and halved
1 cup whole fresh strawberries, raspberries, blackberries and or blueberries

**VANILLA-BUTTERCREAM FROSTING**

½ cup butter, softened
6 cups powdered sugar, divided
3 tablespoons milk plus
   1 or 2 teaspoons if needed

2 teaspoons vanilla bean paste or vanilla extract

Preheat oven to 350°. Grease bottoms of 2 (8 inch) round cake pans. Line bottoms with parchment paper; grease and lightly flour pans. Set aside. In a large bowl stir together flour, cornstarch, baking powder and salt. Add water, oil, milk and vanilla. Beat with a wired whisk until smooth. In a medium bowl combine egg whites and cream of tartar. Beat with an electric mixer on medium speed until soft peaks form (tips curl). Gradually add sugar, beating on high until stiff peaks form (tips stand straight). Fold beaten egg whites into batter. Pour batter into prepared pans, spreading evenly. Bake for 22-25 minutes or until a toothpick inserted in center comes out clean. Cool in pans on wire racks for 10 minutes. Remove from pans; cool completely on racks. In a medium bowl beat softened butter with an electric mixer on medium to high for 30 seconds. Gradually add 3 cups powdered sugar, beating well. Beat in 3 tablespoons milk and vanilla. Gradually beat in 3 cups additional sugar. If needed, beat in milk 1 teaspoon at a time to make easier to spread. To assemble, use a serrated knife to cut cake layers in half horizontally. Place 1 cake layer, cut side down, on serving plate. Spread with ¾ cup frosting and ¼ cup jam. Top with 1 cup of sliced berries. Repeat with two more cake layers. For top layer, place final layer cut side down and spread with remaining frosting, ¼ cup of jam and 1 cup whole berries.

*SERVES 12*

# Stuffed Filet Mignon with Merlot Mushroom Sauce

4 ounces cream cheese, softened
½ cup grated Parmigiano-Reggiano cheese
½ teaspoon minced garlic
1½ teaspoons fresh basil, chopped
2 (8 ounce) beef tenderloin steaks
3 tablespoons olive oil

1 cup sliced baby portabella mushrooms
1 teaspoon garlic, minced
½ cup merlot or dry red wine
¼ cup beef broth
⅛ teaspoon ground black pepper
1 tablespoon butter

Preheat oven to 400°. Line a baking sheet with parchment paper; set aside. In a small bowl, combine cream cheese, cheese, garlic and basil; set aside. Cut a pocket into side of each steak. Spoon cheese mixture evenly into steak pockets. In a large sauté pan, heat olive oil over medium heat. Cook steaks 2-3 minutes on each side or until browned. Remove steaks, reserving drippings in pan, place on prepared baking sheet. Move to oven and cook 15-20 minutes, or until desired degree of doneness. Let steaks rest 2 minutes before serving. Spoon any melted cheese mixture back into the pockets. Add mushrooms to drippings in pan and cook 2 minutes. Add garlic and cook 1 minute. Add wine; cook 3-5 minutes, or until almost dry. Add beef broth and pepper and cook 1 minute. Remove from heat and stir in butter until melted. Spoon sauce over steaks.

*SERVES 2*

# Prosciutto-Melon Bites with Lime Drizzle

16 (1 inch) cubes cantaloupe
16 (1 inch) cubes honeydew melon
16 very thin slices prosciutto, cut in half lengthwise
1 tablespoon fresh lime juice

2 teaspoons extra virgin olive oil
¼ teaspoon crushed red pepper flakes
2 tablespoons thinly sliced fresh mint
16 (4 inch) skewers

Wrap each cantaloupe cube and each honeydew cube with ½ prosciutto slice. Thread 1 wrapped cantaloupe cube and 1 wrapped honeydew cube onto each of 16 skewers. Arrange skewers on a serving platter. Combine juice, oil and pepper, stirring with a whisk; drizzle evenly over skewers. Sprinkle evenly with mint

*SERVES 8 (2 SKEWERS EACH)*

# Parmesan Polenta Cakes

3½ cups milk
¾ teaspoon salt
½ teaspoon ground black pepper
1 cup yellow stone-ground cornmeal

½ cup grated Parmigiano-Reggiano
cheese
2 tablespoons butter
Garnish: shaved Parmigiano-Reggiano
cheese, fresh basil leaves

Line bottom of 9x5 inch loaf pan with waxed paper; set aside. In a medium saucepan over medium heat, combine milk, salt and pepper; carefully bring to a boil, stirring frequently. Gradually whisk in cornmeal until well mixed. Reduce heat to low, cover, cook 30 minutes, stirring frequently. Stir in cheese until melted. Cool slightly, spread evenly into prepared pan; refrigerate 1-2 hours, or until set completely. Remove from pan and cut into four equal pieces. In a large non-stick skillet, melt 2 tablespoons butter over medium heat. Cook polenta squares 2 minutes on each side, or until golden brown. Garnish with Parmigiano-Reggiano cheese and basil.

*SERVES 4*

# Peanut Butter and Banana Bread

2 cups all-purpose flour
1 teaspoon baking soda
¼ teaspoon salt
½ cup butter, softened
½ cup firmly packed brown sugar

½ cup sugar
½ cup peanut butter
2 eggs
2 bananas, mashed
½ cup chopped walnuts

Preheat oven to 350°. Grease a 9x5 inch loaf pan, set aside. In a medium bowl, whisk together flour, baking soda and salt; set aside. In a large bowl, cream together butter, sugars, peanut butter and eggs. Stir bananas into creamed mixture until combined. Add the flour mixture and nuts. Mix well. Pour batter into prepared pan. Bake for 55-60 minutes or until a toothpick inserted in the center comes out clean. Cool for 15 minutes. Remove bread from pan and cool on a wire rack.

*SERVES 10-12*

# Maple French Toast and Bacon Cupcakes

## CUPCAKES

1 cup all-purpose flour
1 cup cake flour
1 (3.4 ounce) box instant vanilla
   pudding mix
1 teaspoon baking powder
1 tablespoon cornstarch
1 teaspoon cinnamon
1 teaspoon freshly grated nutmeg
½ teaspoon salt

½ cup unsalted butter, at room
   temperature
¾ cup firmly packed light brown sugar
¾ cup sugar
1½ teaspoons vanilla extract
4 egg whites, at room temperature
¼ cup maple syrup
½ cup half and half, at room
   temperature
5 strips cooked bacon, crumbled

## FROSTING

1 (8 ounce) package cream cheese, at
   room temperature
2 tablespoons unsalted butter, at room
   temperature
2 cups sifted powdered sugar

¼ cup maple syrup
2 teaspoons ground cinnamon
3 strips bacon, cooked and chopped,
   optional

Preheat oven to 350°. Place paper liners in 12 cup muffin tin. In a bowl, whisk flours, pudding mix, baking powder, cornstarch, cinnamon, nutmeg and salt. In another bowl, cream butter and sugars with a mixer on low speed until combined 6-8 minutes. Gradually mix in the vanilla and egg whites. Scrape down the sides of the bowl; mix until light and fluffy. Add flour mixture in 3 batches, alternating with the maple syrup and half and half, mixing after each addition and ending with flour mixture. Mix until the ingredients are just combined, do not overmix. Fold in the bacon. Pour the batter into muffin tin, filling each cup about three-quarters of the way. Bake until a toothpick inserted in the center comes out clean, about 40 minutes. Cool completely. Prepare the frosting by beating the cream cheese and butter with a mixer on medium speed until creamy. Add the powdered sugar, maple syrup and cinnamon; beat until combined. Spread on the cooled cupcakes: top with chopped bacon, if desired.

*SERVES 12*

Bacon won't curl when being cooked if it is dipped into cold water prior to cooking.

# Peanut Butter Banana Cream Pie

1 baked deep dish pie shell
⅓ cup sugar
1½ tablespoons cornstarch
⅛ teaspoon salt
1 cup whipping cream
½ cup whole milk

2 egg yolks
1 vanilla bean, split lengthwise
1 tablespoon unsalted butter
4 firm but ripe bananas, peeled, divided
3 tablespoons orange juice, divided

**PEANUT BUTTER LAYER**

1 (3 ounce) package cream cheese, room temperature
½ cup powdered sugar

1 teaspoon vanilla extract
⅓ cup creamy peanut butter
⅔ cup chilled whipping cream

Whisk sugar, cornstarch and salt in heavy medium sized saucepan until no lumps remain. Gradually whisk in cream, then milk. Add yolks and seeds from vanilla bean; whisk to blend. Cook over medium heat, whisking constantly, until pudding thickens and boils, about 5 minutes. Add butter and stir until melted. Spread warm pudding in cooled crust. Chill until filling is cool, about 1 hour. Thinly slice 3 bananas on diagonal. Combine banana slices and 2 tablespoons orange juice in medium bowl; toss to coat. Transfer banana slices to paper towel, pat dry. Arrange enough banana slices in single layer over vanilla custard filling to cover completely. For the peanut butter layer using an electric mixer, beat cream cheese and powdered sugar in medium bowl until smooth. Beat in vanilla, then peanut butter. Beat cream in another medium bowl until firm peaks form. Fold large spoonful of whipped cream into peanut butter mixture to loosen then fold in remaining cream in 2 additions. Spread peanut butter layer evenly over bananas. Chill at least 3 hours. Thinly slice remaining banana on diagonal. Toss with remaining orange juice, then pat dry with paper towels. Arrange banana slices around top edge of pie.

*SERVES 8*

Peanut butter layer can be made 8 hours ahead. Keep chilled.

# Sweet Pea Casserole

¼ cup butter
1 (8 ounce) container sliced baby bella
  mushrooms
1 cup chopped onion
2 cloves garlic, minced
2 tablespoons all-purpose flour
1 teaspoon sugar
¾ teaspoon salt
¼ teaspoon ground black pepper

¼ teaspoon ground nutmeg
1 cup milk
1 cup whipping cream
2 cups grated fontina cheese
1 cup grated Parmesan cheese
2 (16 ounce) packages frozen green
  peas, thawed and drained
1 (16 ounce) can french-fried onion
  rings

Preheat oven to 350°. In a Dutch oven melt butter over medium heat. Add mushrooms, onions and garlic; cook for 5-6 minutes, or until tender. Stir in flour, sugar, salt, pepper and nutmeg; cook, stirring constantly, for 2 minutes. Gradually stir in milk and cream; cook, stirring constantly, for 6-8 minutes, or until slightly thickened. Add cheese, stirring until melted and smooth. Add peas, stirring to combine. Spoon mixture into a 9x13 inch baking dish; bake for 30 minutes. Top evenly with french-fried onion rings, bake for 5 minutes. Serve immediately.

*SERVES 12*

# Hash Brown Cakes

1½ cups shredded ham
½ cup green onions, chopped
2½ tablespoons all-purpose flour
¼ teaspoon salt

1 (20 ounce) bag refrigerated
  shredded hash browns
2 eggs, lightly beaten
¼ cup canola oil

Combine ham, green onions, flour, salt and hash browns. Add eggs, toss well. Scoop mixture by ¼ cupfuls into 1 tablespoon hot canola oil per batch in a large nonstick skillet over medium heat; flatten slightly and cook 5 minutes on each side or until browned.

*SERVES 8*

# Baked Ravioli Bites

1 (9 ounce) package refrigerated ravioli, prepared according to directions

2 eggs, beaten

1 cup Italian bread crumbs

7 ounces pesto or pesto with sun-dried tomatoes

Cooking spray

Assorted toppings to garnish (see below)

Preheat broiler and grease baking sheet. Dip the cooked ravioli into beaten eggs, making sure both sides are coated. Then dredge in bread crumbs so that both sides are covered. Place on baking sheet and lightly spray with cooking spray. Broil for 1-2 minutes or until edges begin to brown. Turn ravioli over and spray again. Broil for about 1 additional minute until edges begin to brown. Remove from broiler and top each with 1 teaspoon pesto and your choice of toppings.

*MAKES 45 APPETIZERS*

Topping choices could include your choice of olives, small mozzarella balls, pepperocini pepper slices, fresh basil or artichoke hearts.

# Sweet Potato Risotto

1 tablespoon olive oil

½ onion, chopped

1 clove garlic, minced

¼ cup jalapeño pepper, finely chopped

1 cup arborio rice

3 cups chicken stock, divided

1 cup sweet potato, diced and blanched

4 tablespoons orange flavored liqueur

½ cup fresh spinach, chopped

½ cup fontina cheese, grated

Salt and pepper to taste

Heat olive oil in large skillet over medium heat. Add onions and cook until translucent. Add garlic, jalapeños and rice. Cook for 5 minutes, stirring occasionally. Stir in 1 cup chicken stock, cook and stir until it is absorbed. Repeat 2 times with the stock. Stir in remaining ingredients. Serve immediately.

*SERVES 4*

# Pork Loin with Fontina, Prosciutto and Sun-Dried Tomato

5 ounces pork loin, divided in half

Salt and pepper to taste

4 sage leaves

2 ounces fontina cheese, thinly sliced

2 ounces prosciutto, thinly sliced

Flour for dredging

1 tablespoon cooking oil

2 tablespoons Marsala wine

4 tablespoons butter, browned

1 tablespoon sun-dried tomatoes, diced

Pound pork to 1 inch thickness and sprinkle lightly with salt and pepper. Place 2 sage leaves, 1 thin slice of fontina cheese and prosciutto on top of each piece of pork. Roll the loin and secure with a toothpick. Dredge in flour. Put oil in a hot skillet and sauté each side of the pork starting with the cheese side. This cooking process will take 4-5 minutes on each side. Remove pork from pan and deglaze the pan using the Marsala wine. Stir in browned butter and sun-dried tomatoes. To serve, place pork on the plate and top with the tomato sauce.

*SERVES 2*

To brown butter place butter in a saucepan; carefully heat until brown, then remove from heat immediately.

Freeze leftover red wine in sealable plastic freezer bags or in ice cube trays. It is wonderful to have on hand to add to soups and sauces. You can also use this trick with tomato paste.

# Skinny Fettuccini Alfredo

9 ounces dried fettuccini

1½ teaspoons flour

1 cup plus 2 tablespoons fat free half and half

1 cup reduced fat Parmesan cheese

½ teaspoon garlic powder, or more to taste

⅛ teaspoon salt, or to taste

3 tablespoons light butter (stick not tub)

Chopped fresh parsley

Prepare fettuccini as directed on the package. Set aside. In a medium bowl mix flour with enough half and half to form a paste. Add remaining half and half, stirring continuously to remove any lumps. Heat a non stick skillet over medium heat. Place the half and half mixture, ½ cup Parmesan cheese, garlic powder and salt in the pan. Cook for 5-7 minutes until the mixture becomes a thick gravy. Add the butter and stir constantly until it is incorporated into the mixture. Toss the cooked fettuccini in and stir until coated. Divide among 4 servings and top with remaining Parmesan and a sprinkle of parsley. Serve immediately.

*SERVES 4*

# Mesclun Green Salad with Camembert Cheese

¼ cup fine bread crumbs

¼ cup sesame seeds, toasted

1 Camembert cheese wheel with rind

1 egg white, slightly beaten

2 tablespoons oil for sautéing

1 tablespoon white truffle oil

¼ teaspoon Fleur de Sel French salt

Freshly cracked black pepper to taste

1 (6 ounce) package Mesclun green salad

Combine bread crumbs and sesame seeds in a small bowl. Cut cheese into 1 inch wedges; dip into beaten egg white, coat with the bread crumb mixture, then sauté both sides quickly in a small skillet with oil over high heat. Remove from heat, cool and refrigerate. Can be done ahead. Place mesclun greens in a medium sized bowl drizzle with truffle oil, add salt and pepper. Serve on individual plates with a sautéed Camembert wedge.

*SERVES 6-8*

# Hazelnut, Ricotta & Lemon Pesto

1 garlic clove, peeled
½ cup hazelnuts, toasted, husked (about 2 ounces)
½ cup fresh basil, coarsely chopped
5 tablespoons extra virgin olive oil, divided
1½ cups whole milk ricotta cheese

3 tablespoons fresh lemon juice
½ teaspoon packed finely grated lemon zest
3 tablespoons freshly grated Pecorino Romano cheese
Fine sea salt and ground black pepper to taste

With food processor running, drop garlic clove into machine and blend until finely chopped. Add hazelnuts, basil and 2 tablespoons olive oil; process until hazelnuts and basil are finely chopped. Add ricotta cheese, lemon juice, lemon zest and remaining 3 tablespoons olive oil; process until well blended. Transfer mixture to small bowl and stir in Pecorino Romano cheese. Season to taste with sea salt and freshly ground black pepper.

*SERVES ABOUT 2⅓ CUPS*

Can be made up to 2 days ahead. Cover and refrigerate. This can be tossed with a pound of pasta served warm or chilled, used as a topping for grilled chicken or spread on toasted slices of baguette or focaccia.

# Puff Pastry Pizza with Chorizo

1 sheet frozen puff pastry, thawed
Flour as needed
1 tablespoon garlic, puréed
3 ounces chorizo sausage, cooked and crumbled
1 small eggplant, roasted

4 cherry tomatoes, sliced
½ cup arugula, loosely packed
1 roasted red pepper, thinly sliced
4 ounces mozzarella cheese
Basil leaves for garnish

Preheat oven to 400° or to temperature shown on puff pastry package. Unfold puff pastry on lightly floured work surface. Place on baking sheet and pierce thoroughly with a fork. Spread garlic purée around the pastry leaving a 1 inch border around the edge uncovered. Layer all ingredients on the pastry with the cheese placed on the very top. Bake for 10-15 minutes or until the cheese has melted and the pastry is lightly browned. Garnish with fresh basil. Serve immediately.

*SERVES 4-6*

# Fresh Tomato-Olive Sauce

1½ pounds plum tomatoes, cored, cut lengthwise into thin wedges

12 Kalamata olives, pitted and sliced

½ cup extra virgin olive oil

½ cup diced roasted red or yellow bell peppers from jar

¼ cup finely chopped red onion

3 garlic cloves, minced

2 tablespoons drained capers, coarsely chopped

2 tablespoons fresh lemon juice

2 tablespoons fresh Italian parsley, chopped

2 tablespoons fresh oregano, chopped

½ teaspoon dried crushed red pepper flakes

Salt and pepper to taste

Combine ingredients in a large bowl; sprinkle with salt and pepper. Let stand at room temperature for at least 1 hour and up to 2 hours to let the flavors blend. Taste and adjust seasonings as needed. Serve with pasta of choice.

*MAKES 5 CUPS*

For the best flavor use very ripe tomatoes. May cut this in half to serve as an appetizer and serve with baked ravioli bites or toasted baguette slices.

When using a garlic press it isn't necessary to peel the garlic first. Simply place the clove in the press, squeeze and then remove the papery peel which is left behind.

# Short Ribs with Tagliatelle

3 tablespoons olive oil

2 ounces chopped pancetta (about ½ cup)

2½ pounds short ribs

Salt

Freshly ground black pepper

¼ cup all-purpose flour

1 medium onion, chopped

1 carrot, chopped

½ cup fresh parsley leaves

2 cloves garlic

1 (14.5 ounce) can tomatoes, whole or diced

1 tablespoon tomato paste

1 teaspoon fresh rosemary leaves, chopped

1 teaspoon dried thyme

½ teaspoon dried oregano

1 bay leaf

2½ cups beef broth

¾ cup red wine

1 pound fresh or dried tagliatelle (pasta in long narrow ribbons)

4 to 6 teaspoons shaved bittersweet chocolate

Place the olive oil in a large heavy soup pot over medium heat. Cook the pancetta until golden and crisp, about 4 minutes. Meanwhile, season the short ribs with salt and pepper and dredge in the flour. Using a slotted spoon, remove the pancetta from the pan and set aside. Add the short ribs to the pan and brown on all sides, about 7 minutes total. Combine the onion, carrot, parsley and garlic in a food processor and blend until finely minced. Then add the tomatoes and tomato paste and pulse. Once the short ribs are browned, carefully add the mixture from the food processor to the pot. Return the pancetta to the pot and stir. Add the rosemary, thyme, oregano, bay leaf, beef broth and wine. Bring the mixture to a boil. Reduce the heat and simmer, covered, for 1 hour 15 minutes. Remove the lid and simmer for another hour and a half, stirring occasionally. Remove the bay leaf and the meat and bones from the pot. Discard the bay leaf and bones. Shred the meat and return it to the pot. Season with ½ teaspoon salt and ¾ teaspoon pepper, or to taste. Bring a large pot of salted water to a boil over high heat. Add the pasta and cook until tender but still firm to the bite, stirring occasionally, about 8-10 minutes for dried pasta and 2-3 minutes for fresh. Drain the pasta, reserving 1 cup of the cooking liquid. Add the pasta to the pot and stir to combine. Add the reserved pasta liquid ¼ cup at a time, if needed, to moisten the pasta. Transfer to serving bowls, top each bowl with 1 teaspoon of chocolate shavings. Serve immediately.

*SERVES 4-6*

# Berry Tiramisu

## MASCARPONE CREAM

1½ cups raspberries, rinsed and patted dry

1 cup blueberries, rinsed and patted dry

1 cup strawberries, rinsed and patted dry, hulled and quartered

2 tablespoons sugar

½ cup plus 3 tablespoons Chambord or other raspberry flavored liqueur or ruby port

2 cups whipping cream

½ cup powdered sugar, divided

1 pound mascarpone

## POUND CAKE

1 teaspoon vegetable shortening, for the pan

2 cups plus 2 teaspoons all-purpose flour

1 teaspoon baking powder

¼ teaspoon salt

1 cup unsalted butter, room temperature

1 cup sugar

4 eggs

1 teaspoon vanilla extract

Fresh mint for garnish

## RASPBERRY COULIS

2 cups raspberries, rinsed

¾ cup simple syrup

1½ tablespoons fresh lemon juice

½ tablespoon cornstarch

For the pound cake, preheat the oven to 325°. Prepare an 8½x4½x2½ inch loaf by coating the pan with the shortening and 2 teaspoons of the flour, tapping off the excess. Sift the remaining 2 cups flour, baking powder and salt into a medium bowl. Cream the butter and sugar in a medium bowl with an electric mixer on high speed, scraping down the sides of the bowl as needed, until light and fluffy, about 3 minutes. On low speed, in 3 additions, beat in the flour, alternating with 1 egg at a time, scraping down the sides of the bowl as needed. Beat in the vanilla just until blended. Spread evenly in the prepared pan. Bake until the cake is golden brown and a cake tester or toothpick comes out clean, about 1 hour 10 minutes. Cool on a wire rack for 10 minutes in the pan. Turn the cake out onto the rack, turn right side up, and let cool for at least 30 minutes. Serve warm or at room temperature. Cut pound cake into ½ inch thick slices, making 8 slices. To make the raspberry coulis; bring the raspberries, syrup and lemon juice to a simmer in a heavy medium saucepan over low heat. Simmer, stirring occasionally, until the berries are very soft, about 10 minutes. Sprinkle the cornstarch over 2 teaspoons cold water and stir to dissolve. Pour into the simmering raspberry mixture. Cook, stirring occasionally, until the sauce thickens, about 3 minutes. Strain through a fine-mesh wire sieve into a medium bowl. Discard the seeds. Cool completely, then

## Berry Tiramisu, continued

cover and refrigerate until ready to use.(Freeze any leftover coulis in a plastic container for up to 1 month.) For the berries; gently stir raspberries, blueberries and strawberries in a bowl with the sugar, 2 tablespoons of the Chambord, and ½ cup of the raspberry coulis. Whip the cream in a large bowl with an electric mixer on high speed or a whisk until it thickens and almost doubles in volume. Add ¼ cup of the powdered sugar and 1 tablespoon of the Chambord and whip until stiff peaks form. In medium bowl, whip the mascarpone with the remaining ¼ cup powdered sugar with an electric mixer on low speed until smooth. Fold in half of the whipped cream. To assemble, spread half the pound cake slices in the bottom of a 6x9 inch pan. Drizzle the remaining ¼ cup Chambord over the cake and cover with half of the berry mixture. Cover the berries with half of the mascarpone cream, gently spreading it into a smooth layer with a rubber spatula. Repeat with the remaining ingredients and top with a smooth layer of the remaining whipped cream. Cover tightly with plastic wrap. Refrigerate for at least 2 hours and up to 1½ days. Spoon into bowls and garnish with mint sprigs Serve with the remaining raspberry coulis spooned over each serving or passed on the side.

*SERVES 6-8*

Simple syrup is made with 1 cup sugar and 1 cup water, boiled until sugar dissolves, and cooled.
To reduce the time needed, purchase a good quality pound cake and use frozen whipped topping

# Focaccia Versiliese

2 teaspoons dried yeast

1 cup warm water

1 tablespoon olive oil

1 tablespoon rosemary, chopped

4 sage leaves, torn

3½ ounces ripe olives, pitted

2 tablespoons garlic, minced

2 cups all-purpose flour

1 cup corn flour

2 teaspoons salt

2 teaspoons olive oil

Stir yeast into a large mixing bowl with the water and let sit for 10 minutes. Stir in the 1 tablespoon oil, rosemary, sage, olives and garlic. Using a wooden spoon, add the flours and salt. Stir until the dough is thick and smooth. Knead by hand for 8-10 minutes until the dough is firm and elastic. Set the dough in a lightly oiled container, cover with plastic wrap and let rise until doubled. Turn the dough onto an oiled 10½x5½ inch baking pan and stretch it to fit. (If it won't fit, let rest for 10 minutes and try again.) Cover with a towel and let rise for about 30 minutes. Thirty minutes before baking, preheat oven to 400°F. Just before baking, dimple the top of the dough with your fingertips and sprinkle with some extra salt and 2 teaspoons of oil. Bake for 25 to 30 minutes until golden brown.

Slices of focaccia are like finger food, Italian style. Eat with the main dish or as an appetizer. A bowl of extra virgin olive oil with freshly ground pepper on top makes a wonderful dip.

# Tonga Mai Tai

1 ounce dark rum
½ ounce light rum
¼ ounce orgeat (almond flavored) syrup
2 ounces orange juice

2 ounces pineapple juice
¼ ounce triple sec
Pineapple wedge and maraschino cherry for garnish

Mix the dark and light rum, orgeat syrup, orange and pineapple juice in a cocktail shaker with ice cubes or crushed ice. Pour into a glass. Float the triple sec on top by pouring it over the back of a spoon. Garnish with the pineapple wedge and cherry.

*SERVES 1*

Orgeat, almond flavored syrup, can be found where coffee flavor syrup is located.

# Shrimp Pâté

**PÂTÉ**

4 (7.5 ounce) cans shrimp, rinsed and drained
1 small onion, minced
½ cup butter, melted

⅓ cup mayonnaise
2 tablespoons fresh lemon juice
Dash of hot sauce

**SAUCE**

1 cup ketchup
2 tablespoons horseradish

2 teaspoons fresh lemon juice

For the pâté, mash shrimp well and add onion. Pour butter over shrimp and onion. Add mayonnaise, lemon juice and hot sauce. Mix and pack into a mold. Refrigerate for 3 hours. Blend the ketchup, horseradish and lemon juice to form the sauce. Unmold the pâté and pour the sauce over it. Serve with crackers.

*SERVES 2½ CUPS*

# Tomato Relish Salad

3 medium tomatoes, sliced

1 cup sliced cucumbers

1 medium onion, sliced thinly

½ cup thinly sliced carrots

½ cup thinly sliced celery

**DRESSING**

½ cup tarragon vinegar

⅓ cup water

¼ cup sugar

1 teaspoon paprika

1 teaspoon dried basil

½ teaspoon salt

¼ teaspoon black pepper

Alternate rows of vegetables on a large platter, overlapping. Mix the dressing thoroughly and pour over vegetables. Cover and refrigerate 4 hours or overnight.

*SERVES 4-6*

# Spring Peas with Dates and Walnuts

Kosher salt

2 cups shelled fresh English peas or thawed frozen peas (about 10 ounces)

1 pound sugar snap peas, trimmed

¼ pound snow peas, trimmed and thinly sliced

1 tablespoon extra virgin olive oil

1 medium shallot, thinly sliced

¼ cup chopped walnuts

¼ cup chopped pitted dates

Pinch of cayenne pepper

2 teaspoons walnut oil

Bring a large pot of salted water to a boil over high heat. Fill a large bowl with ice water. If using fresh English peas, add to the boiling water and cook until tender, about 1 minutes, add the snap peas and cook until bright green, about 2 minutes, then add the snow peas and cook 30 seconds. Drain the peas and plunge into the ice water to cool. Heat the olive oil in a large skillet over medium-high heat. Add the shallot and cook until soft, about 2 minutes. Add the walnuts, dates and cayenne and cook until the nuts are slightly toasted, about 1 minute. Drain the peas, then add to the skillet (if using frozen peas, add them here). Add 1 teaspoon salt and cook, stirring until heated through, about 3-5 minutes. Add walnut oil and toss. Season with salt to taste.

*SERVES 6-8*

# Herbed Rice with Raisins

| | |
|---|---|
| 1 cup basmati, jasmine or jasmati rice | 1 medium carrot, grated |
| ½ cup golden raisins | 1 (3.5 ounce) package pea shoots |
| Grated zest and juice of 1 lemon | 3 tablespoons rice vinegar |
| ¼ cup chopped fresh chervil | 2 teaspoons sugar |
| ¼ cup chopped fresh basil | Kosher salt and freshly ground black |
| ¼ cup chopped fresh parsley | pepper |
| ¼ cup chopped fresh cilantro | ⅓ cup extra virgin olive oil |

Cook the rice as the label directs. Spread out on a baking sheet and let cool completely. In a cup, soak the raisins in the lemon juice for 10 minutes. Meanwhile, toss the rice with the chervil, basil, parsley, cilantro and carrot in a large bowl. Chop the pea shoots, reserving some whole for garnish and add to the bowl. Drain the raisins, straining the lemon juice into a separate bowl. Add the vinegar, lemon zest, sugar, ¼ teaspoon salt and pepper to taste to the lemon juice. Whisk in the olive oil. Add the rice mixture along with the raisins and toss. Season with salt and pepper. Top with reserved pea shoots.

*SERVES 6*

# Lemon-Peppered Broiled Fish

| | |
|---|---|
| 2 pounds any fresh fish or 2 (12 ounce) packages frozen perch or trout fillets | ½ teaspoon thyme leaves |
| | ½ teaspoon paprika |
| | ⅛ teaspoon celery seed |
| 1 tablespoon butter, melted | 2 teaspoons lemon juice |
| 1 teaspoon lemon and pepper seasoning | 1 tablespoon parsley flakes |

If using frozen fillets, thaw just enough to separate. Combine butter, lemon and pepper seasoning, thyme, paprika and celery seed. Brush on fish. Place fish with skin side down on oiled grill rack or broiler pan. Grill or broil 4-5 inches from heat for 10 minutes or until fish is easily flaked with fork. Sprinkle lemon juice and then parsley flakes over fish. Serve immediately.

*SERVES 4-6*

# Cedar Plank Salmon with Maple-Ginger Glaze

2 to 3 pounds skin-on center-cut salmon fillet (about 1½ inches thick)

2 teaspoons ground coriander

Kosher salt and freshly ground pepper

¼ cup pure maple syrup

1 (2 inch) piece ginger, peeled and grated

Grated zest and juice of 1 lemon

2 tablespoons unsalted butter

Fill baking dish with water. Soak 1 large cedar grilling plank (15x6 inches) in baking dish, about 2 hours; put a plate on top to keep the plank submerged. Preheat the oven to 425°. Sprinkle the salmon with the coriander, 1 teaspoon salt and ½ teaspoon pepper. Let stand at room temperature about 15 minutes. Meanwhile, heat the maple syrup, ginger, lemon zest and butter in a small saucepan over medium heat until slightly thickened, about 7 minutes. Stir in the lemon juice and set aside. Remove the cedar plank from the water and pat dry. Place the plank directly on the oven rack and preheat about 15 minutes. Using tongs or oven mitts, remove the plank from the oven and place the fish, skin-side down, on the wood. Brush the fish with half of the ginger glaze. Transfer the fish on the plank to the oven, put a baking sheet on the rack below to catch any drips. Cook until the salmon is just firm and slightly golden on top, about 12 minutes. Remove the fish from the oven and change the oven setting to broil. Brush the remaining ginger glaze over the salmon and broil until golden, 2-3 minutes more. Remove from the oven and let rest 5 minutes on the plank before serving. Serve warm or at room temperature.

*SERVES 6-8*

# Oven-Fried Fish

1½ to 2 pounds filet of fish (for example sole or orange roughy)

½ teaspoon garlic powder

¼ cup flour

1 egg

¼ cup milk

2 cups crushed cheese crackers

2 tablespoons Parmesan cheese

2 tablespoons parsley

¼ cup butter, melted

Mix garlic powder and flour. Coat fish with mixture. Mix egg and milk. Dip fish in mixture. Mix cheese cracker crumbs. Parmesan cheese and parsley. Dip fish again. Place filets in glass baking dish with melted butter; bake until fish is white and flaky, about 25-30 minutes.

*SERVES 4*

# Grilled Citrus Salmon

1½ tablespoons fresh lemon juice

2 tablespoons olive oil

1 tablespoon butter

2 dashes salt

1 teaspoon dried dill

3 pounds salmon fillets

1 tablespoon Dijon mustard

4 cloves garlic, minced

2 dashes ground red pepper

1 teaspoon dried basil

2 teaspoons capers

In a small pan over medium heat, combine the lemon juice, olive oil, butter, mustard, garlic, red pepper, salt, basil, dill and capers. Bring to a boil and stir. Reduce heat and simmer for 5 minutes. Place the salmon fillets, skin side down, on a piece of heavy-duty foil with the edges folded up, to make a pan. Pour the sauce evenly over the fish. Put the fish on the grill and cover. Cook over medium hot coals for 10-15 minutes. The fish will be flaky and light pink in color when cooked.

*SERVES 6*

# Glacé Fruit

1 (20 ounce) can pineapple chunks, drained (save juice)

1 (30 ounce) can apricots, drained (save juice)

1 (11 ounce) can Mandarin oranges, drained (save juice)

1 small package instant vanilla pudding

Mix drained fruit together. Mix pudding with 1½ cups of the reserved juices. Pour over fruit. Chill. May use any type of fruits desired, peaches are delicious.

*SERVES 8*

# Easy Roasted Asparagus

Preheat oven to 375°. Wash asparagus and break off the base. Pour olive oil in a glass baking dish. In a bowl, toss asparagus in 3 tablespoons olive oil. Combine equal amounts of bread crumbs and shredded Parmesan cheese. Toss asparagus with the bread mixture. Place asparagus in the pan with the oil. Bake around 20 minutes, depending on the thickness of the asparagus stalks.

# Butterhorns

1 cup butter

12 ounce carton cottage cheese

2 cups flour

Dash of salt

**GLAZE**

1 cup powdered sugar

2 tablespoons milk

½ teaspoon vanilla extract

Cream butter and cottage cheese. Add flour and salt. Chill 4 hours or overnight. Divide into 3 parts. Roll each in circle and cut into 12 wedges. Roll into crescents. Bake in a 350° oven for 30-40 minutes. Mix glaze ingredients in a small bowl; it should be a thin consistency, adjust sugar and milk accordingly.

*MAKES 3 DOZEN*

# Marinated Vegetables

1 medium head cauliflower, cut into flowerets

1 medium bunch fresh broccoli, cut into bite-size pieces

3 medium zucchini, cut into ¼ inch slices

1 pint cherry tomatoes

1 (7.25 ounce) can black olives

1 (16 ounce) bottle Italian dressing

1 package dry Italian dressing

2 teaspoons salt

½ teaspoon pepper

Early in the day, or the day before, place all the ingredients in a large bowl and mix well. Cover and refrigerate at least 6 hours, tossing occasionally. Best if it sets overnight.

*SERVES 12*

# Bits 'n Pieces

# Kids Stuff

## Substitutions

# Sensational Starts

# Extra Touches

Cape Cod Cooler, page 260
Cherry Limeade, page 261
Spanish Coffee, page 260
Poinsettia Cocktail, page 260
Mock Champagne, page 262
Mistletoe and Holly Cocktail, page 261
Sausage-Stuffed Jalapeño Peppers, page 262
Cranberry-Nectarine Salad, page 263
It's the Berries Salad, page 262
Grand Oranges and Strawberries, page 263
Make and Forget Tossed Salad, page 264
Tomato Salad with Cheese Crisps, page 265
Strawberries in Red Wine, page 264
Cookie Dough Truffles, page 265

# Lovin' from the Oven

Pumpkin Pie Crunch, page 266
Glazed Apple Pie Squares, page 266
Pineapple Cake, page 267
Simple Coffee Cake, page 267
Indiana Heath Brunch Coffeecake, page 268
Melt in Your Mouth Pumpkin Cookies, page 268
Foothill House Sweet Dream Cookies, page 269
Sugar Cookies, page 270
Raspberry Coconut Layer Bars, page 271
Millionaire's Shortbread, page 272
Delicious Apple Bread, page 270
Sixty Minute Rolls, page 272
Lemon-Glazed Banana Scones, page 273
White Chocolate Apricot Scones, page 274
Baked Caramel Apples, page 275
Go Nuts, page 271

# Savory Sauces

# Blow Out The Candles

## Substitutions

# As The Cookie Crumbles

# How Sweet It Is

# Potluck

Beef Salami, page 297
No Risk Artichoke Bisque, page 296
Watercress, Avocado and Orange Salad, page 296
Rainbow Chopped Salad, page 299
Mediterranean Potato Salad, page 298
Pork Chops with Apple-Walnut Mix, page 297
Swiss Vegetable Medley, page 297
Amy's Meatloaf, page 299
Chili Con Carne, page 300

# Poultry Potpourri

Baby Drumsticks Oriental, page 301
Chicken Dijon, page 301
Puerto Rican Style Chicken Salad, page 302
Healthy Savory Chicken Chowder, page 303
Healthy Crisp Cobb Salad, page 302
Slow Cooker Coq au Vin, page 304
Chicken and Dressing, page 303
Robin's Chicken Salad, page 304

# All Dressed Up

De La Croix Salad Dressing, page 305
Miso-Sesame Vinaigrette, page 306
Sour Cream Buttermilk Dressing, page 305
Cardamom Dressing, page 306
A Flurry of Curry Dressing, page 307
Feta Dressing, page 307
Jalapeño Cilantro Dressing, page 308
Parmesan Dressing, page 307
Plum Delicious Asian Dressing, page 308

# Hot Dog On A Stick

1 (11 ounce) can refrigerated
  breadstick dough
12 bun length hot dogs

Vegetable cooking spray
Wooden picks, optional

Unroll and divide breadstick dough along perforation marks, creating 12 strips. Gently stretch each strip to the length of 8 inches. Wrap 1 dough strip lengthwise completely around hot dog and, if necessary, secure with a wooden pick. Coat lightly with cooking spray. Place on a lightly greased baking sheet. Bake at 400° for 15 minutes or until golden brown. Let stand 5 minutes then remove wooden picks before serving.

*SERVES 12*

# Dip Sticks with Fruit

Maraschino cherries, reserve juice
Pineapple chunks
Watermelon cubes
Banana, sliced in ½ to ¾ inch pieces
Strawberries

Kiwi, sliced
Red or green seedless grapes
Long bamboo skewers
Fruit yogurt diluted with maraschino
  cherry juice

Choose your favorite fruits from the selection above. Thread 4-5 pieces of fruit on a bamboo skewer. Serve with dip.

To limit "double dipping", all children should have their own bowls of dipping sauce.

# Bite-Size Sour Cream Pound Cake with Vanilla Buttercream Frosting

## CUPCAKES

½ cup butter, softened

4 ounces cream cheese, softened

2 cups sugar

4 eggs

1 teaspoon vanilla extract

3 cups all-purpose flour

1 teaspoon baking powder

½ teaspoon baking soda

½ teaspoon salt

1 (8 ounce) container sour cream

## VANILLA BUTTERCREAM FROSTING

½ cup butter, softened

1 (3 ounce) package cream cheese, softened

2 teaspoons vanilla extract

1 (16 ounce) package powdered sugar

3 to 4 tablespoons milk

Preheat oven to 350°. Beat butter and cream cheese at medium speed with an electric mixer until creamy. Beat in sugar until light and fluffy. Add eggs, one at a time, beating until blended after each addition. Stir in vanilla. Combine flour, baking powder, baking soda and salt. Gradually add to butter mixture alternating with sour cream, beating until blended. Spoon batter by rounded tablespoonfuls into lightly greased miniature muffin pans. Bake for 13-15 minutes or until a wooden pick inserted in the centers of the muffins comes out clean. Cool in pans on a wire rack for 5 minutes. Remove from pans to wire racks, and cool completely (about 30 minutes). Spread cupcakes with frosting. For frosting, beat butter, cream cheese and vanilla at medium speed with an electric mixer until creamy. Gradually add powdered sugar alternately with 3 tablespoons milk, beating at low speed until blended and smooth after each addition. If desired, beat in remaining 1 tablespoon milk, 1 teaspoon at a time, until desired consistency.

*SERVES 6 DOZEN MINI OR 2 DOZEN REGULAR CUPCAKES, BAKED FOR 22 TO 24 MINUTES.*

# M&M Cream Cheese Dip

2 (8 ounce) packages cream cheese, softened
1 cup butter, softened
1½ cups powdered sugar
4 tablespoons firmly packed brown sugar

1 teaspoon vanilla extract
1½ cups mini-chocolate-coated candies
Caramel and chocolate toppings, optional
Graham crackers or graham cracker sticks, optional

Beat together cream cheese and butter. Add powdered sugar, brown sugar and vanilla. Stir in chocolate candies. Cover and chill 2 hours. If desired, pour a topping over and use graham crackers to dip.

*SERVES 3 CUPS*

# Mini Corn Dogs

1 cup reduced-fat milk
1 package active dry yeast
2 tablespoons extra virgin olive oil, plus more for greasing
2 tablespoons firmly packed light brown sugar
1 cup fine yellow cornmeal
1¼ cups all-purpose flour, plus more for dusting and kneading

1 teaspoon salt
¼ teaspoon baking soda
¼ teaspoon cayenne pepper or paprika
9 reduced-fat hot dogs, halved crosswise
1 egg, beaten
Small wooden skewers
1 tablespoon black sesame seeds, optional

Warm the milk to about 110° in a saucepan; pour into a medium bowl. Sprinkle in the yeast and let soften for about 2 minutes. Stir in the olive oil, brown sugar and cornmeal with a wooden spoon. Add the flour, salt, baking soda and cayenne pepper; stir to make a sticky dough. Turn the dough out onto a lightly floured surface and knead, adding more flour if needed, until smooth but still slightly tacky, about 5 minutes. Shape the dough into a ball, place in a lightly oiled bowl and cover with plastic wrap. Let rise in a warm spot until doubled in size, 45-60 minutes. Meanwhile, insert a wooden stick or small skewer into each hot dog half, about 1 inch deep; set aside. Preheat oven to 450°. Turn the dough out onto a lightly floured surface; divide into 18 pieces. With your palms, roll each piece into a 10 inch length. Wrap each piece around a hot dog, tucking and pressing the edges to seal; place on a lightly oiled, large baking sheet. Brush the dough wrapped dogs with the beaten egg; sprinkle with sesame seeds if desired. Bake until golden brown about 15 minutes.

*SERVES 9 OR 18 MINI-CORN DOGS*

# Sweet and Sassy Snack Mix

6 cups crispy rice cereal squares
6 cups crispy corn cereal squares
4 cups crispy wheat squares
2 cups unsalted pecans or mixed nuts
2 cups pretzels, any shape

1¼ cups unsalted butter
1½ cups firmly packed brown sugar
½ teaspoon cayenne pepper
1 teaspoon cinnamon

Preheat oven to 350°. In a large roaster, toss together cereals, pecans and pretzels. In a medium saucepan, melt butter. Add brown sugar, cayenne, and cinnamon to butter, stirring over medium high heat until mixture comes to a boil. Cook at a moderate boil for 1 minute. Remove from heat and immediately pour over cereal mixture. Toss and mix gently to coat cereal evenly with rubber spatula. Pour into a roasting pan. Place roaster into oven and bake for 8 minutes. Remove from oven, stir gently and return to oven for another 12 minutes. Remove from oven, pour out on a clean towel and allow the mixture to cool completely. After completely cool it may be stored in an airtight container for up to 2 weeks.

# Almond Crunch Cookies

Graham crackers (at least 12 doubles)
2 sticks unsalted butter

½ cup sugar
6 ounces or more sliced almonds

Preheat oven to 350°. Line a baking sheet with foil. Cover with graham crackers. Melt butter and sugar. Bring to a boil for 2 minutes. Pour melted butter and sugar over graham crackers. Smooth it all out, then sprinkle sliced almonds over the top of the graham crackers until completely covered. Bake for 20 minutes. Remove from oven and let stand 5 minutes. Remove from pan, turning it upside down onto wax paper. Cool then break or cut apart while still warm.

*MAKES 4 DOZEN*

# Sugar and Nut Glazed Brie

¼ cup firmly packed brown sugar
¼ cup broken walnuts, pecans,
  almonds, macadamia nuts or
  filberts.
1 tablespoon whiskey or brandy

1 (14 ounce) round Brie cheese
  (about 5 inches in diameter)
Apple wedges, seedless grapes and
  crackers
Lemon juice

Preheat oven to 500°. In a small bowl or wide mouthed jar, stir together sugar, nuts and whiskey. Cover and refrigerate up to 1 week. Place cheese on a large round ovenproof platter or 9 inch pie plate. Bake in oven for 4-5 minutes or until cheese is slightly softened. Sprinkle sugar mixture over top; bake 2-3 minutes or more until sugar is melted and cheese is heated through but not melted. Brush apple wedges with lemon juice. Arrange fruit and crackers around cheese.

*SERVES 16-20*

# Flakey Reuben Slices

1 (8 ounce) can crescent rolls
¼ pound thinly sliced corned beef
⅓ cup shredded Swiss cheese

⅓ cup well-drained sauerkraut
½ cup thousand island dressing
1 tablespoon milk

Preheat oven to 375°. Unroll dough into 2 long rectangles. Press each to form 12 inch long rectangles. Press perforations to seal. Layer ½ of corned beef on each rectangle. Top with ½ of cheese and ½ of sauerkraut. Starting at long side, roll up each rectangle tightly. Seal long edges. Place seam side down on ungreased baking sheet. Bake for 12-14 minutes or until golden brown. Cut warm rolls into 1 inch slices. Make dipping sauce by combining thousand island dressing and milk. Mix and serve with Reuben Slices for dipping.

*SERVES 2 DOZEN SLICES*

# Mini-Ham Puffs

2 (2.5 ounce) packages processed ham or smoked turkey, finely chopped
4 tablespoons finely chopped onion
1 cup shredded Swiss or Cheddar cheese
2 eggs
2 tablespoons snipped fresh parsley
1 tablespoon Dijon mustard
¼ teaspoon ground black pepper
1 (8 ounce) package refrigerated crescent rolls

Preheat oven to 350°. Combine meat, onion, cheese, eggs, parsley, mustard and black pepper. Mix well. Unroll crescent dough and press into 1 large rectangle. Cut into 24 squares using pizza cutter. Spray a mini-muffin pan with oil. Press 1 square of dough into each muffin cup. Using a 1 tablespoon scoop, fill each muffin cup with a scant scoop of ham or turkey mixture. Bake for 12-14 minutes or until puffs are light golden brown. Remove from mini-muffin pan and serve immediately.

*SERVES 24 APPETIZERS*

# Cranberry Cheese Box

5 ounces Cheddar cheese, shredded
¼ cup mayonnaise
½ cup chopped onions
¼ teaspoon salt
¼ teaspoon black pepper
¼ to ½ teaspoon ground red pepper
1 cup chopped pecans
1 (8 ounce) can whole cranberry sauce
Garnishes: green onion strips, fresh cranberries and orange curls

Beat cheese, mayonnaise, chopped onions, salt, pepper and red pepper until well blended. Stir in pecans. Shape into a 5x2 inch square. Cover and chill 8 hours or up to 2 days. Spoon cranberry sauce over cheese. Blanch green onion tops and use as ribbons to decorate box. Top with fresh cranberries and orange curls to look like ribbon on a package. Serve with crackers.

*SERVES 6-8*

# Corn Dip

1 can Mexican corn
2 (4 ounce) cans jalapeño peppers, chopped
1 tablespoon picante sauce
½ cup mayonnaise

Dash of cumin
1 (4 ounce) can chopped green chilies
1 tablespoon green onions, chopped
¾ cup grated Cheddar cheese
½ cup sour cream

Mix together and serve with corn chips.

# Chocolate Grape Clusters

½ cup unsalted butter
½ cup milk
½ cup ground almonds or pecans
1 cup cocoa powder
2 cups sugar

2 cups oatmeal (not instant)
1 teaspoon vanilla extract
4 ounces semisweet chocolate (for grape leaf, stem and tendril)

Lightly grease a baking sheet or large pan with sides. Combine the butter, sugar and milk in a saucepan. Let mixture come to a boil over medium heat, then continue cooking at a slow boil for 3 minutes. Remove pan from the heat and immediately stir in ½ cup cocoa, then oatmeal, ground nuts and vanilla. Mix well. Pour batter into the prepared pan. Cool briefly, then refrigerate until the candy hardens somewhat and you can handle it. Scoop up portions of the candy and roll it between the palms of your hands until it is perfectly smooth and in the shape of balls (the size of grapes). Make some slightly smaller than others for a variety of sizes. Roll the balls in the remaining cocoa and chill completely. Arrange the balls to resemble the cluster of grapes on a small serving platter with the smallest of balls at the bottom and the largest stacked toward the top. In a double boiler, melt 4 ounces of semisweet chocolate. Line a cookie sheet with aluminum foil. Select a very large, clean ivy or grape leaf, and brush the melted chocolate over the back of the leaf. Place the leaf on a cookie sheet. Scoop the remaining melted chocolate into a small piping bag and make a rough grape stem 3 inches long and ¾ inches wide with a slight curve to it. Pipe out a long spiraling tendril. Place the cookie sheet in the refrigerator to harden, about 5 minutes. Peel off the leaf from the chocolate and remove the stem and tendril. Arrange them at the top of the cluster.

*MAKES 36 CHOCOLATE GRAPES*

# Reuben Dip

1 (8 ounce) package cream cheese, softened
½ cup sour cream
1 cup sauerkraut, drained and chopped

½ pound lean corned beef, cooked and chopped fine
2 tablespoons onion, finely chopped
2 teaspoons spicy brown mustard
1 cup grated Swiss cheese
Rye crackers or pumpernickel bread

Preheat oven to 375°. Combine all ingredients and bake covered for 30 minutes. Uncover and bake 5 more minutes. Serve with rye crackers or pumpernickel bread or buns.

*SERVES 6-10*

# Tuxedo Strawberries

1 (6 ounce) white chocolate baking square
24 large fresh strawberries, cleaned and dried

6 (1 ounce) semisweet chocolate squares

Melt white chocolate in heavy saucepan or double boiler, stirring constantly. Dip each strawberry into melted white chocolate to just below stem and place on wax paper-lined cookie sheets. Chill until firm. Melt semisweet chocolate in heavy saucepan or double boiler, stirring constantly. Dip 1 side of each strawberry halfway into chocolate; then dip half of opposite side of strawberry in chocolate forming a V with semisweet chocolate. Chill until firm. Spoon remaining melted semisweet chocolate into a small heavy duty zip-top plastic bag and seal. Prick tiny hole in 1 corner of plastic bag and pipe a bow tie and 3 buttons onto each strawberry to resemble a miniature tuxedo. Chill until chocolate is firm.

*SERVES 24*

May be made the night before. Let sit out 15-20 minutes before serving.

# Kahlúa Dip

1 (8 ounce) package cream cheese
1⅔ cups frozen nondairy whipped
   cream, thawed
¾ cup firmly packed brown sugar

1 cup sour cream
⅓ cup Kahlúa
⅓ cup chopped pecans
Fruit of choice

Mix together cream cheese, whipped cream, brown sugar, sour cream and Kahlúa. Add chopped pecans just before serving. Serve as a dip for bite-size pieces of any variety of fruit you wish.

*SERVES 6-8*

# Caramelized Onion Dip

2 tablespoons olive oil
2 medium-sized Vidalia onions,
   chopped
¾ cup mayonnaise

¾ cup sour cream
Salt and pepper to taste
1 bag sweet potato chips

Heat oil in large skillet. Stir in chopped onions and caramelize by cooking for 20 minutes over medium heat stirring frequently. Cool completely. Mix the mayonnaise, sour cream and a pinch of salt and pepper. Then add the cooled caramelized onions. Mix thoroughly. Refrigerate several hours or overnight. Taste, add salt and pepper if needed. Serve with chips.

*SERVES 8*

If you wish to kick up the heat a little, substitute in 1 tablespoon of oil infused with red pepper and 1 tablespoon of regular olive oil for the 2 tablespoons of olive oil above. If time is short you may substitute 1 bag of frozen chopped onions for the Vidalia onions above. You may substitute light mayonnaise and light sour cream, but not fat free.

# Cape Cod Cooler

1 (48 ounce) bottle cranberry juice
cocktail
1½ cups vodka
⅓ cup sweetened lime juice

1 (1 liter) bottle ginger ale, chilled
Ice cubes
Fresh cranberries for garnish
Lime wedges on swizzle sticks

Stir together cranberry juice cocktail, vodka and sweetened lime juice. Stir in ginger ale just before serving. Serve over ice and garnish if desired.

*SERVES 20*

# Spanish Coffee

Coffee (make enough to cover the
amount of servings desired)
Lemon (enough juice of the lemon in
which to dip the rim of cups)
Sugar (enough to coat rim of cup)
Rum

Coffee-flavored liqueur
Triple sec
Nutmeg
(enough for a pinch in each cup)
Cinnamon

Use glass coffee cups with handles. Mix the nutmeg and cinnamon together. Rim cups with juice of lemon dipped in sugar. Fill cups half full with hot coffee. Mix equal amounts of each liqueur together (the amount depends on how much you are making). In a saucepan warm the liqueur slightly until it is hot enough to light with a match (do not boil as it will boil out the alcohol). With the help of a friend, light the alcohol with a fireplace lighter. Pour the flaming liqueur on top of coffee. Before the flame dies throw in a pinch of cinnamon/nutmeg into each flaming cup. The cinnamon/nutmeg will shoot up sparks making a nice presentation.

# Poinsettia Cocktail

1.5 ounces triple sec
¼ cup cranberry juice

½ cup Prosecco or champagne

Pour triple sec and cranberry juice into a chilled champagne flute. Top with Prosecco or champagne.

*SERVES 2*

# Cherry Limeade

¾ cup lime juice
Non-nutritive sweetener, equal to
1 cup sugar
2 liters lime carbonated water, chilled

½ cup maraschino cherry juice
8 maraschino cherries with stems
8 lime slices

In a large bowl, combine lime juice and non-nutritive sweetener. Cover and refrigerate. Just before serving, stir lime carbonated water into lime juice mixture. For each serving, place 1 tablespoon cherry juice in a glass. Add crushed ice and about 1 cup of lime juice mixture. Garnish with a maraschino cherry and a lime slice.

*SERVES 8*

# Mistletoe and Holly Cocktail

12 fresh cranberries for garnish
1½ cups cranberry juice
(100 percent juice)
¼ cup (2 ounces) white crème de cacao
¼ cup (2 ounces) 100-proof
peppermint schnapps

¼ cup whipping cream, lightly
whipped with 1 teaspoon sugar for
garnish
Pinch of matte green Matcha powder
for garnish

Spear 3 cranberries each onto 4 bamboo skewers or heat proof swizzle sticks. Pour cranberry juice into a small saucepan over medium heat and bring to a simmer. Lower heat, add crème de cacao and peppermint schnapps and stir to blend and release some of the alcohol. Continue to cook over low heat for exactly 1 minute. Pour the hot beverage into footed glass mugs and place a small dollop of whipped cream on each. Garnish with cranberry skewers and use a fine mesh sieve to gently tap a light dusting of Matcha over the whipped cream. Serve hot.

*SERVES 4*

Replace the fresh cranberry garnish with an old-fashioned candy cane if you wish.

# Mock Champagne

1 small can frozen lemonade, diluted as instructed on container

2 large bottles white grape juice
1 liter bottle ginger ale

Mix all ingredients together. Use pink lemonade for a blush look. You can adjust the look and taste by changing the proportions of ingredients.

*SERVES 10*

# Sausage-Stuffed Jalapeño Peppers

1 pound ground sausage, cooked and drained
1 (8 ounce) package cream cheese

½ cup (4 ounces) grated Parmesan cheese
20-22 large jalapeño peppers, halved and seeded

Mix sausage and cheese then stuff into pepper halves. Bake at 425° until brown and bubbly. Be careful, the peppers are very hot right out of the oven.

*SERVES 20*

# It's the Berries Salad

1 pound fresh spinach, washed and torn
1 pint strawberries, hulled and sliced
¼ to ½ cup sugar
2 tablespoons sesame seeds
¼ teaspoon paprika

¼ teaspoon Worcestershire sauce
¼ cup cider vinegar
1 tablespoon poppy seeds
1½ teaspoons minced onion
½ cup oil

In blender (or food processor) mix sugar, sesame seeds, Worcestershire sauce, vinegar, poppy seeds, onion and paprika. With machine running slowly, add oil. Blend well. Toss with strawberries and spinach just before serving.

*SERVES 4-6*

# Cranberry-Nectarine Salad

1 (3 ounce) package Oriental flavored
   dry noodle soup mix
½ cup dried cranberries
1 cup hot water
⅓ cup canola oil
1 tablespoon firmly packed light
   brown sugar
2 tablespoons balsamic vinegar
2 tablespoons rice wine vinegar

1 tablespoon soy sauce
1 (10 ounce) package mixed salad
   greens, washed thoroughly
3 large nectarines, peeled and cut into
   wedges
½ cup coarsely chopped walnuts
1 (4 ounce) package crumbled feta
   cheese

Preheat oven to 350°. Reserve flavor packet from the soup mix. Crumble noodles and place in a single layer in a shallow pan. Bake for 5 to 6 minutes or until toasted, stirring occasionally. Cool completely in pan on a wire rack (about 15 minutes). Place cranberries in a small bowl; add hot water. Let stand 5 minutes; drain. Whisk together reserved soup flavor packet, canola oil, brown sugar, balsamic vinegar, red wine vinegar and soy sauce in a large bowl. Add noodles from dry noodle soup mix, cranberries, salad greens, nectarines, walnuts and feta cheese tossing gently to coat evenly. Serve immediately.

*SERVES 4*

# Grand Oranges and Strawberries

½ cup orange marmalade
1½ cups sparkling white grape juice,
   chilled
¼ cup orange liqueur

10-12 large navel oranges, peeled and
   sectioned
2 cups sliced fresh strawberries
Fresh mint for garnish

Melt marmalade in a small saucepan over low heat, stirring constantly. Remove from heat and let cool slightly. Stir together marmalade, white grape juice and orange liqueur in a large serving dish or bowl until blended. Add orange sections and stir gently. Cover and chill 8 hours. Add strawberries to oranges in serving dish and gently toss to coat. Garnish if desired.

*SERVES 10-12*

# Make and Forget Tossed Salad

3 tablespoons oil

1 tablespoon lemon juice

Beau Monde Seasoning

1 bunch green onions, chopped

1 bunch romaine lettuce, torn

1 avocado, sliced

Fresh Parmesan cheese

In bottom of large bowl mix together oil and lemon juice. Sprinkle liberally on top Beau Monde seasoning-do not mix. Without mixing, sprinkle green onion on top. Add romaine lettuce on top. Seal tight with plastic wrap and refrigerate overnight. Add avocado and toss salad, making sure you get to the bottom of the bowl to the dressing. Sprinkle with the desired amount of Parmesan cheese and mix thoroughly. Serve immediately.

*SERVES 4-6*

# Strawberries in Red Wine

2 quarts fresh strawberries

1 bottle dry red wine

2 cups sugar

1 tablespoon fresh lemon juice

Zest from 2 lemons

Zest from 2 oranges

2 cinnamon sticks, approximately 3 inches long

10 whole black peppercorns

Pinch of kosher salt

Vanilla ice cream or whipped cream, for garnish

Clean strawberries and cut into desired size. In a heavy saucepan combine wine, sugar, lemon juice, lemon zest, orange zest, cinnamon sticks, peppercorns and salt. Cook over medium high heat, stirring occasionally, until the sauce is reduced by at least half about 15 minutes. Strain and serve warm or at room temperature over the strawberries and garnish with vanilla ice cream or whipped cream.

*SERVES 8*

This sauce is amazingly versatile. Drizzle over pound cake or chocolate cake. Reduce it even further, spoon into a fine tipped plastic squirt bottle and use it decoratively to 'paint' dessert plates. Keeps well in the refrigerator and makes a thoughtful gift in a decorative jar.

# Tomato Salad with Cheese Crisps

4 thick slices Italian bread, cut into cubes

¼ cup extra virgin olive oil, divided

Kosher salt and freshly ground black pepper

1 tablespoon Dijon mustard

1 tablespoon fresh lemon juice

2 tablespoons white wine vinegar

2 pounds mixed heirloom tomatoes, cut into chunks

1 bunch green onions, sliced

2 tablespoons fresh dill, chopped

¾ cup Gruyère cheese, grated

1 tablespoon all-purpose flour

Preheat oven to 400°. Toss the bread with 2 tablespoons olive oil on a baking sheet and season with salt and pepper. Bake until golden, about 8 minutes. Let cool slightly. Whisk mustard, lemon juice and vinegar in a large bowl and season with salt and pepper. Slowly whisk in the remaining 2 tablespoons of olive oil. Add the tomatoes, onions, dill and season with salt and pepper. Add the bread cubes and toss to coat. Set aside while you make the crisps. In a large bowl toss the cheese with the flour and pepper to taste. Arrange the mixture in 4 mounds on a baking sheet and flatten slightly. Bake until golden, about 10 minutes. Cool slightly, then remove with a spatula to a rack and let cool. Serve with the tomato salad.

*SERVES 4*

# Cookie Dough Truffles

½ cup butter, softened

½ cup firmly packed brown sugar

¼ cup thawed egg substitute

1 teaspoon vanilla extract

1¼ cups all-purpose flour

1 cup miniature semisweet chocolate chips

¾ cup chopped pecans or walnuts

1 (12 ounce) package semisweet chocolate chips

1½ tablespoons solid shortening

Beat butter at medium speed until creamy. Gradually add brown sugar beating well. Add egg substitute and vanilla, beat well. Add flour to mixture and beat well. Stir in miniature chocolate chips and nuts. Cover and chill 30 minutes. Shape mixture into 1 inch balls. Cover and freeze until very firm. Place package of semisweet chocolate chips and shortening in a 1 quart glass bowl and melt in the microwave, according to package directions. Using two forks, quickly dip frozen truffles into melted chocolate mixture, coating completely. Place on wax paper to harden. Store truffles in refrigerator for 2-3 days.

*MAKES 4½ DOZEN*

# Pumpkin Pie Crunch

1 (15 ounce) can pure pumpkin
1 (15 ounce) can evaporated milk
3 eggs
1½ cups sugar
4 teaspoons pumpkin pie spice

½ teaspoon salt
1 (18.5 ounce) box yellow cake mix
1 cup pecans, coarsely chopped
1 cup melted butter
Frozen nondairy whipped topping

Preheat oven to 350°. Combine pumpkin, evaporated milk, eggs, sugar, pumpkin pie spice and salt in a bowl. Pour into a greased 9x13 inch pan. Sprinkle the dry cake mix over the pumpkin mixture, then sprinkle the pecans on. Pour the melted butter over the mixture. Bake for 50-55 minutes. Serve warm or cool with whipped topping.

*SERVES 12*

# Glazed Apple Pie Squares

2½ cups all-purpose flour
1 teaspoon salt
1 cup cold butter
1 egg, separated
3-4 tablespoons milk
1 cup crushed cornflakes

9 cups (about 10 medium sized) tart
   apples, peeled and thinly sliced
1 cup plus 2 tablespoons sugar, divided
2 teaspoons ground cinnamon, divided
½ teaspoon ground nutmeg

GLAZE
1 cup powdered sugar
½ teaspoon vanilla extract

1-2 tablespoons milk

Preheat oven to 350°. In a large bowl, combine flour and salt; cut in butter until mixture resembles coarse crumbs. In a measuring cup combine egg yolk and enough milk to measure ⅓ cup. Gradually add to flour mixture, tossing with a fork until dough forms a ball. Divide dough in half. Roll 1 portion into a thin 15x10 inch rectangle. Transfer to the bottom of an ungreased 15x10 inch baking pan. Sprinkle with cornflakes. In a large bowl, combine the apples, 1 cup sugar, 1½ teaspoons cinnamon and nutmeg; toss to coat. Spoon over crust. Roll remaining dough into a thin 15x10 inch rectangle; place over apple filling. Beat egg white; brush over pastry. Combine remaining sugar and cinnamon; sprinkle over the top. Bake for 45-50 minutes or until golden brown. For glaze, combine powdered sugar, vanilla and enough milk to achieve a drizzling consistency. Drizzle over warm pastry. Cool completely on a wire rack. Cut into squares.

*SERVES 2 DOZEN*

# Pineapple Cake

**CAKE**

2 cups all-purpose flour

2 cups sugar

2 eggs

1 (14.5 ounce) can crushed
   pineapple

2 teaspoons baking soda

**ICING**

½ cup butter

1 (8 ounce) package cream cheese

1¾ cups powdered sugar

Preheat oven to 350°. Mix flour, sugar, eggs, pineapple and baking soda together. Bake on a greased baking sheet for 35 minutes. For icing mix butter, cream cheese and powdered sugar together; spread over cooled cake.

*SERVES 18*

# Simple Coffee Cake

**COFFEE CAKE**

1 (18.5 ounce) box yellow cake mix

½ cup sugar

4 eggs

1 cup sour cream

¾ cup oil

**TOPPING**

1 cup firmly packed brown sugar

4 teaspoons cinnamon

**ICING**

2 tablespoons milk

½ teaspoon vanilla extract

1 cup powdered sugar

Preheat oven to 350°. Mix cake mix, sugar, eggs, sour cream and oil together. For topping, mix powdered sugar and cinnamon together. Put ½ of cake mixture in a 9x13 inch greased pan. Sprinkle ⅔ of topping over cake mixture. Top with the remaining cake mixture. Sprinkle the rest of the topping over this. Take a knife and swirl blade back and forth through mixture to marbleize. Bake for 45-55 minutes. For icing; mix the milk, vanilla and powdered sugar until smooth. Spread over the cake while it is still hot.

*SERVES 12-15*

# Indiana Heath Brunch Coffeecake

½ cup butter
2 cups all-purpose flour
1 cup firmly packed brown sugar
1 cup buttermilk
1 teaspoon baking soda

1 egg
1 teaspoon vanilla extract
2 (1.125 ounces) chocolate-covered
toffee candy bars, finely chopped
¼ cup pecans or almonds, chopped

Preheat oven to 350°. Cut butter into flour and brown sugar. Reserve ½ cup of mixture. To remaining mix; add buttermilk, baking soda, egg and vanilla. Blend. Pour into greased 9x13 inch pan. Mix candy bars, nuts and reserved mixture. Sprinkle over top of batter. Bake for 30 minutes.

*SERVES 12-15*

# Melt in Your Mouth Pumpkin Cookies

2½ cups butter, softened and divided
2 cups sugar
2 teaspoons baking powder
2 teaspoons baking soda
1 teaspoon salt
1 teaspoon ground cinnamon
1 teaspoon ground nutmeg
2 eggs

3 teaspoons vanilla extract, divided
1 (15 ounce) can pumpkin
4 cups all-purpose flour
½ cup firmly packed brown sugar
¼ cup milk
2¾ cups powdered sugar
Ground cinnamon, optional

Preheat oven to 350°. In a large bowl beat 2 cups butter with an electric mixer on medium to high speed for 30 seconds. Add sugar, baking powder, baking soda, salt, cinnamon and nutmeg. Beat until combined, scraping bowl occasionally. Add eggs and 2 teaspoons vanilla; beat until combined. Stir in pumpkin. Beat in as much of the flour as you can with the mixer. Using a wooden spoon, stir in any remaining flour. Drop dough by heaping teaspoonfuls 2 inches apart on an ungreased cookie sheet. Bake for 10-12 minutes or until tops are set. Transfer cookies to a wire rack; let cool. In a small saucepan, heat ½ cup butter and brown sugar until melted and smooth. Transfer to a medium bowl. Stir in milk and 1 teaspoon vanilla. Beat in powdered sugar until smooth. Spread frosting on cookies. If desired sprinkle with additional cinnamon.

*SERVES 5 DOZEN*

# Foothill House Sweet Dream Cookies

1 cup unsalted butter

1½ cups firmly packed light brown sugar

1 egg, at room temperature

1 teaspoon vanilla extract

2½ cups all-purpose flour

1 teaspoon baking soda

1 teaspoon cinnamon

1 teaspoon ginger

½ teaspoon salt

1 (12 ounce) package semisweet chocolate chips

1 cup walnuts, chopped

1 cup powdered sugar

Cream butter, beat in brown sugar, egg and vanilla. Combine flour, baking soda, cinnamon, ginger and salt. Blend into butter mixture. Fold in chocolate chips and walnuts. Refrigerate until firm. Preheat oven to 375°. Lightly grease baking sheets. Make dough into 1 inch round balls. Dredge balls in powdered sugar. Arrange balls on baking sheet, spacing at least 2 inches apart. Bake for 10 minutes. Let cool 5 minutes on sheets. Transfer to racks and cool. Store in an airtight container.

*SERVES 2-3 DOZEN*

The dough may be made a day ahead to save time.

# Sugar Cookies

**COOKIE**

1 cup butter, softened

1 cup powdered sugar

1 cup sugar

1 teaspoon vanilla extract

2 eggs

1 cup cooking oil

4 cups all-purpose flour

1 teaspoon baking soda

1 teaspoon cream of tartar

½ teaspoon salt

**FROSTING**

3 cups powdered sugar

½ cup butter, softened

1½ teaspoons vanilla extract

2 tablespoons milk

Using cookie ingredients, cream butter, powdered sugar and sugar together. Add vanilla, eggs and cooking oil. Blend well. In a separate bowl combine flour, baking soda, cream of tartar and salt. With a mixer on the lowest speed, slowly add the flour mixture by spoonfuls to dough mixture. Refrigerate overnight or at least 2 hours. Preheat oven to 350°. Roll the dough out on a floured surface and use a cookie cutter of your favorite shapes. Transfer onto an ungreased cookie sheet. Bake 9-11 minutes Make the frosting by combining in a mixer the butter, vanilla and milk. Beat until creamy. Add the powdered sugar slowly, then beat the mixture until it is smooth. Wait until the cookies have cooled completely before frosting.

*SERVES 3 DOZEN*

# Delicious Apple Bread

3 cups all-purpose flour

3 teaspoons baking powder

½ teaspoon salt

2¾ cups sugar, divided

1 cup oil

4 eggs

2 tablespoons orange juice

2½ teaspoons vanilla extract

4 large apples, chopped

2 teaspoons cinnamon

Preheat oven to 350°. Sift together the flour, baking powder and salt, put aside. Blend together 2½ cups sugar and oil. Add the eggs, orange juice and vanilla and beat well. Spoon the flour mixture slowly into the batter and beat until smooth. In separate bowl mix the apples with the cinnamon and ¼ cup sugar until coated. Fold the apples into the batter. Place in a loaf pan and bake for 45 minutes.

*SERVES 1 LOAF*

# Raspberry Coconut Layer Bars

1⅔ cups graham cracker crumbs
½ cup butter, melted
2⅔ cups (7 ounce) package flaked coconut
1¼ cups (14 ounce) can sweetened condensed milk
1 cup red raspberry jam or preserves
⅓ cup walnuts, finely chopped and toasted
½ cup semisweet chocolate chips, melted
¼ cup white milk chocolate pieces, melted

Preheat oven to 350°. In a medium bowl, combine graham cracker crumbs and butter. Spread evenly over bottom of 9x13 inch baking pan; pressing to make a compact crust. Sprinkle coconut over crust. Pour sweetened condensed milk evenly over coconut. Bake for 20-25 minutes or until lightly browned. Cool. Spread jam over coconut layer. Sprinkle with walnuts. Chill 3-4 hours. Drizzle separately the semisweet and white milk chocolate over the top layer, making a lacy effect. Chill. Cut into 24 bars.

*SERVES 24*

# Go Nuts

1 egg white
1 tablespoon water
⅔ cup sugar
Kosher salt
1 teaspoon pumpkin pie spice or chai spice blend
¼ teaspoon cayenne pepper
3 cups assorted mixed nuts
2 dashes Worcestershire sauce

Preheat oven to 275°. Line a large baking sheet with parchment paper. Whisk the egg white with water in a large bowl until frothy. In a small bowl, combine sugar, salt, spice blend and cayenne pepper. Toss the nuts in the egg white mixture, then stir in the sugar spice mixture and Worcestershire sauce. Spoon the nuts onto the prepared baking sheet in small clusters. Bake until golden, 30-35 minutes. Cool completely, then break into pieces.

*SERVES 3 CUPS*

Turn store bought waffle cones into mini cornucopias: just fill the cones with spiced nuts and put one at each place setting.

# Sixty Minute Rolls

2 packages active dry yeast
¼ cup lukewarm water
3 tablespoons sugar
1¼ cups milk

1 teaspoon salt
¼ cup butter, divided
4 cups all-purpose flour

Preheat oven to 400°. Soak yeast in water for about 5 minutes. Place sugar, milk, salt and 2 tablespoons butter in a large saucepan. Heat until lukewarm. Remove from heat. Add yeast mixture. Gradually add flour and mix well. Cover with a dish towel and place the pan in a warm place, about 15 minutes. Turn onto a floured board and pat until ¾ inch thick. Cut with a biscuit cutter or a glass. Fold each circle of dough in half and place a pat of butter inside the fold. Put rolls on a baking sheet, cover with a dish towel and let rise in a warm place for 15 minutes. Bake for 10 minutes or until golden brown.

*SERVES 2 DOZEN*

# Millionaire's Shortbread

**SHORTBREAD**
1 cup butter, cut into small pieces
2 cups all-purpose flour

⅔ cup sugar
½ teaspoon salt

**CARAMEL LAYER**
2 (14 ounce) cans sweetened
   condensed milk

2 tablespoons butter

**TOPPING**
¾ pound good quality milk chocolate

Preheat oven to 350°. Butter 2 (8 or 9 inch) square nonstick pans and coat with flour, tapping off excess. Place flour, sugar and salt in a food processor and pulse once. Add butter and pulse until mixture resembles peas. Press the shortbread mixture into prepared pans and bake until golden brown around the edges, about 20 minutes. Remove from oven and cool completely. For the caramel layer, in a heavy bottomed saucepan over medium- low heat, combine the condensed milk and butter. Slowly bring the mixture to a boil, stirring continuously. Continue stirring over medium-low heat until mixture becomes thick and amber in color; about 15-20 minutes. Pour the caramel over the cooled shortbread and spread evenly. Cool to room temperature..Melt the chocolate in a glass bowl over simmering water, double boiler or microwave oven. Pour melted chocolate over the cooled caramel layer. Cool at room temperature for about 10 minutes and then place in refrigerator to cool completely. Cut into 2 inch squares.

*SERVES 24*

# Lemon-Glazed Banana Scones

## SCONES

2 cups all-purpose flour; more as needed

¼ cup sugar

2¼ teaspoons baking powder

1 teaspoon finely grated lemon zest

⅜ teaspoon salt

5½ tablespoons cold unsalted butter, cut into pieces

1 small ripe (but not mushy) banana, diced into ¼ inch pieces (½ cup)

1 tablespoon minced crystallized ginger

¾ cup plus 2 tablespoons heavy cream, more for brushing

Coarse white sanding sugar, optional

## GLAZE

¾ cup powdered sugar

1½ tablespoons fresh lemon juice

1 tablespoon unsalted butter, softened

Pinch of salt

Preheat oven to 375°. Stack two rimmed baking sheets and line the top one with parchment paper. Position a rack in the top third of the oven. In a large bowl, whisk the flour, sugar, baking powder, lemon zest and salt. With your fingers, rub the butter into the flour mixture until a few pea size lumps remain. Stir in the banana and ginger. Add cream with a fork, gradually stir until the mixture just comes together. Turn the dough onto a lightly floured surface and pat gently into a 7 inch circle about 1 inch thick. Cut the dough into 8 wedges. Transfer to the baking sheet, spacing the wedges 1-2 inches apart. Brush the tops with heavy cream and sprinkle liberally with sanding sugar if you wish. Bake until the tops are golden, 19-25 minutes. Rotate the baking sheet halfway through baking for even browning. Transfer the scones to a wire rack and cool slightly, 3-4 minutes. In a small bowl, stir the powdered sugar, lemon juice, butter and salt until smooth. Drizzle the warm scones with the glaze. Serve warm or at room temperature.

*SERVES 8*

# White Chocolate Apricot Scones

2 cups all-purpose flour
⅓ cup sugar
2 teaspoons baking powder
½ teaspoon salt
¼ cup unsalted butter
½ cup whipping cream

1 egg
1 teaspoon vanilla extract
6 ounce bar white chocolate, cut into small chunks
1 cup dried apricots, chopped

Preheat oven to 350°. In large bowl, stir together flour, sugar, baking powder and salt. Cut butter into ½ inch cubes, cut into flour until it resembles coarse crumbs. In a small bowl, stir together cream, eggs and vanilla. Add cream mixture to flour mixture and knead until combined. Knead in the apricots and white chocolate chunks. With a lightly floured hand, pat dough into small circles (about 3 inches). Place circles on an ungreased cookie sheet. Bake approximately 15-20 minutes.

*SERVES 8-10*

Don't work dough too much as it will make your scones more dense.

To make self-rising flour, add 1 teaspoon baking powder and ¼ teaspoon salt to every cup of all-purpose flour, mixing thoroughly.

# Baked Caramel Apples

Unsalted butter to coat pan
Enough sugar to coat pan
¼ cup apple cider
⅛ cup brandy or apple cider
1 teaspoon vanilla extract
1 teaspoon ground cinnamon
¼ teaspoon ground cloves
4 tablespoons unsalted butter, melted

¼ cup sugar
½ cup firmly packed brown sugar
4 apples, cored and peeled
1 regular package refrigerated sugar cookie dough
¼ cup whipping cream
2 tablespoons cinnamon sugar (2 tablespoons sugar with 2 teaspoons cinnamon)

Preheat oven to 350°. Coat a shallow roasting pan with butter and sugar. In a bowl, combine apple cider, brandy, vanilla, cinnamon, cloves, melted butter, sugar and brown sugar. Mix well. Cut each apple into 4 large wedges. Coat well in sugar mixture. Place sugared apples in pan. Pour remaining sugar mixture in pan to cook into caramel sauce. Dot the apples with the cookie dough until about ¾ of the apple surface is covered. Lightly brush cookie dough with whipping cream and sprinkle with cinnamon sugar. Bake until dough is golden brown and apple sugar begins to bubble, 10-15 minutes. Serve apples warm with a bowl of ice cream.

*SERVES 15*

If preferred, substitute additional apple cider for the brandy. Try butter pecan ice cream instead of vanilla.

We like to have fun and increase our Ways & Means earnings at the same time. Over the years we have had funfests such as Las Vegas Nights, auctions, bridge tournaments, themed dinners, Jeans and Martini Nights and Trivia Nights.

# Blender Hollandaise

4 egg yolks
4 tablespoons lemon juice
¼ teaspoon salt

¼ teaspoon ground cayenne pepper
1 cup butter, melted

Put egg yolks, lemon juice, salt and cayenne in a blender. While blending, slowly add melted butter until well mixed. Store in refrigerator. Great for vegetables and Eggs Benedict.

*SERVES 2 CUPS*

# White Horseradish Sauce

1½ cups mayonnaise
Juice of ½ lemon
¼ cup cider vinegar
¼ cup water
1 tablespoon horseradish

1 teaspoon salt
1 teaspoon black pepper
1 teaspoon sugar
1 teaspoon cayenne pepper

Blend well and refrigerate. This is great with meats.

*SERVES 2 CUPS*

# Lemon Mint Dressing

½ cup unflavored honey
¼ cup water
½ teaspoon ground cardamom
½ teaspoon ground coriander
1 teaspoon lemon zest

Juice of 1 lemon
¼ cup fresh mint, finely chopped
⅛ teaspoon salt
¼ cup olive oil

In a small saucepan, combine honey, water, cardamom and coriander and bring to a boil. Reduce the heat to simmer for 2 minutes. Add lemon zest, lemon juice, mint, salt and olive oil. Stir until mixture is smooth. Refrigerate until needed.

*SERVE 1 CUP*

This is a fantastic dressing for fruit.
1 tablespoon of dried mint may be substituted for the fresh mint.

# Pesto

1 cup firmly packed fresh basil leaves
½ cup torn spinach leaves
¼ cup grated Parmesan or Romano cheese
¼ cup almonds

2 cloves garlic, quartered
2 tablespoons olive oil
½ teaspoon salt, divided
2 tablespoons water

Put cheese, basil, spinach, nuts, garlic and salt in a food processor. Cover and blend several times. Scrape the sides then slowly add oil and water. Blend until it is the consistency of soft butter. If it is too thick add a little more oil or water. Cover and store in the refrigerator for 2 days.

*SERVES 1½ CUPS*

This may be frozen in ice cube trays or sandwich bags until you need it.

# "Nick & Jakes" Red Wine Vinaigrette

2 cups olive oil
1 cup red wine vinegar
1 teaspoon salt
1 teaspoon sugar
1 teaspoon black pepper, finely ground
1½ tablespoons lemon juice

1 tablespoon garlic powder
1 tablespoon oregano
1 teaspoon thyme
¼ cup Dijon mustard
½ cup Parmesan cheese, grated
1 tablespoon garlic, chopped

Combine vinegar, sugar, salt, pepper, lemon juice, garlic powder, oregano, thyme, mustard, cheese and chopped garlic in a blender. Blend at medium speed; very slowly add the olive oil in a gentle stream. Refrigerate.

*MAKES 1 QUART*

# Bolognese Sauce

2 pounds hot Italian sausage

2 pounds ground beef

½ cup unsalted butter

1 large yellow onion, cut into ½ inch dice

1 medium green pepper, seeded, cored and diced

2 ribs celery, cut into ¼ inch dice

2 (28 ounce) cans Italian plum tomatoes, broken up

1 bay leaf (can use dried)

3 tablespoons dried oregano

2 tablespoons dried basil

2 teaspoons salt

1 teaspoon freshly ground black pepper

1 cup dry red wine

2 (6 ounce) cans tomato paste

⅛ teaspoon ground cinnamon

Cut the sausage into ¼ inch pieces and brown in heavy skillet. Drain and set aside. Brown ground beef in same skillet, drain and set aside. Melt butter in large saucepan over medium heat. Add onion, green pepper and celery and sauté until limp, about 5 minutes. Stir in sausage, beef, tomatoes with liquid, bay leaf, oregano, basil, salt and pepper. Simmer covered for 30-40 minutes. Stir in the wine, tomato paste, and cinnamon and simmer covered for 15 minutes or more. Take out bay leaf and let stand for at least 30 minutes before serving, but preferably overnight to enhance the flavor. Serve over your choice of pasta.

*SERVES A CROWD*

Italian turkey sausage may be substituted for the regular Italian sausage. Try doubling the cinnamon, it adds a unique flavor.

Store that bumper crop of fresh herbs for use all year long. Chop the fresh herbs and store in zip-top plastic gags. Freeze for future use.

# Tequila Salad Dressing

1 teaspoon cumin seed, toasted and
   mashed
4 cloves garlic, minced
1 cup safflower oil
½ cup red wine vinegar

2 tablespoons sugar
1 teaspoon salt
¼ cup tequila
Juice of 1 lime

Combine cumin, oil, garlic, vinegar, sugar, salt, tequila and lime juice and mix well. Refrigerate until serving.

*APPROXIMATELY 2 CUPS*

One teaspoon of ground cumin may be substituted for the cumin seed.

# Pork Rub Seasoning

4 tablespoons brown sugar
2 tablespoons onion powder
2 tablespoons garlic powder
2 tablespoons dried thyme
2 tablespoons dried oregano
1 tablespoon mild paprika
1 tablespoon hot paprika

2 teaspoons cayenne pepper
2 teaspoons ground coriander
1 teaspoon freshly ground black
   pepper
1 teaspoon freshly ground white
   pepper
1 tablespoon kosher salt

Combine sugar, onion and garlic powders, thyme, oregano, paprika (both mild and hot), cayenne, coriander, peppers (both black and white) and salt in a bowl and mix together. Rub ribs with seasoning.

# Best Grilled Cheese Ever

½ cup softened butter
½ cup fresh Parmesan cheese, grated
16 slices Italian bread

16 slices Provolone cheese
Marinara sauce for dipping, warmed

Blend butter and Parmesan cheese. Spread onto 1 side of each slice of bread. Heat griddle on medium-high heat. Put butter side down on griddle. Put 2 slices of Provolone on each. Top with an additional slice of bread with buttered side up. Grill until lightly browned on each side. Cut in thirds and serve with the warm marinara sauce for dipping.

*8 SANDWICHES*

# Salad Shooters

1 green pepper, sliced into strips
1 red pepper, sliced into strips
1 carrot, sliced into strips

2 ribs celery, sliced into strips
1 bottle ranch dressing
   (or your choice, such as blue cheese)

Pour 2 tablespoons of dressing into bottom of short juice glass. Place strips lengthwise into the glass.

*SERVES 8*

# Peanut Butter Sticks

1 loaf dense bread, not thinly sliced
1 cup creamy peanut butter

1 scant cup vegetable oil

Preheat oven to 300°. Remove the crusts from each slice of bread. Place crusts on a cookie sheet and toast in oven until golden brown and dry. Remove from oven and roll with a rolling pin to make very fine crumbs. Cut bread slices into 5-6 strips. Preheat oven to 400°. Place strips on cookie sheet. Brown until golden, approximately 5 minutes. Flip slices over and continue another 5 minutes or so until this side is also golden brown. Melt peanut butter in a double boiler. Add oil and mix together. Place toasted bread strips in a bowl and pour in the peanut butter mixture. Toss until all strips are coated with mixture. Remove strips from bowl; roll into crumbs of crusts. Cool. Store in an airtight container.

*SERVES ABOUT 5 DOZEN*

# White Chocolate Snack Mix

1 (10 ounce) package mini twist
  pretzels
5 cups toasted oat cereal
5 cups crispy corn cereal
2 cups salted peanuts

1 (14 ounce) package candy-coated
  milk chocolate pieces
2 (11 ounce) packages white chocolate
  chips
3 tablespoons vegetable oil

Line 3 baking sheets with waxed paper or parchment paper. Set aside. In a large bowl, combine pretzels, oat cereal, corn cereal squares, peanuts and candy-coated chocolate pieces. Set aside. In a microwave safe bowl, heat white chocolate chips and oil on medium high for (approximately 2 minutes), stirring once. Microwave on high for 10 seconds; stir until smooth. Pour over cereal mixture and mix well. Spread onto prepared baking sheets. Cool completely; break apart. Store in an airtight container.

*SERVES 15 CUPS*

# Caramel Apple Dip

1 (8 ounce) package cream cheese
¾ cup lightly packed light brown sugar

1 tablespoon vanilla extract

Mix the cream cheese, sugar and vanilla in a food processor or blender until smooth. Serve as a dip for apple slices.

*SERVES 1 CUP*

# Party Mix

2 cups O-shaped oat cereal
3 cups bite-sized rice cereal
2 cups bite-sized shredded wheat
  cereal
1 cup peanuts, pecans or cashews
1 cup thin pretzel sticks, optional

½ teaspoon onion salt
½ cup butter, melted
4 tablespoons Worcestershire sauce
Dash of hot pepper sauce
½ teaspoon seasoned salt
½ teaspoon garlic salt

Combine oat, rice and wheat cereals with nuts and pretzels in a crock-pot. Mix butter with onion salt, Worcestershire sauce, hot pepper sauce, salt and garlic salt; pour over cereal mixture. Toss lightly to coat. Do not cover crock-pot. Cook on high setting for 2 hours, stirring well every 30 minutes. Turn to low setting for 2-6 hours. Store after cooling in airtight container.

*MAKES 10 CUPS (2½ QUARTS)*

# Candy Bar Cookies

1 cup firmly packed brown sugar
⅔ cup butter
¼ cup dark or light corn syrup
¼ cup peanut butter plus ⅔ cup
    peanut butter
1 teaspoon vanilla extract

3½ cups quick-cooking rolled oats
2 cups (12 ounces) semisweet
    chocolate pieces
1 cup butterscotch pieces
1 cup peanuts, chopped

Preheat oven to 375°. In a medium saucepan, stir brown sugar, butter and corn syrup over medium-low heat until combined. Remove the saucepan from the heat. Stir in the ¼ cup of peanut butter and vanilla until smooth. Place rolled oats in a very large bowl. Pour brown sugar mixture over the oats, stirring gently until combined. Press oat mixture evenly onto bottom of ungreased 9x13 inch baking pan. Bake for 10 minutes or until edges are lightly browned. Let layer cool slightly in pan on a wire rack. In the same saucepan, stir chocolate and butterscotch pieces together over low heat until melted. Stir in remaining ⅔ cup peanut butter until chocolate mixture is smooth. Sprinkle half of the peanuts over oat layer in pan. Slowly pour chocolate mixture over the peanut-topped oat layer, spreading evenly. Sprinkle rest of peanuts on top of the chocolate. Cool cookies in the pan on a wire rack for several hours or until chocolate layer is firm. Cut into 1 inch squares.

*SERVES 50 PIECES*

# Teriyaki Chicken Wings

3 to 3½ pounds chicken wings, about
    20 wings
¾ cup ketchup
¼ cup soy sauce

2 tablespoons sugar
1 teaspoon salt
½ teaspoon ground ginger
1 clove garlic, crushed

Preheat oven to 375°. Cut each chicken wing at joint to make 3 pieces and discard tip. Place chicken into an ungreased 9x13 inch baking dish. Mix ketchup, soy sauce, sugar, salt, ground ginger and garlic and pour over wings. Cover and refrigerate, turning chicken occasionally, for at least 1 hour. Drain chicken, reserving marinade (set aside). Place chicken on rack in a roasting pan lined with foil. Bake for 30 minutes; brush with reserved marinade. Turn chicken and bake, brushing occasionally with reserved marinade until tender; approximately 30-40 minutes.

# Haystacks

2 cups sugar
½ cup milk
½ cup butter
½ cup cocoa powder
3 cups quick cooking oats

½ cup coconut, optional
2 tablespoons peanut butter
1 teaspoon vanilla extract
¼ teaspoon salt

Combine sugar, milk, butter, salt and cocoa powder in a large saucepan. Bring to a boil and boil for 1 minute. Remove from heat and cool 1 minute. Stir in oats, coconut, peanut butter and vanilla. Drop by teaspoonfuls onto waxed paper. Allow to cool and harden. Store covered.

*SERVES 48*

½ cup chopped nuts (pecans or walnuts) may be substituted for the coconut and/or sprinkled on top of hot cookies.
These may be poured onto a greased baking sheet and cut when cool.

# Butterscotch Chip Cookies

1 cup sugar
1 cup firmly packed brown sugar
1 cup shortening (or ½ cup butter and
    ½ cup shortening)
2 eggs
2 cups oats
1 teaspoon baking soda

½ teaspoon baking powder
½ teaspoon salt
2 tablespoons vanilla extract
2 cups all-purpose flour
1 (12 ounce) package butterscotch
    chips

Preheat oven to 350°. Cream together sugar, brown sugar and shortening. Add eggs and beat well. Set aside. In small bowl mix together flour, baking soda, baking powder and salt. Stir oats, dry ingredient mixture and vanilla into sugar mixture. Stir in butterscotch chips. Drop by teaspoonfuls onto greased baking sheet and bake for 9-11 minutes or until barely brown. Let cool on wire racks.

*3 DOZEN*

# Super Delicious Brownies

2 cups sugar

1 cup butter, melted

2 teaspoons vanilla extract

1 teaspoon salt

¼ cup cocoa powder

4 eggs

1½ cups all-purpose flour, sifted

½ cup chopped pecans or walnuts, optional

**ICING**

1 cup powdered sugar

1 teaspoon vanilla extract

¼ cup cocoa powder

2 tablespoons milk

Preheat oven to 375°. Mix together sugar and cocoa. Stir in butter; then add eggs and vanilla. Beat well. Sift flour and salt together and stir into wet mixture. Fold in nuts. Place into 9x13 inch greased pan and bake for 25 minutes or until sides begin to pull away from the pan and the center is still slightly soft. Mix icing ingredients together. This will be a fairly thin mixture. Pour over hot brownies and allow to cool.

*SERVES 18*

# Grandma's Sugar Cookies

½ cup butter

¾ cup oil

1 cup sugar plus extra for garnish

1 cup powdered sugar

2 eggs

4 cups all-purpose flour, sifted

1 teaspoon cream of tartar

1 teaspoon salt

1 teaspoon baking soda

2 teaspoons vanilla extract

Preheat oven to 350°. Cream together butter, oil and sugars. Stir in eggs and vanilla. Add dry ingredients gradually and mix until well blended. Roll dough into small balls and flatten with the bottom of a glass. Bake for about 10 minutes. Remove from pan and place on wire rack. Sprinkle with sugar while warm. Allow to cool and then store in tightly covered container.

*SERVES 36*

Look for a glass with a decorative bottom; it will make a nice design on the cookie.

# Coconut Butterballs and Ruby Sparklers

2 cups all-purpose flour, sifted
¼ teaspoon salt
1 cup butter, softened
½ cup sugar
1 teaspoon vanilla extract
1 teaspoon almond extract

48 candied cherries, well drained
½ cup sweetened flaked coconut
1 (6 ounce) package semisweet
   chocolate chips
Colored sugars as desired

Preheat oven to 325°. Stir flour and salt together. Cream butter and sugar until light and fluffy, beat in vanilla and almond extracts. Stir in flour mixture a third at a time, blending well after each to make stiff dough. Press dough, a level teaspoonful at a time, around a candied cherry to make a small ball. Roll in coconut. Place 1 inch apart on ungreased baking sheet. Press remaining dough, a level teaspoonful at a time, around 3 chocolate chips to make a small ball. Roll in decorating sugars (or sprinkle sugar on top). Place 1 inch apart on an ungreased cookie sheet. Bake for 25 minutes, or until firm. Carefully remove from pan and cool completely on wire racks. To store cookies, layer them between waxed paper in tightly covered container.

*SERVES 7-8 DOZEN*

These may be made 2 to 3 weeks ahead and stored tightly covered.

# Sand Cookies

1 cup butter, softened
4 tablespoons powdered sugar,
   plus extra

3 cups flour
1 cup finely chopped pecans

Preheat oven to 325°. Cream butter and powdered sugar together. Gradually add flour and pecans and continue to mix. When dough holds together shape into small rolls about 1½ inches long. Place on an ungreased cookie sheet and bake about 50 minutes or until golden brown. Roll in powdered sugar while still warm. Cool on wire rack and store in tightly covered container.

*SERVES 60*

# Snickerdoodles

1 cup shortening or butter
1½ cups plus 2 tablespoons sugar
2 eggs
2⅓ cups all-purpose flour

2 teaspoons cream of tartar
1 teaspoon baking soda
½ teaspoon salt
2 teaspoons cinnamon

Preheat oven to 400°. Sift together flour, cream of tartar, baking soda and salt. Cream shortening and 1½ cups sugar; add eggs and dry ingredient mixture. Mix together 2 tablespoons sugar and cinnamon. Roll dough into about 1½ inch balls and then into cinnamon sugar mixture. Place 2 inches apart on an ungreased baking sheet and bake for 8-10 minutes.

*SERVES 60*

# Brown Sugar Drops

1 cup butter, softened
2 cups firmly packed brown sugar
2 eggs
½ cup buttermilk or soured milk

3½ cups all-purpose flour
1 teaspoon baking soda
1 teaspoon salt

Preheat oven to 400°. Cream butter and sugar, add eggs and beat well. Stir in buttermilk. Sift together flour, baking soda and salt and stir into wet mixture. Chill dough for at least 1 hour. Drop rounded teaspoonfuls about 2 inches apart on lightly greased baking sheet. Bake about 8-10 minutes or until set.

*SERVES 72*

To sour milk, measure ½ cup milk, remove ½ tablespoon, stir in ½ tablespoon lemon juice and allow to sit for about 5 minutes.

# Chocolate Crispies

2½ cups unsifted all-purpose flour
1 teaspoon baking soda
½ teaspoon salt
1 cup butter, softened
2 cups sugar

2 eggs
2 teaspoons vanilla extract
4 cups crispy rice cereal
1 (12 ounce) package chocolate chips

Preheat oven to 350°. Stir together flour, soda and salt, set aside. Cream butter and sugar until smooth. Beat in eggs and vanilla. Mix in flour mixture. Stir in cereal and chocolate chips. Drop by level tablespoonfuls onto greased baking sheets. Bake about 10 minutes or until lightly browned. Cool on wire rack and store in tightly covered container.

*SERVES 84*

# Best Ever Cookies

1 cup sugar
1 cup firmly packed brown sugar
1 cup shortening (may use butter)
3 eggs
1 teaspoon baking soda
1 teaspoon baking powder
½ teaspoon salt

3 cups all-purpose flour
½ teaspoon cinnamon
½ cup chopped nuts, pecans or
  walnuts
1 teaspoon vanilla extract
½ cup raisins
1 cup sweetened flaked coconut

Preheat oven to 350°. Cream sugars and shortening. Add eggs and beat well. Add remaining ingredients, blending well. Drop by teaspoonfuls onto a greased baking sheet. Bake for 10-12 minutes or until slightly underdone. Cool on wire racks and store in tightly covered container.

*SERVES 60*

# Fruity Sugar Cookies

1 cup sugar
1 box (3 ounce) gelatin, any flavor
¾ cup shortening (use part butter)
2 eggs

3 cups all-purpose flour
1 teaspoon baking powder
1 teaspoon salt

Preheat oven to 375°. Mix sugar and dried gelatin together. Add shortening and eggs, blend well. Sift flour, baking powder and salt and add to mixture. Roll ¼ inch thick on floured surface. Cut with desired cookie cutters. Place on ungreased baking sheet and bake for 5-8 minutes.

*SERVES APPROXIMATELY 48*

May alter gelatin for seasons, i.e. green St. Patrick's Day, lemon for Easter.

# Cherry Bars

1 cup butter, softened
1¾ cups sugar
4 eggs
3 cups all-purpose flour

1½ teaspoons baking powder
½ teaspoon salt
2 cans cherry pie filling

Preheat oven to 350°. In a large bowl, combine butter, sugar, eggs, flour, baking powder and salt. Set aside about 1½ cups of batter. Spread remaining batter in greased 9x13 inch baking pan. Gently spread pie filling over dough and drop remaining dough on top by teaspoonfuls, this will spread as it bakes. Bake for 40-45 minutes. Cool and cut into bars. Store covered. This may be sprinkled with chopped nuts while warm or frosted with a simple powdered sugar glaze.

*SERVES 48*

# White Texas Sheet Cake

1½ cups butter, divided
1 cup water
2 cups sugar
2 cups all-purpose flour
1 teaspoon baking soda

½ cup sour cream
2 teaspoons almond extract, divided
2 eggs, beaten
¼ cup milk
4½ cups powdered sugar, sifted

Preheat oven to 375°. Place 1 cup of butter and water in large saucepan and bring to a boil. Then remove from heat and stir in sugar, flour, baking soda, almond extract, sour cream and eggs. Stir until mixture is smooth. Pour into a prepared 10x15 inch baking pan. Bake 20-22 minutes. Prepare frosting while cake is baking by combining ½ cup butter and milk in a saucepan. Bring to a boil. Remove from heat and add powdered sugar and 1 teaspoon almond extract. Mix until smooth and spread over warm cake.

*SERVES 15*

# Layered Chocolate Bars

½ cup butter, softened
¼ cup sugar
3 eggs, divided
1½ teaspoons vanilla extract, divided
1 cup flour plus 4 tablespoons, divided

⅝ teaspoon salt, divided
1½ cups firmly packed brown sugar
½ teaspoon baking powder
1½ cups semisweet chocolate chips

**ICING**

1½ cups powdered sugar
1 teaspoon orange zest, grated

½ teaspoon orange juice

Preheat oven to 350°. Combine butter and sugar. Add 1 egg and ½ teaspoon vanilla. Beat well and then add 1 cup plus 2 tablespoons flour and ⅛ teaspoon salt. Once this mixture is combined, press evenly into a 9x13 inch ungreased pan. Bake for 10-15 minutes until light golden brown. While the crust is baking, combine brown sugar, 2 eggs, 2 tablespoons flour, baking powder, ½ teaspoon salt and 1 teaspoon vanilla. Mix well and add chocolate chips. Mix well and then pour onto baked crust. Bake for about 25 minutes. When bars are cool, frost with icing that is made with the powdered sugar, orange juice and orange zest.

*SERVES 20-24 BARS*

# Orange Tart

| | |
|---|---|
| 1 (9 inch) baked pie shell | 2 tablespoons fresh lemon juice |
| 1½ tablespoons orange marmalade | 2 tablespoons orange juice |
| 1 large navel orange | 1½ tablespoons triple sec |
| 4 eggs | 6 tablespoons butter, melted |
| ⅓ cup sugar | |

Preheat oven to 425°. Brush warm baked pie shell with marmalade. Peel the orange, remove all white pith and slice into 8 thin, even slices making "wheels." Set aside. Beat eggs with sugar until light and then add in the lemon juice, orange juice, liqueur and melted butter. Gently pour this mixture into the pie shell. Arrange the 8 orange "wheels" on top. Bake in the oven for 25 minutes until custard is set and barely beginning to brown.

*SERVES 6-8*

The tart can be served warm or at room temperature. It is best if it has not been refrigerated.

# It's the Frosting!!!

| | |
|---|---|
| 2 cups whipping cream, chilled | 2 tablespoons crème de cacao |
| ½ cup chocolate syrup | |

Mix frosting ingredients and then chill until cold. Remove from refrigerator and whip for about 10 minutes until mixture is firm.

*RECIPE WILL FROST A TWO LAYER CAKE OR 9X13 INCH CAKE*

# Chocolate Crescents

1 (8 ounce) tube refrigerated crescent rolls
⅔ cup semisweet chocolate morsels plus 1 tablespoon morsels

4 tablespoons sugar, divided
1-3 teaspoons cinnamon
2 tablespoons butter, divided
3 tablespoons all-purpose flour

Preheat oven to 375°. To make streusel topping, combine flour and 3 tablespoons sugar in a small bowl. With a fork, cut in 1 tablespoon of butter until the mixture is crumbly. Set aside. Open crescent roll tube and roll out to form a 12x8 inch rectangle. Press firmly to eliminate perforation marks. Sprinkle with ⅔ cup of chocolate morsels, 1 tablespoon sugar, cinnamon and half the streusel topping. Starting at the long side of the rectangle, roll up and pinch the edge to seal. Join the two ends to create a ring and pinch to seal the ring. Gently twist ring to create a figure eight. Place on greased and floured cookie sheet. Brush with melted butter, sprinkle with remaining streusel topping and chocolate morsels. Bake for 20-22 minutes.

*SERVES 8*

# Frozen Strawberry Margarita Pie

1¼ cups finely crushed pretzels
8 tablespoons butter, melted
¼ cup sugar
1 (14 ounce) can sweetened condensed milk
1½ cups strawberries, fresh or frozen (thawed and well drained)

⅓ cup bottled lime juice
¼ cup tequila
2 tablespoons triple sec
1½ cups whipping cream, whipped with 2 tablespoons powdered sugar

In a medium bowl, combine pretzel crumbs, butter and sugar. Press into 9 inch pie plate. Set aside. In a large bowl, combine remaining ingredients except for the whipped cream. Pour mixture into crust and freeze for 4 hours or overnight. Before serving, remove from freezer for 10-20 minutes. Top with whipped cream and serve.

*SERVES 6-8*

# Fresh Peach Pie

1 cup sugar
3 tablespoons cornstarch
⅛ teaspoon salt
3 tablespoons light corn syrup
1 cup water

3 tablespoons lemon gelatin, not
   sugar-free
1 quart fresh peaches, sliced
½ tablespoon lemon juice
10 inch pie shell, baked
Whipped cream for garnish

Combine sugar, cornstarch, salt and syrup in a saucepan. Add water, stir and cook until mixture thickens, about 5 minutes. Add gelatin and blend into mixture. Set aside and cool. Toss peaches with the lemon juice and place into the cooled, baked pie shell then spoon the gelatin mixture over the peaches. Chill thoroughly and serve with whipped cream.

*SERVES 8*

# Frosted Lemon Squares

2 cups all-purpose flour
1 cup butter, divided
½ cup powdered sugar
4 eggs

4 tablespoons flour
2 cups sugar
2 tablespoons lemon juice
¼ teaspoon salt

**ICING**
3 cups powdered sugar, sifted
3 tablespoons whipping cream
1½ teaspoons vanilla extract

4 ounces cream cheese, softened
½ cup butter

Preheat oven to 350°. Cream together the flour, 1 cup butter, and ½ cup powdered sugar in a food processor. Press this mixture into an ungreased 9x13 inch pan. Bake for 20 minutes or until a light, golden brown. While the crust is baking, beat together 4 eggs, lemon juice, flour, sugar and salt. Pour over the baked crust and bake for an additional 25 minutes. Cool completely before icing. The icing is made by combining ½ cup butter, sifted powdered sugar, whipping cream, vanilla and cream cheese.

*48 SQUARES*

# Mocha Cream Freeze

1 quart chocolate ice cream
2 tablespoons Kahlúa
2 tablespoons dark rum

½ cup coffee candies, pulverized
½ cup freeze dried, decaffeinated
    coffee crystals

Soften ice cream and stir in Kahlúa and rum. After mixing well, cover and place in freezer for a minimum of 4 hours. To serve, scoop ice cream into individual bowls or wine glasses and sprinkle with the candy chips and coffee crystals.

*SERVES 6-8*

# Orange Sherbet with Chocolate Sauce

1 quart orange sherbet

1 (8 ounce) jar chocolate sauce, or
    chocolate flavored liqueur

Scoop out ice cream into individual serving dishes or martini glasses. Drizzle with chocolate sauce. This dessert is easy and refreshing.

*SERVES 6-8*

# Pineapple and Passion Fruit Syllabub

1 cup whipping cream
4 tablespoons powdered sugar
4 tablespoons rum
10 ounces Greek yogurt

4 passion fruits
1 pineapple, peeled and cut into very
    small pieces

Combine the powdered sugar, cream and rum in a medium bowl. Whisk until thick and fold in the yogurt. Cut 4 passion fruit in half, scoop out the pulp, reserve ½ cup pulp for garnish and add remainder to yogurt mixture. Place half the pineapple into the mixture and fold again. Put into individual ramekins and freeze for a minimum of 30 minutes. When serving, garnish with remaining passion fruit pulp and pineapple chunks.

*SERVES 8*

# Poached Peaches in Raspberry Sauce

5 large firm peaches, unpeeled and
    cut in half
½ cup water

3 tablespoons sugar
1 pint raspberries, divided
1 (8 ounce) container sour cream

In a pan large enough to hold 10 peach halves, place the peaches, sugar, water and half the raspberries. Bring to a slow boil, cover and let the fruit mixture simmer for 2-3 minutes. Turn peaches over to make sure they have cooked through but are still firm. Remove peaches from the pan and remove the skin. Continue to simmer the liquid mixture until it has become thick. Place peaches in a dish and then pour the liquid mixture through a strainer to cover the peaches. Refrigerate the peaches and turn them occasionally. When serving, add a dollop of sour cream and garnish with reserved raspberries.

*SERVES 5*

# Lemon Chess Pie

2 cups sugar
1 tablespoon all-purpose flour
1 tablespoon cornmeal
4 eggs
½ cup butter, melted

¼ cup milk
2 tablespoons lemon zest
⅓ cup lemon juice with pulp
1 (9 inch) pie shell
Whipped cream for garnish

Preheat oven to 375°. In a large bowl, combine sugar, flour and cornmeal. Blend well. Add eggs and mix well. Add milk and stir. Add butter and stir. Add lemon juice and zest; combine well. Pour into pie shell. Cover edges of pie shell with aluminum foil strips to prevent overbrowning. Make sure not to touch the filling with the foil strips. Bake for 45 minutes, removing the foil strips after 30 minutes. Cool the pie several hours before serving. Garnish with whipped cream.

*SERVES 8*

# Apple-Oatmeal Crisp

3 cups peeled and sliced apples
1 cup sugar

½ teaspoon cinnamon

**TOPPING**

½ cup all-purpose flour
½ cup firmly packed brown sugar
½ cup uncooked oats

¼ cup butter
Whipped cream or ice cream,
optional

Preheat oven to 350°. Spread apples in a buttered 9x13 inch baking dish. Cover with sugar and cinnamon which have been mixed together. Mix the topping of flour, brown sugar, oats and crumbled butter. Sprinkle the topping over the apple mixture. Bake for 45 minutes. Serve with whipped cream or ice cream.

*SERVES 8-10*

# Peanut Butter Pie

**CRUST**

¼ cup light corn syrup
2 tablespoons brown sugar

3 tablespoons butter
2½ cups crispy rice cereal

**PIE**

¼ cup smooth peanut butter
¼ cup fudge sauce plus additional
    for topping

3 tablespoons corn syrup
1 quart vanilla ice cream

For the crust, combine brown sugar, syrup and butter in medium saucepan. Cook over low heat until mixture begins to boil. Remove from heat and add cereal, stir until blended. Press into a 9 inch pie pan. Freeze until firm. For the pie, stir peanut butter, fudge sauce and corn syrup together. Spread over the frozen crust. Freeze overnight. Soften ice cream and spread over the readied pie crust. Freeze until firm. Top with fudge sauce and serve.

*SERVES 8*

# Watercress, Avocado and Orange Salad

¼ red onion, thinly sliced

¼ cup orange juice

1 lime, juiced

1 tablespoon honey

2 teaspoons Dijon mustard

½ teaspoon salt and black pepper to taste

3 tablespoons olive oil

2 bunches watercress

2 avocados, sliced

2 oranges, peeled and segmented

Hazelnuts, chopped and toasted for garnish

Soak the red onion in cold water for 10 minutes. Whisk orange juice, lime juice, honey, mustard, salt and pepper in a bowl. Whisk in olive oil. Drain the onion, toss with the watercress, avocados and oranges. Toss with the dressing from the bowl and top with hazelnuts.

*SERVES 6*

# No Risk Artichoke Bisque

4 tablespoons butter

1 yellow onion, chopped

32 ounces marinated artichoke hearts (undrained)

1 quart non-fat half and half

¼ pound Gruyère cheese, shredded

In a large, heavy pot, sauté onions in butter. Add all remaining ingredients. Purée with an immersion blender until the bisque reaches a smooth consistency. Cook over medium low heat for 1 hour. Blend again with immersion blender. This wonderfully decadent bisque is ready to serve.

*SERVES 6-8*

If you don't have an immersion blender, you can get the same result by putting ingredients in a food processor or blender. For an alternative bisque recipe, substitute a total of 2 pounds of yellow squash and zucchini for the artichoke hearts.

# Beef Salami

2 tablespoons curing salt
¼ teaspoon onion powder
⅛ teaspoon garlic powder
1½ teaspoons liquid smoke

1 cup water
2 pounds hamburger (medium fat)
Condiments, cream cheese and
    crackers

Mix salt, onion and garlic powders, liquid smoke and water together and add to hamburger. Mix well. Form into log. Wrap in foil or plastic wrap and refrigerate for 24 hours. Remove wrap and bake in pan for 45 minutes at 350°. Serve with plain or horseradish flavored cream cheese and whole grain, rye or wheat crackers. This freezes well.

*MAKES 3 ROLLS*

# Pork Chops with Apple-Walnut Mix

4 medium thick pork chops
2 tablespoons olive oil
4 tablespoons butter
2 cups sliced Fuji apples

½ cup raisins
½ cup button mushrooms, sliced
½ cup firmly packed brown sugar
½ cup walnuts

Season the pork chops with salt and pepper. Heat olive oil in a pan, add the chops, then brown on both sides. In another pan, melt the butter, add the apples, raisins, button mushrooms, brown sugar and walnuts. Stir. Sauté in the pan for a few minutes. Add the apple/walnut mix to the pork chops and sauté for about 20 minutes until the pork chops are done and the apples are soft.

*SERVES 4*

# Swiss Vegetable Medley

1 (16 ounce) bag frozen broccoli,
    carrots and cauliflower
    combination, thawed and drained
1 (10.75 ounce) can condensed cream
    of mushroom soup
1 cup (4 ounces) shredded Swiss
    cheese, divided

⅓ cup sour cream
¼ teaspoon black pepper
1 jar (4 ounces) chopped pimiento,
    drained
1 (2.8 ounce) can French fried onions,
    divided

Preheat oven to 350°. Combine vegetables, soup, ½ cup cheese, sour cream, pepper, pimiento and ½ can French fried onions. Pour into a greased 1 quart casserole. Bake covered for 30 minutes. Top with remaining cheese and onions. Bake uncovered 5 minutes longer.

*SERVES 8-10*

# Mediterranean Potato Salad

### DRESSING

¼ cup fresh lemon juice

2 teaspoons Dijon mustard

1 teaspoon kosher salt

½ teaspoon freshly ground black pepper

¼ cup extra virgin olive oil

2 large cloves garlic, mashed to a paste

2 teaspoon chopped fresh marjoram

½ teaspoon crushed red pepper flakes

### SALAD

¼ cup plain rice vinegar

2 tablespoons plus 2 teaspoons kosher salt

3¼ pounds baby red potatoes, scrubbed clean

1 tablespoon extra virgin olive oil

2 cups frozen artichoke hearts, thawed, patted dry and cut into ¾ inch wedges

1 cup halved or quartered black olives

¾ cup chopped fresh mint

Salt and black pepper to taste

For the dressing, whisk the lemon juice, mustard, salt and pepper in a small bowl. Slowly whisk in the oil until combined. Whisk in the garlic, marjoram and red pepper flakes. To make the salad, combine the vinegar and 2 teaspoons salt in a large bowl. Let sit to dissolve the salt. Put the potatoes and 2 tablespoons salt in a 6 quart pot then add enough cold water to cover the potatoes by 1 inch. Bring to a boil over high heat and reduce the heat to maintain a simmer. Cook the potatoes until fork tender, about 5-10 minutes. Gently drain the potatoes in a colander and set aside until cool enough to handle. Cut the potatoes into ¾ inch chunks. Add the potatoes to the bowl with the rice vinegar and gently stir with a spatula to coat. Pull apart any pieces that are stuck together. In a large skillet heat the olive oil over medium high heat. Add the artichoke hearts and a sprinkle of salt, cook turning once, until browned on both sides. Gently fold the browned artichokes, olives and chopped mint into the potatoes. Whisk the vinaigrette back together and fold enough of it into the potatoes to generously coat them (you may not need all of the dressing). Season to taste with salt and pepper. Serve while still slightly warm, or at room temperature.

*SERVES 8*

Our membership averages between 275 to 300 dedicated women.

# Rainbow Chopped Salad

**DRESSING**

¼ cup red wine vinegar

1½ tablespoons finely chopped shallot

½ tablespoon honey

¼ cup hazelnut oil or extra virgin olive oil

Salt and black pepper to taste

**SALAD**

6 cups chopped romaine hearts

4 cups sliced red cabbage

1 large Fuji apple, halved, cored, diced

1 Asian pear, halved, cored, diced

1 mango, peeled, diced or 2 Fuyu persimmons, peeled, seeded, diced

¾ cup hazelnuts, toasted, husked, coarsely chopped

½ cup pomegranate seeds

½ cup crumbled blue cheese, optional

For the dressing whisk vinegar, shallot and honey in small bowl to blend. Gradually whisk in oil. Season dressing to taste with salt and freshly ground pepper. In a large bowl, combine the romaine, cabbage, apple, pear, hazelnuts and pomegranate seeds. Add dressing and toss to coat. Divide salad among plates and sprinkle with blue cheese.

*SERVES 8*

# Amy's Meatloaf

½ cup bread crumbs

2 tablespoons extra virgin olive oil

½ medium onion, diced

2 cloves garlic, minced

2 teaspoons dried oregano

1½ teaspoons kosher salt

½ teaspoon black pepper

1 pound ground pork

1 pound ground beef

⅓ cup grated Parmesan cheese

2 teaspoons Worcestershire sauce

2 eggs, beaten

Preheat oven to 350°. Toast the bread crumbs in a dry skillet over medium heat until browned and fragrant, about 1 minute. Transfer to a large mixing bowl and set aside. Add the olive oil, onions, garlic, oregano, salt and pepper to the skillet and cook until onions are tender, about 8 minutes. Let cool slightly. Add the onions to the bread crumbs along with the meat, cheese and Worcestershire sauce. Toss and mix gently. Add the eggs and stir to coat the meat completely. Transfer to a foil-lined sheet pan and gently press into desired shape. Bake until an instant read thermometer registers 160° in the center of the loaf; it can take anywhere from 45-60 minutes.

*SERVES 4*

# Chili Con Carne

1 tablespoon whole cumin seeds

2 teaspoons whole coriander seeds

1 tablespoon ground ancho chile

1 teaspoon ground chipotle chile

1½ teaspoons dried oregano, preferably Mexican

2 pounds boneless beef chuck, trimmed of all visible fat and cut into ½ inch cubes

Salt

2 tablespoons canola oil, divided

1 medium yellow onion, chopped

1 medium poblano, seeded and chopped

1 large jalapeño, seeded and finely chopped

3 medium cloves garlic, minced

1 (14.5 ounce) can no-salt added diced tomatoes

2 tablespoons fresh lime juice, divided

1 (15 ounce) can low-sodium pinto beans, drained and rinsed

1 avocado, cut into medium dice

¼ cup finely diced red onion

¼ cup coarsely chopped fresh cilantro

Toast the cumin and coriander in a small dry skillet over medium heat, stirring frequently until fragrant, about 30 seconds. Transfer to a spice grinder and grind into a powder. Transfer to a small bowl and add the ancho, chipotle and oregano. Season the meat with ¼ teaspoon salt. Heat 2 teaspoons of the oil in a 6 quart pot or Dutch oven over medium-high heat. Add half of the meat and cook until well browned on all sides, about 5 minutes total. Transfer the meat to a plate. Repeat with another 2 teaspoons oil and the remaining meat. After transferring the second batch of meat to the plate, add the remaining 2 teaspoons oil to the pot. Add the onion, poblano and jalapeño and cook, stirring until softened, about 4 minutes. Add the garlic and cook until fragrant, about 1 minute more. Add the spice mixture and cook until fragrant and well blended, 1-2 minutes more. Return the beef to the pot along with any accumulated juice. Add 2½ cups water, the tomatoes and their juice, 1 tablespoon of the lime juice, and 1 teaspoon salt. Bring to a boil over medium-high heat; then reduce the heat to low and simmer, covered, for 1½ hours. Remove the lid and simmer until the meat is tender, about 30 minutes more. Add the beans, raise the heat to medium-high and stir until the beans are heated through, about 5 minutes. Add the remaining 1 tablespoon lime juice and season to taste with additional salt.

*SERVES 4*

This is much better if prepared ahead of time and frozen. Serve the chili garnished with the avocado, red onion and cilantro.

# Baby Drumsticks Oriental

3 pounds chicken wings
¼ cup soy sauce
½ cup sugar
½ cup firmly packed brown sugar

¼ cup white or rice vinegar
Freshly ground black pepper
1 cup chicken broth

Separate each wing into 3 pieces; discard tips. Place wings in shallow baking dish which has been sprayed with nonstick spray. Blend remaining ingredients to make sauce. Cover chicken with mixture; let stand for 60 minutes, turning, so all pieces are marinated. Preheat oven to 350°. Bake for 1½ hours or a bit longer, watch to prevent burning. Turn during baking after 1 hour. Serve hot or cold with Chinese mustard.

Other chicken pieces can be cooked this way. May use a zip-top plastic bag while marinating.

# Chicken Dijon

3 tablespoons butter
4 boneless, skinless chicken breasts
2 tablespoons flour
1 cup chicken broth

½ cup light cream
2 tablespoons Dijon mustard
2 tomatoes, cut in wedges
2 tablespoons minced fresh parsley

Melt butter in a large skillet. Add chicken breast and cook until done and lightly browned, about 20 minutes. Remove chicken to a warm serving platter. In the skillet, add flour, cook 1 minute, then add broth to thicken and deglaze the skillet. Next add the cream and mustard. Return the chicken to the skillet and cover and heat for 10 minutes. Garnish with tomatoes and sprinkle with parsley.

*SERVES 4*

# Puerto Rican Style Chicken Salad

2 pounds boneless, skinless chicken breasts, cut into large cubes

Juice of 2 limes or lemons (about 6 tablespoons)

3 tablespoons orange juice

2 tablespoons reduced-sodium soy sauce

1 teaspoon ground turmeric, optional

1 tablespoon snipped fresh oregano

4 cloves garlic, minced

1 to 2 tablespoons olive oil, or as needed

¼ cup all-purpose flour

6 cups torn mixed salad greens

½ cup cucumber slices

¼ cup sliced pitted ripe olives

1 tomato, halved and thinly sliced

1 small red onion, thinly sliced

Reduced-fat vinaigrette, purchased

½ cup crumbled feta cheese, optional

Place the chicken in a large glass bowl. Combine the lime or lemon juice, orange juice, soy sauce, turmeric, oregano and garlic. Cover the chicken and marinate overnight in the refrigerator. Drain chicken, discarding marinade. Place all-purpose flour in a zip-top plastic bag. Add chicken pieces, a few at a time, and shake to coat each piece. Heat oil in a very large skillet over medium heat. Add the pieces, half at a time and cook, stirring occasionally, until cooked through and tender. Keep warm. For salad, toss greens with cucumber, olives, tomato, onion and vinaigrette in a large salad bowl. Serve chicken with salad and sprinkle with cheese if desired.

*SERVES 8*

# Healthy Crisp Cobb Salad

1 ounce cooked turkey breast, chopped

3 thin slices of cucumber

1 radish, sliced

2 cherry tomatoes, halved

2 cups crisp salad greens

1 ounce skim milk Swiss cheese

Fat free dressing of choice

Mix all the ingredients together in a bowl. When ready to serve, drizzle the fat-free dressing of your choice over the salad.

*SERVES 1*

# Healthy Savory Chicken Chowder

2½ cups fat-free chicken broth, divided
1¼ cups chopped carrots
1¼ cups chopped celery
1¼ cups diced turnips
¾ cup chopped onion
2 (16 ounce) cans diced tomatoes with juice

¼ teaspoon dried thyme leaves
¼ teaspoon dried rosemary leaves
¼ teaspoon black pepper
¼ teaspoon garlic powder
2 cups chicken, cooked and diced

Preheat oven to 350°. Pour ½ cup chicken broth into large baking pan. Cut chicken into bite-size pieces and put into the baking pan with broth. Bake for 15 minutes. Put cut-up vegetables and remaining chicken broth into a large saucepan. Cover and boil gently on the stovetop until vegetables are tender, about 10 minutes. Add tomatoes and chicken to cooked vegetables. Cover and simmer for 10 minutes to blend flavors. If desired, more broth may be added.

*SERVES 8*

# Chicken and Dressing

4 cups chicken, cooked, deboned, cut into large pieces
½ cup plus 2 tablespoons butter
½ cup celery, chopped
½ cup chopped onion
1 (10 ounce) can cream of mushroom soup

1 (10 ounce) can cream of chicken soup
1 (8 ounce) package stuffing mix
2 (10 ounce) cans chicken broth
Salt and pepper to taste

Sauté celery and onion in 2 tablespoons butter. Add both cans of soup and ½ cup chicken broth. Add chicken pieces and stir, then place in a 9x13 inch buttered pan. Combine 1 cup chicken broth, ½ cup melted butter, salt, pepper and dressing. Spread over the chicken. Cover and refrigerate overnight. Before baking, let stand at room temperature for 1 hour. Preheat oven to 350°. Bake covered for 20 minutes and uncovered for 40 additional minutes.

*SERVES 8*

# Slow Cooker Coq au Vin

3 slices (4 ounces) thick cut bacon, cut into ¼ inch pieces

2 medium onions, minced

8 medium garlic cloves, peeled and crushed

2 tablespoons tomato paste

2 teaspoons fresh or dried thyme minced

Salt

1 (750 ml) bottle dry red wine

⅓ cup soy sauce

3 tablespoons minute tapioca

2 bay leaves

4 pounds bone-in chicken pieces (thighs are best), skinned and trimmed

Black pepper

2 cups frozen pearl onions, thawed

½ cup water

3 tablespoons unsalted butter

2 teaspoons sugar

10 ounces cremini mushrooms, halved

Cook bacon in a 12 inch non-stick skillet over medium heat until crisp, about 8 minutes. Transfer to a paper-lined plate, leaving fat in the skillet. Refrigerate bacon until serving time. Pour off all but 2 tablespoons bacon fat and place over medium heat until shimmering. Add onions, garlic, tomato paste, thyme and ¼ teaspoon salt and cook until onions are soft and lightly browned, 8 minutes. Stir in wine and cook until reduced by 3 cups, 10 minutes. Transfer to crock-pot and stir in the soy sauce, tapioca and bay leaves. Season chicken with salt and pepper and nestle in the crock-pot. Cover and cook on low for 4-5 hours. About 20 minutes before serving, bring pearl onions, water, butter and sugar to a boil in a non-stick skillet. Cook until onions are thawed, 8 minutes, and water has evaporated. Add mushrooms and ¼ teaspoon salt and cook without stirring for about 2 minutes. Stir until all vegetables are browned and remove from heat. Skim fat from slow cooker, removing as much as possible. Discard bay leaves, stir in onion mixture and season with salt and pepper to taste. Reheat the bacon in the microwave and sprinkle on individual portions while serving.

*SERVES 8*

# Robin's Chicken Salad

1 cup celery, chopped

½ cup almonds, slivered

3 hard-boiled eggs, chopped

1 (10 ounce) can cream of chicken soup

¾ cup mayonnaise

2 tablespoons onion, chopped

1 tablespoon lemon juice

2 cups rice, cooked, may use brown

2 cups chicken, cooked and cut up (may use rotisserie)

Potato chips, crushed, optional

Preheat oven to 350°. Mix all the ingredients together. Place in a lightly greased, 9x13 inch pan. Bake for 15 minutes. Can place crushed potato chips on top and cook another 5 minutes.

*SERVES 8-10*

# De La Croix Salad Dressing

1 pint mayonnaise
½ cup creole mustard
Dash cayenne pepper
Salt to taste

2 tablespoons lemon juice
Hot sauce to taste
1 tablespoon parsley, chopped

Mix all ingredients together and adjust seasonings to taste. Refrigerate until serving.

*SERVES 2½ CUPS*

This dressing is the perfect finish to a salad made of shrimp, hearts of palm, capers, green onion tops and romaine lettuce.

# Sour Cream Buttermilk Dressing

¼ cup sour cream
¼ cup buttermilk

1 garlic clove, minced
⅛ teaspoon oregano

Combine all ingredients and refrigerate.

*SERVES ½ CUP*

This dressing works well with green salads and a sprinkling of crumbled blue cheese on top.

# Miso-Sesame Vinaigrette

½ cup rice wine vinegar, divided

3 tablespoons white miso

3 tablespoons sugar

2 egg yolks

2 tablespoons smooth peanut butter

2 teaspoons fresh ginger, minced

1 clove garlic, minced

1 fresh red chile, minced

2 teaspoons Dijon mustard

1 cup vegetable oil

2 teaspoons dark sesame oil

2 teaspoons white sesame seeds, lightly toasted

Water as needed

Mix ¼ cup vinegar, ¼ cup water, miso and sugar in a medium sized glass bowl and stir until the sugar is dissolved. Place the remaining vinegar, yolks, peanut butter, ginger, garlic, chile, and mustard in a blender. Process until ingredients are blended. Leave the blender running and slowly drizzle the vegetable oil until it is incorporated. Repeat with the sesame oil. Add the toasted sesame seeds to the vinaigrette. If it is too thick, add enough water to create a pouring consistency. Add this mixture to the bowl and stir until the two are well combined. Refrigerate until serving time.

*SERVES ABOUT 3 CUPS*

Raw egg yolks are used in this recipe so be certain that the eggs are fresh. Some suggest that this recipe not be made for pregnant women or young children.

# Cardamom Dressing

1 tablespoon vegetable oil

1 tablespoon lemon juice

1 tablespoon apple juice

1½ teaspoons honey

1 teaspoon soy sauce

½ teaspoon cardamom, grated

Combine all ingredients and chill until serving time. This dressing has a special flavor and does not require a great amount to make a great impact!

*SERVES ABOUT ½ CUP*

# A Flurry of Curry Dressing

½ cup plain yogurt
½ cup mayonnaise

2 tablespoons curry powder
Salt and pepper to taste

Combine all ingredients and chill until serving time.

*SERVES 1 CUP OR ENOUGH FOR 6 SERVINGS*

This dressing is ideal for chicken or suitable for a quick dip for raw vegetables.

# Feta Dressing

½ cup plain yogurt
⅓ cup sour cream
¾ cup feta cheese, crumbled

½ garlic clove, finely minced
⅓ teaspoon dried oregano
⅛ teaspoon black pepper

Mix all ingredients thoroughly and serve chilled over green salad.

*SERVES 6-8*

# Parmesan Dressing

1 cup mayonnaise-type salad dressing
1 tablespoon lemon juice
½ teaspoon lemon zest
1 garlic clove, finely minced

3 tablespoons Parmesan cheese, grated
1 cup whipping cream

Place all ingredients in a medium bowl and mix thoroughly. Chill until it is time to dress the salad. The dressing can be combined with the salad ingredients or served on top of each serving.

*SERVES 8*

# Jalapeño Cilantro Dressing

1 tablespoon white wine vinegar
1 tablespoon Worcestershire sauce
⅓ cup cilantro, chopped
2 tablespoons lime juice
1 teaspoon lime zest
3 green onions, both white and green parts chopped

2 jalapeño peppers, seeded and chopped
1 cup mayonnaise
1 cup sour cream
Salt and pepper to taste

Place vinegar, Worcestershire, lime juice, zest, cilantro, green onions and jalapeños in a food processor. Process until the mixture is smooth. Add the mayonnaise and sour cream and process until all ingredients are incorporated. Be sure to scrape down the sides of the bowl. Chill until serving time.

*SERVES 20*

This dressing is terrific on fish tacos. Another option would be to include in a scalloped potatoes recipe.

# Plum Delicious Asian Dressing

3 cups plum sauce
½ teaspoon red pepper flakes

½ teaspoon light sesame oil
1-2 tablespoons light soy sauce

Combine all ingredients and serve over salad made with greens and fruit. It is also good in a pasta salad that includes fresh vegetables of your choice.

*SERVES ABOUT 3 CUPS*

JCYM and the cookbook committee are grateful to all who have supported us in producing this golden anniversary book. Whether you submitted your favorite dishes, tested recipes, typed, proofed, sold cookbooks, served on a committee or performed any of the many tasks required to make *Punch Bowl Optional* a reality, we thank you. If we have omitted anyone we apologize; we've been as diligent as we could in creating this list. For everyone, we appreciate you.

Judy Adams
Lisa Adams
Phyllis Alber
Revelyn Alpaugh
Bonnie Anderson
Margaret Anderson
Cindy Anderson
Marcie Artman
Jennifer Bain
Emily Baker
Suzie Baker
Doris Barnds
Lyn Barr
Margo Bartling
Janet Bash
Karen Basler
Orlanda Bazin
Brenda Beachey
Carolyn Beauchamp
Sally Bechard
Nancy Beck
Ophelia Behee
Pat Benson
Nancy Bentz
Winky Bergeson
Julie Berggren
Karen Bernhard
Donna Bloecker
Connie Boles
Beverly Booe
Joyce Bottiger
Cassie Braxdale
Stephanie Breedlove
Bette Brown
Betty Brown
Lynne Brown
Margaret Ann Brown
Kathy Brunk-Reed
Cindy Bundschuh
Cheryl Bunton
Jolene Burke
Jane Burton
Candy Byrne
Lucero Calderon
Donna Calvert
Shannon Cannata
Mary Martha Carrico
Patricia Caruso
Kay Chandler

Linda Chartier
Kaye Cillessen
Kim Cohen
Sheila Cohenour
Beth Cole
Lisa Collins
Louise Connor
Carlene Couch
Ruth Cousins
Jill Crockett
Jane Crow
Mary Cullen
Kay Davis
Linda Davis
Sue Davis
Anne Debus
Donna Dehn
Shirley Derryberry
Linda Dibbern
Sybille Dickey
Suzy Dissinger
Ginger Dohrmann
Jane Dooley
Jessica Dupriest
Karen Eberting
Emily Eblen
Sharon Eckert
Jan Eilert
Shirley Ellenberger
Deidre Ellis
Sue Ernst
Debbie Erskine
Kathy Euston
Pat Fairchild
Melanie Falbe
Carole Faltermeier
Betsy Fellers
Jan Fischer
Patty Fisher
Eileen Fitzpatrick
Lori Foderberg
Delores Forland
Carole Franklin
Linda Frazer
Jeanne Gates
Patty Gay
Pat Gies
Joan Goebel
Shirley Goetz

Maryln Golub
Cathy Graham
Donna Grant
Martha Graves
Toni Gray
Liz Grimes
Jo Ann Gundersen
Kathy Gupta
Darla Hajinian
Anne Hall
Lillian Hall
Lana Hansen
Margie Harden
Mary Lou Hardinger
Roberta Harris
Betty Harrison
Lou Hartwig
Marjorie Haub
Debbie Hedenkamp
Susan Hellstern
Dawn Hennig
Marian Herre
Pat Herrin
Sarah Herster
Kathy Hetu
Marjorie Hickey
Nancy Hiler
Pat Hipp
Nancy Hirschman
Marilyn Hodges
Judi Holloway
Gloria Holmes
Gaye Hosier
Susan Houdek
Mindy Householder
Susan Howard
Sandy Howell
Joyce Howes
Carole Huggins
Linda Hughes
Paula Humphries
Sherry Hutchison
Sharry Huyser
Betty Jackson
Judy Jaso James
Linda Janowitz
Kathy Jayroe
Patti Jefferies
Jan Jensen

Deepa Johnson
Diane Johnson
Vicki Johnston
Melena Keeth
Lesley Kennedy
Sue Kennedy
Natalie Kenny
Sarah Kesler
Cherry Klaassen
Judi Knight
Dottie Knobel
Carol Knott
Emma Jane Lang
Megan Leathers
Vida Leming
Donna Limbaugh
Dawn Linscott
Peggy London
Cathy Lorino
Sherry Love-Hunter
Carol Lucas
Sandra Luetje
Candace Lyles
Mary Lynam
Lyn Lynch
Nancy MacCready
Sandra Machtley
Trish Mack
Ellie Maddox
Carolyn Mankellow
Melissa Mann
Dottie Marr
Ellen Marsee
Diane Marshall
Jeanne Maurer
Jessie McCaffree
Karon McCready
Joan McFadden
LaVonne McGinty
Leslie McKee
Paulette McKee
Patti McMurray
Charee McWilliams
Judy Meinholdt
Marilyn Mellor
Donna Mertz
Sara Meyers
Vicki Miano
Julie Micek
Cheryl Miller
Desi Miller
Marti Miller
Cathy Misemer
Mary Jo Moore
Cynthia Moosbrugger
Naomi Muha
Jayne Nash
Becky Neese
Carol Neill
Sheila Nettels

Robin O'Hara
Wendy Orlando
Teri Orr
Joy Ottenad
Diana Owens
Joy Padley
Bea Palmer
Sue Park
Linda Parkins
Julie Pass
Lou Patton
Kathy Pelz
Cheryl Perry
Alice Petersen
Lori Peterson
Nancy Pinnell
Ann Pisani
Rosemary Pittman
Judy Plath
Nancy Popek
Jacqueline Pouppirt
Liz Quade
Sue Rassette
Margie Ray
Barbara Reda
Shirley Reed
Jane Reintjes
Carmela Rejba
Phyllis Rick
Nancy Riley
Sharilyn Robben
Barbara Rolander
Laveigh Rooney
Dee Roosa
Jan Rosche
Maria Rozman
Linda Rumsey
Betty Rutherford
Judy Saale
Michelle Salzman
Marina Samples
Ruth Sanders
Sheila Sanders
Burks Scarborough
Mary Schaefer
Sharon Schick
Kathryn Schmidt
Joanne Schottman
Sandy Schumacher
Jacqueline Schweiker
Cindy Scott
Suzanne Sedgwick
Dianne Seltzer
Anna Mae (Johnnie) Schaeffer
Donetta Shaner
Marty Shaw
Kay Shepherd
Diane Sheppard
Judy Sjoberg
Carolyn Smell

Elsie Smith
Judy Smith
Suellen Smith
Tam Smith
Marilyn Spraetz
Jean Spreen
Doris Squibbs
Marion St. Clair
Anita Starke
Frankie Stealey
Walda Stevens
Karen Stewart
Susan Strongman
Suzy Svoboda
Vicki Tennissen
Mary Textor
Carolyn Thomas
Linda Thomas
Mary Jean Thomas
Carol Thurman
Carol Tinklepaugh
Judy Tremblay
Diane Trotter
Frances Truman
Patty Turner
Libby Tyrrell
Kathryn Urbanek
Carol Van Walleghem
Joyce Vancrum
Emily Venteicher
Bonnie Veskerna
Cathy Vicklund
Diane Wall
Frances Walters
Ginger Waters
Leigh Watkins
Karen Way
Kay Webb
Ellen White
Jessica White
Joyce Whitehead
Susan Wiens
Christie Williams
Diana Willman
Margaret Willson
Barbara Wilson
Sharman Wilson
Martha Wofford
Marcia Woodhouse
Pauly Woodworth
Judy Woolfolk
Linda Wright
Doris Yantis
Barbara Yeokum
Karen Yungmeyer
Grace Zimmerman
Connie Zuck
Poppy Zurcher

# INDEX

315

# INDEX

# INDEX